CESCA'S DIAR
1913–1916

Where Art and Nationalism Meet

1. *Photo of Sadhbh Trínseach, c.1917*

CESCA'S DIARY

1913–1916

Where Art and Nationalism Meet

Hilary Pyle

With a Foreword by
DOUGLAS HYDE SEALY

The Woodfield Press

This book was typeset by
Datapage Private Limited for
THE WOODFIELD PRESS
17 Jamestown Square, Dublin 8
www.woodfield-press.com
e-mail: terri.mcdonnell@ireland.com

Publishing Editor
Helen Harnett

Publisher
Terri McDonnell

A catalogue record for this title
is available from the British Library.

ISBN 0-9534293-7-7

Printed in Ireland
by Colour Books, Dublin

SUPPORTED BY THE HERITAGE COUNCIL

LE CUIDIÚ AN CHOMHAIRLE OIDHREACHTA

For Muiris
with love

'Hearts with one purpose alone'

W.B. Yeats, 'Easter 1916'

CONTENTS

Part Four: 'Everything Normal is Abnormal'

LIST OF ILLUSTRATIONS

Black and White Illustrations

CREDITS

Acknowledgements and thanks to the following for permission to reproduce images (those not listed are in private ownership):

Colour Plates: 1 (National Museum of Ireland); 3 (National Gallery of Ireland); 12 (National University of Ireland, Galway); 13, 14 (Coláiste Eoin Uí Chomhraí, Carrigaholt).

Black-and-White Illustrations: 48 (Blackrock Historical Society); 5 (Father Nenor, Tue Brook Church, Liverpool); 27, 28, 35, 39, 78, 92, 94–7 (National Gallery of Ireland); 2–3, 8, 12–23, 25–6, 29, 30, 40–3, 45, 49, 54–5, 58–9, 61–6, 68, 72–3, 76–7, 79–84, 88–91, 93, 98, 101 (National Library of Ireland); 85 (National University of Ireland, Galway).

2. *Page of Sketchbook, 1916*

FOREWORD

"What ish my nation?" Captain MacMorris famously asks in *Henry the Fifth*. Frances Georgiana Chenevix Trench, born in Liverpool in 1891, would have had no hesitation in answering: "Irish". And for her "Irish" was no mere label: it involved learning the language, joining the Gaelic League, altering her name from the familial "Cesca" to Sadhbh, being present at the Howth gun-running, joining Cumann na mBan, the women's equivalent of the Irish Volunteers, and carrying a gun. Various branches of the Trench family had settled in Ireland down the centuries and they were proud of being Irish but their patriotism did not extend to breaking the union with England. Cesca and her sister Margot, inspired by their cousin Dermot Trench (also born in England), a prominent member of the Gaelic League, were exceptions to the family tradition.

The name Cesca meant nothing to me until I discovered that I had long known about her under the name of Sadhbh Trínseach, the artist who had supplied the frontispiece for Diarmid Cobhthaigh's book about Douglas Hyde, my grandfather, and who had also made a drawing of my mother's sister Nuala. Nuala had died not long afterwards, of TB, though that was never mentioned. Two years later Sadhbh herself was dead having succumbed to the Spanish 'flu.

Hilary Pyle has made skilful use of Cesca's and Diarmid's letters and family papers in order to narrate, as far as possible in the subject's own words, Cesca's brief life of 27 years. One gets an impression of a friendly girl of great intelligence, excitable but level-headed, eager and adventurous, artistically gifted, beautiful and charming; a charm enhanced by the colourful clothes she designed for herself in a lavish Celtic style. Much of the time it must have seemed that she had stepped out of one of her own pageants or tableaux. A talent for painting was not unusual among the Trenches but it was more marked in Cesca and when she and her mother settled in Dublin in 1914 she became more active than ever, working at her art, deeply involved in the political movement for Irish freedom.

Sadhbh first met Douglas Hyde in 1913 and wrote, "I am so scared of that man..."; she soon became acquainted with his family. His daughter Úna, my mother, was 7 years younger than Sadhbh, but both came from families with a strong clerical background, both were talented artistically, and could speak Irish. They got on well together. Úna, being the daughter of the President of the Gaelic League, would have been at an advantage when it came to speaking Irish. But she lacked his affability and gregariousness; and her German mother, Lucy, who had admired the academic achievements of Douglas Hyde and had looked forward to a life in the upper echelons of urban society, never learned Irish. She resented the inroads on his time made by the Gaelic League and had nothing but disdain for the native Irish speakers with whom he associated. She disliked living in Co. Roscommon far from what she considered a civilised centre of culture and could be quite acid in expressing her feelings. As for those enthusiastic Gaeilgeoirs who spoke Irish in a refined Oxford accent and refused to speak English, Claud Chevasse in particular, at one time a suitor of Sadhbh, she would refuse to have them in the house. Some of her attitude must have rubbed off on Úna, who despite her fondness for her father, never showed any missionary zeal in furthering Irish.

Úna was educated in Alexandra College, studied art at Miss Marsh's studio, went on a sketching trip to Brittany, illustrated (with K. Verschoyle) an Irish translation by Pádraic Ó Cadhla of *Alice in Wonderland* in 1923, and a book of Irish folktales, and at the age of 29 married a widower with 6 children, James Sealy from an old Wexford family, 22 years her senior. Úna would have had few opportunities to speak Irish but she did make some attempt to teach her own children the Irish for please, thank you, I would like some more, and good night.

Sadhbh describes a visit in 1916 to Hyde's house where she did drawings of Hyde, Nuala and Úna. Sadhbh could now regard Hyde without being scared as she was when she first met him. I do not know what became of the drawing of Úna; with her habitual reserve, which she inherited along with her artistic talent from Lucy, she may well have hidden it away, as she did her portrait by Sarah Purser, saying it made her look like a barmaid.

Sadhbh's candid account of life at Ratra is the only one I can think of and it has the freshness and vivacity of all her writing, whether she is recording her time in Paris, or attending Irish school in Achill, or trying to decide between Claud Chevasse and Diarmid Coffey, her rival suitors. The confusion attendant on the Easter Rising is brilliantly recreated. Sadhbh was not engaged in the fighting and had only rumour to tell what was happening. She may have had a gun but it might as well have been a toy for all the use she made of it;

there is an innocence in her whole approach to war, as if the bloody slaughter on the battlefields of Europe were an irrelevance. Despite her romanticism she considered the Easter Rising ill conceived and ill timed; she wrote about the leaders as "high-minded but utterly lacking in judgement, poets, or they wouldn't have run us into such idiocy." The death that affected her most was not that of any of the leaders but that of her brother Reggie, in March 1918, while fighting for the English army.

Cesca's diaries give many intriguing glimpses of the prominent people of her time, but it is the picture she gives of herself, characterful, warm-hearted and volatile, that will stay longest in the mind. And for that our warmest thanks must go to Hilary Pyle.

Douglas Hyde Sealy

Cesca

CHRONOLOGY

1891 Frances Georgiana Chenevix Trench born 3 February in St. John the Baptist's Vicarage, Tue Brook, Liverpool, fourth of five children of the Reverend Francis Trench and his wife Isabel.

1900 Death of Reverend Francis Trench while Vicar of Orpington, Kent. The family spent long periods with elderly relatives in England and Ireland, and Cesca (as she was now known) and Margot attended school for a time in Switzerland.

1906 Cesca sent to Malvern, where she distinguishes herself at drawing. Isabel Trench takes a house for 7 years at Radnor Park, Folkestone. Friendship begins with Uncle Henry Butcher, Conservative MP for Cambridge.

1907 First lessons in Irish from Cousin Dermot Trench.

1908 Cesca and her sister Margot join the Gaelic League (Conradh na Gaeilge) in London. Visit to Dresden.

1909 Cesca and Margot go to Aran and then Achill to practice speaking Irish. Reading nationalist papers, *Sinn Féin* and *An Claidheamh Soluis*. Collecting Irish traditional poetry and songs.

1910 Cesca first wears national dress designed by Deora Frínseach. With Margot attends the Celtic Congress in Brussels. Begins signing herself 'Proinsíos' (Frances), then 'Saidhbh', later 'Sadhbh Trínseach'. Death of Uncle Henry, whose bequest includes a small legacy for each of the young Trenches.

1911 Cesca writing in English and Irish – essays, dramatic scenes and debates on nationalism versus unionism in the form of conversations. She and Margot attend Scoil Acla (Mrs Weddall's new Irish college) in Achill with Claud Chevasse, An Paorach and other nationalists. Friendships with Pádraic Ó Conaire, Diarmid Coffey and artists Lily Williams, Neilí Ní Bhriain and Ella Young begin about now. In December travels to India for five months with her mother to stay with Bishop of Calcutta and to visit brother Arthur.

1912 Cesca sketches at Árd Fheis of Conradh na Gaeilge, and returns to Scoil Acla with Margot. In Belfast Edward Carson builds up opposition to the new Home Rule Bill. Cesca attends Ménard's atelier in Paris during the winter.

1913 Cesca and Margot attend Árd Fheis in Galway in July, where Douglas Hyde wins the first challenge to his Presidency of Conradh na Gaeilge. Cesca begins her diary. Designs Christmas cards for the Conradh before returning to Atelier Ménard in Paris, living in the rue d'Assas with her mother. Her designs for national costume published in *An Claidheamh Soluis*. The manager, The O'Rahilly, asks her for political cartoons.

1914 Cesca attends Colorossi and Désvallières as well as Ménard atelier. English artist Alfred (Fra) Palmer makes five portraits of her. At the Hôtel Drouot Sale preview in February sees paintings by Matisse and cubist artists. Studies Old Irish and Breton at the Sorbonne. Courted by both Claud Chevasse and Diarmid Coffey, who is now Secretary to Col. Cotter, Military Secretary of the Irish National Volunteers. Coffey keeps her informed of political events in Dublin, and of the ensuing rift in the Volunteers. Margot, in Belfast, sends reports of Carson's incitement to political unrest. Cesca returns from Paris in time for the Howth gunrunning in July. Designs cover for Pádraic Ó Conaire's new book, *An Chéad Cloch*. She and Margot join Cumann na mBan and are active in the newly formed Cumann Gaelach na Eaglaise. When War is declared, Cesca's brothers join up. Her mother decides to settle in Dublin. On 2 November Cesca signs up for a five month course at the Metropolitan School of Art.

1915 Cesca, on the executive of Conradh na Gaeilge, makes illustrated language reading charts. A gap of fourteen months in her journals from February of this year. Actively recruiting for Cumann na mBan and attending National Volunteer reviews, where she meets Pearse. Friendly with James Stephens, whose new collection of poems, *Songs from the Clay*, is published. She exhibits at the Oireachtas exhibition and frequents the Abbey Theatre, the Arts Club and the Dublin Hermetic Society.

1916 Cesca draws Celtic antiquities in the National Museum and at Cashel. She resumes her journal on Easter Monday and records the events of Easter week in detail. Her brother Reggie sent with his regiment to the Curragh to put down the insurrection. In July she stages a pageant at the Carrigaholt Irish college, Co. Clare, where Claud falls in love with Móirín Fox. Cesca visits Douglas Hyde and his family in Roscommon to draw their portraits. Her journal ends on 24 August. In the aftermath of the Rising she is detained as a spy. In December commissioned by the Irish Nation League to design their logo.

1917 In January Reggie goes to the Front. Diarmid Coffey proposes to Cesca and is accepted. Cesca draws many small portraits in pastel and charcoal, and expands her oil painting. In May and July painting murals in Carrigaholt College. De Valera, released from prison, wins Sinn Féin seat in the general election. She tells Diarmid, 'he reads like a man of sense in the middle of talkers'. The Irish Convention meets at Raheen, Co. Clare. Diarmid becomes secretary to the Convention. Æ paints Cesca's portrait.

1918 Cesca orders her trousseau from the Cuala Industries. Reggie is killed in action. Cesca and Diarmid marry in April. They live at the Trench home, Temple Hill, where Cesca paints portraits and landscapes, and continues her association with Cumann na mBan and Cumann Gaelach na hEaglaise. In June she is published in *Colour* Magazine. She paints Cecil Salkeld's portrait in August. A victim of the 'flu epidemic, Cesca (Sadhbh Trínseach) dies in Dublin on 30 October.

3. *At Carrigaholt: Page of Sketchbook, 1916*

A NOTE ON SOME PROMINENT CHARACTERS IN THE DIARY

The Trench Family

CESCA, Frances Georgiana Chenevix, alias 'Sadhbh Trínseach'
Margot, Margaret Isabella Chenevix, her sister, called 'Máighréad' or 'the Goat'
Isabel, Cesca's mother, known as Isabella
Arthur, Arthur Henry Chenevix, eldest brother, called 'Art' by Cesca
Reggie, Charles Reginald Chenevix, brother, called 'Raghnall' by Cesca
Herbert, Herbert Chenevix, youngest brother, called 'Eireamháin' by Cesca

The Coffey Family

DIARMID, occasionally Dermot, always referred to as 'Diarmuid' (the Irish form of his name) by Cesca and Margot; active Home Ruler, author, assistant to Colonels Cotter and Moore in organising the Irish National Volunteers
George, Diarmid's father, called 'Fid' by the family; archaeologist, ex-Keeper of Antiquities at the National Museum of Ireland
Jane (née L'Estrange), Diarmid's mother; she ran the City of Dublin Workingmen's Club, and helped Edward Martyn set up the National Theatre, etc.

At the Achill School and Coláiste Uí Comhraidh, Carrigaholt

Mrs Weddall (Bean an Uadallach), founder of Scoil Acla
Dónal Ó Riordáin, co-founder of Scoil Acla, and tutor
An Paorach (Francis Power), tutor
Claud Chevasse, Oxford scholar and Irish language tutor
Ella Young, mystic and author
Móirín Nic Shionnaigh (Maureen Fox), writer and Irish language enthusiast

In Paris

Máire (Marie Palmer), fellow student at the atelier
Alfred Palmer, English painter married to Máire

Georges Cornélius, fellow student from Alsace
Róisín (Rosa Blaud), fellow student from Switzerland
Jean Malye (Seán Maillidhe), writer
Liam Mac Giolla Bhrighde (Lord Ashbourne), Irish language tutor at the Sorbonne

In Dublin

Maria, Fanny and Jane Trench at Lios an Uisce, Blackrock, cousins
Wilbraham Trench, cousin
An Craoibhín Aoibhinn (Douglas Hyde), President of the Gaelic League
The O'Rahilly, Manager of An Claidheamh Soluis
Jennie Wyse-Power, President and Chairman of Cumann na mBan
Kathleen Clarke, Cumann na mBan, wife of Tom Clarke, executed in 1916
Neilí Ní Bhriain (Nelly O'Brien), founding member of Cumann Gaelach na hEaglaise and founder of Coláiste Eoghain Uí Chomhraidhe at Carrigaholt

PREFACE

The Irish artist, Sadhbh Trínseach, whose drawings are preserved in the National Gallery of Ireland and in the National Library of Ireland, and whose semblance looks out from among other contemplative faces in the National Portrait Collection, has always been a mysterious and appealing character. The invitation to translate (which also meant to decipher) her personal journal was a challenge, and a tempting challenge. The manuscript notebooks are written in Irish, English and French, the latter language while she was at art school in Paris, and sometimes she resorts to a mixture of the three. The content is fascinating. The final volume describes at first hand the day-to-day events of the Rising of 1916 and its aftermath, and it is for this, and her record of the events leading up to it, as seen from the inside, that the journal is valued. For nearly ninety years the notebooks have lain hidden from general view in a box where they were put away with other papers and letters associated with the artist.

Cesca Trench, as those outside the Gaelic world knew her, started out to write her historic diary in Irish, not for reasons of secrecy as is one suggestion, but because she believed Irish was the first language of Ireland and that it would be revived as the common tongue. She really believed in the return of 'that big race of "fine tall men & splendid girls" that Seosamh Mac Cathmhaoil talks about', as she told her sister in a letter, and she was filled with enthusiasm for the restoration of the original Celtic nation as a modern state. When the impulse to write down what she remembered was pressing – as in the account of the Rising – she lapsed into English for the most part (while in France, French). She felt it important to record everything that was happening politically prior to the expected restoration of Home Rule. Fortunately for posterity she recorded the events of her private life as well, in a very human and touching way.

Reading her diaries was not easy – her handwriting is especially bad when she writes excitedly on poor paper, and this required not a little interpretation. She was not a native speaker so her Irish, though idiomatic and with a fairly wide vocabulary, is not always accurate. Spelling tends to be old-fashioned – Irish orthography had not yet been regularised; and even in English the meaning may be elusive. She was not particular either about where she put down her thoughts, and she used any notebooks or paper that lay around to write swiftly in the odd moments of what was already a very busy life. Pages here and there in the manuscript have been displaced, or the content is disjointed, so that to find the correct sequence has been another hurdle. But ultimately events fell into place, and letters, of which she wrote many, have helped to fill gaps and broaden out the narrative of a life lived to the full at some of the tensest moments in Irish history.

The diary and some other biographical detail is to be found in the following notebooks, which are privately owned:

Notebook 1. Small black notebook with 'P. Trínseach' in Gaelic characters on the cover. It dates from 1910 and has been used later as well. There are notes on Mohammedanism, notes of personal finance, and many drawings of events the artist attended, or places visited, which are seldom dated.

Notebook 2. A large mottled notebook, signed with the name 'S. Trínseach' in Gaelic characters, dating from 1911–1914. Miscellaneous writings appear amidst the gun and artillery notes of one of her brothers. There are excerpts from nationalist literature, stories analysing why she became a nationalist, and drafts of a tale, 'The Planter's Son' and a play about the Civil War in seventeenth century England. The drawings are of Celtic people, including Cuchulain, and the people of India, which she visited in 1912.

Notebook 3. Dates from 1913–14. Here the narrative really begins, with the visit to Galway and Achill, and the greater part of her time at the atelier in Paris.

Notebook 4. A small black notebook, dated April 1914, with the account of her visit to Amboise, and many sketches.

Notebook 5. Large writing pad (French), dating from 6 April–11 June 1914, which concludes her time in France.

Notebook 6. Ancient Irish Vellum writing pad, 27 May–18 February 1915. Cesca is in the middle of the political tension in Dublin, writing about the Volunteers, Cumann Gaelach na hEaglaise and Cumann na mBan. At the end of this long narrative she has copied out Susan Mitchell's satirical 'Celtic Renaissance Birthday Book'.

Notebook 7. Hely's Duplicate Order Book, with loose pages inserted, April–August 1916. It records the events of Easter Week, day by day, and the months that followed.

Other primary sources have been the 12 Sadhbh Trínseach notebooks cum sketchbooks in the National Library of Ireland, and family engagement diaries, her sister Margot's writings, and letters and papers belonging to herself and her siblings, all in private ownership.

In so far as is possible, the aim has been to allow Cesca to tell her own story in the words of her diary and letters. In editing the journal I have substituted full words in place of abbreviations to assist the flow of the text, but retained abbreviations when quoting from letters. Personal names jotted down as initials have generally been written in full too, when I know them, with footnotes for more significant personalities. Some Irish or French words have been left so as to keep something of the flavour of the original (with translation where necessary), and for the same reason variant versions of the names of her family and of her immediate circle have been preserved.

I thank the Coffey family, Saive, Dairine, Manus, Petra and Aedan, for their support and cooperation in writing this book, and the late Terry Trench, Professor Anthony Fletcher and other Trench relatives who have helped me so readily. Pádraig Ó Snodaigh has been my mentor in all Gaelic League and political lore of the time, with the generous assistance of Dr Brendan Ó Riordáin and Marie O'Neill; and in various other ways I have been assisted by the late Father Cyril Barrett, Neamhnait de Paor, Sophie Lacour, Gifford Lewis, Seán MacMathúna, Professor Maureen Murphy, Father Nenor, Andrias Ó Cathasaigh and Douglas Hyde Sealy; by Michael Kenny and Felicity Devlin of the National Museum of Ireland, and by my colleagues Elle von Monschaw, Anne Hodge and Marie McFeely at the National Gallery; by Joanne Finnegan, Keeper of Drawings in the National Library; by the librarians of the National Gallery of Ireland, the National Library of Ireland, Trinity College Library, the Representative Body of the Church of Ireland and the British Library; by MacDara Tóibín, Director of the Eoin Uí Chomhraí Summer School; by Patcooke, Director, and Niamh O'Sullivan, Archivist, of Kilmainham Jail Museum; and by Fionnuala Gallagher, Arts Officer, and Alice Hoary of National University, Galway. I am grateful to Brian Phillips and Roy Hewson for their splendid photography, and thank the National Gallery of Ireland, the National Library of Ireland, the National Museum of Ireland and all private owners for permission to reproduce drawings, paintings and photographs from their collections. A special thank you to Douglas Hyde Sealy for his thoughtful and illuminating foreword.

Finally I thank Terri McDonnell for her vital encouragement and assistance, Helen Harnett for her thoughtful editing, and my long suffering family – especially Dúinseach – for sympathy and support at all times. Bail ó Dhia oraibh go léir.

PART ONE

'A Passion for Ireland'

4. *Early Drawing of a Celtic Hero*

1
A Nationalist Artist in the Making

Cesca Trench was reared in a society that depended on acceptable rules and unrelenting standards, but which also valued idealism within certain limits. 'You dear 16 year old daughter,' Isabella Trench wrote to this second youngest of her children in celebration of her sixteenth birthday. 'I remember when you were quite tiny I used to try & picture what you & Margot would be when you were 16 & 17 & I could not succeed at all. I *am* so thankful to have 2 delicious & loving daughters and I pray constantly that God will give you his Grace that you may live as His Soldiers through this very troublesome world, so full of temptations. Be humble-minded; try & take a lowly view of yourself & exalt your neighbours! See that you leave a sweet & fragrant remembrance behind you & make people long for your presence!'[1] While she penned such loving advice she was fully aware of the effect this rapidly maturing temperamental personality was having on those around her at her English boarding school; but she couldn't possibly have anticipated that Cesca, an artist, would live literally as a soldier less than a decade later, carrying a gun, a member of Cumann na mBan, the women's auxiliary of the Irish Volunteers in revolutionary Ireland. In the event, her charismatic daughter did fulfil her mother's ultimate wish, leaving behind a warm and lovable impression on all who knew her, wherever she went.

1. Isabel (alias Isabella) Trench to Cesca, 1 Feb. 1907.

5. *Tue Brook Church and Vicarage, Liverpool, in 1893*

Cesca's parents were both members of the close knit Trench family which claimed to have descended from a seventeenth century Huguenot refugee who fled the St. Bartholomew massacre to find refuge in Northumberland. His children settled in Ireland at different times.[2] Her own grandfather, Richard Chenevix Trench,[3] Archbishop of Dublin, and famous for his pioneer work on the *Oxford English Dictionary,* was remembered by the family for his gesture for political freedom as a student. In 1830 he travelled to Spain, ready to risk his life in the Torrijos uprising, an abortive attempt to restore the 1812 constitution. Fortunately for him, he delayed in Gibraltar. The Constitutionalists' cause was hopeless and all those involved, including one of his college friends, were shot by order of the despotic monarch, Fernando VII. Cesca inherited her passion for justice and political freedom from this grandfather, and from her father, Herbert Francis Chenevix Trench, who also entered the Church.

He was acting as chaplain to his father in Dublin about the time that he married his first cousin, Isabella Catherine, one of the Trenches of Cangort Park in King's County. Disappointed at his lack of preferment in the recently disestablished Irish Church, he went to Liverpool as Perpetual Curate to St. John the Baptist's Church, Tue Brook, which had had rather a stormy history during its short existence. He was welcomed because, as an Irishman, he was not moved to such extremes of ritual as his tractarian predecessors. The church itself, built in 1870, with Burne Jones windows and a magnificent screen added later, gives some idea of what appealed to a father who is an otherwise shadowy character

2. See Thomas Cooke-Trench, *Memoir of the Trench Family* (Privately printed, 1897).
3. J. Bromley, *The Man of Ten Talents* (London, SPCK, 1959).

since he died when Cesca was only nine. That he retained an influence on the family is clear from recurring references years later to his generosity of spirit and lack of prejudice.

Cesca was born in 1890 in the palatial Vicarage that her father had built beside the church. Two years later he became Vicar of Orpington in Kent. From there he moved to St. Peter's Isle of Thanet at Broadstairs, where he died from consumption at the age of fifty in 1900.

Isabella was left to bring up five children on her own: Arthur (b. 1884), with a gap of four years[4] between him and Reggie (b. 1888), Margot (b. 1889), Frances, known as Cesca (b. 1891), and Herbert (b. 1892). With her limited income, a nineteenth century widow had to depend on the wider family for support. One of the merits of the Irish 'big house' was that it was capable of absorbing such ill-fated individuals and other homeless relatives, and the Trenches were loyal to their kin. During their growing years, Isabella's children would spend extended periods with relations who for the most part were elderly. In England there was Aunt Blanche, their mother's sister, who urged them to regard Hurst House in Berkshire as their home. But the girls loved going to Ireland where Cousins Fanny and Tom, unmarried grandchildren of Dean Trench of Kildare, lived at Glenmalyre near Portlaoise, and Cousin Maria and her twin sisters, Frances and Jane, at Lisaniskea,[5] in Blackrock near Dublin, and Cousin Florence and Cousin Gertrude Fiennes at Bowen's Court, in North Cork, to mention a few. Aunt Haddie, Isabella's older unmarried sister who stayed with them during their youth, was musical and unwittingly encouraged Cesca and Margot's fondness for rebel songs such as 'The Wearing of the Green'.[6]

The family spent a long period in Switzerland after Frank's death, the younger members going to school there. During a tour of Italy in early spring they visited Milan and Florence, and Reggie (from whose strong conservative viewpoint she later diverged radically) accompanied Cesca, who was already showing her creative bent, to the Uffizzi and the Bargello. Their mother, if an annoyance with her unflinching unionism, was a positive influence too, nurturing the gifts of all her children, arranging on their return to send the more pious Margot in September 1906 to the Manor House, Brondesbury, in north west London, and the wilder

---

4. There was a second child, Monica Mary (Aug. 1885–Dec. 1886).
5. Since the 1970s Lisaniskea, a house with a very interesting history, has been called by the Irish form of the name, Lios an Uisce, which Cesca used. See 'Lios an Uisce' by Mary Pat O'Malley, *Proceedings of the Blackrock Society*, vol. 4 (1996), pp. 34–53.
6. She sang a loyalist version of this popular lyric. The original words preferred by the girls, and written by the dramatist, Dion Boucicault, celebrate Napper Tandy (1737–1803), a supporter of Catholic Emancipation, and Secretary of the United Irishmen during the years before the Union.

6. *Margot and Cesca*

Cesca to Malvern in Worcestershire, where she had the best possible encouragement in art and quickly became a confident draughtsman, with a particular talent for portraiture. (The boys were destined for military careers. Arthur and Reggie were at Charterhouse and the youngest boy, Herbert, was sent to Dover College.) The Trenches were proud that they were Irish, and Mother made sure they had shamrock for St. Patrick's Day and sent them large barmbracks. She read and discussed with them the parliamentary debates on the Irish situation in the *Times* – 'between Birrell & Redmond[7] the people in England will believe nothing of the real state of things & unless it touches their pockets they do not care 1 straw what becomes of us in Ireland.' However when it was published in 1908, she found Mrs Stopford Green's book *The Making of Ireland and Its Undoing* – the main theme of which was that, prior to the English devastation of the country in the seventeenth century, Ireland had had a fine highly developed civilisation – 'quite *unreliable.*'[8] For Isabella, Unionism did not preclude honouring the national saint and loving

7. Augustine Birrell (1850–1933), follower of Gladstone and friendly with John Redmond (1856–1918), leader of the Irish Party, had been appointed Chief Secretary for Ireland in 1907, and would establish the new National University in 1908.
8. To Cesca and Margot, 2 Mar. 1909. Mrs Green was an active Home Ruler.

7 *Ink drawing of Celtic hero*

things Irish, but it meant accepting the established order and the impeccability of England's dominance in an amalgamation which could only benefit the smaller island; all of which was frustrating to those who, like her daughters, had bypassed the Home Rulers in their dreaming of a totally free Ireland.

According to her letters, Cesca's interest in nationalist politics was growing from the age of fifteen, and two years later she began to study Irish. Her mother gave her brother Herbert and herself a second edition of *The Spirit of the Nation,* a collection of the songs and her brother poems published by Thomas Davis in his nationalist paper. Cesca kept it. Their younger cousin, Elizabeth Bowen, remembered at Folkstone, where Isabella and her small family had finally settled, the indelible impression Cesca and Margot made on her – 'handsome young girls with black hair . . . in blowing-about Celtic robes of scarlet or green, with Tara brooches clamped to their shoulders. I failed to connect this dress with Ireland, and the Trenches' conspicuousness embarrassed me – especially when they swept down on my school crocodile. Even my mother said, a shade tartly, that no Trenches were ever so Irish as all that.'[9]

As adolescents the girls were relatively happy at their respective schools, especially Margot in her 'old monkish abode'[10] under the rule of the compelling and hospitable Miss Soulsby. Deeply spiritual like her ecumenical sister, who found as much inspiration in art and nature as in uplifting liturgy, Margot would have become a missionary had it not been for her beloved Cesca's infectious obsession for the Celtic Revival. Lucy Soulsby, in her New Year's greeting to Old Girls circulated in 1913, printed her address to the National Union of Women Workers Conference in Birmingham of the previous October, in which she approved of 'Women's Work and the whole Woman Question', and counselled, 'You are standing at the door of the most wonderful Woman's

9. *Bowen's Court*. 2nd ed (London, Longman, 1964) p. 420.
10. S.H. Butcher to Margot, 3 Nov. 1907.

Kingdom that the world has ever known – the Kingdom of Service.' 'I care so very much that all my Old Girls should be growing, year by year, into the large-hearted open-minded women I have pictured . . . so full of Public Spirit that they have no room for Party Spirit,' she added. Margot appreciated and absorbed this philosophy. She decided to dedicate herself to social work.

Cesca's experience of school was different, and she was inclined to be rebellious. She lamented to her sister about the absence of a garden at Malvern, and the lack of a school magazine. She complained about the denseness of English girls in understanding Home Rule,[11] and later said that the best way to rear an Irish nationalist was to send an Irish child to an English public school (something that has been the experience of many generations of Irish sent across the water to be educated). However she was a good mixer, and liked sparring with Miss Leather – 'She and I had a huge argument last History lesson about Ireland as it came up. I swore we'd get Home Rule and she swore we wouldn't. Don't you think that it'd be jolly good for us to find out for ourselves that we can't govern ourselves because we'll never believe it otherwise. That's the attitude I take up.'[12]

Reared on Standish O'Grady's tales of epic heroes of the past, *The Coming of Cuchulain,* and *Red Hugh's Captivity,* Cesca and Margot's determination to become true Irish Irelanders in language and culture was whetted by the example of their first cousin Samuel, who took the extra name of 'Dermot' by deed poll in 1905 so that he could be 'Diarmuid Trínseach' when speaking Irish with other lovers of the tongue.[13] Samuel joined the Gaelic Society while a student at Oxford, and became a fluent speaker of Irish, teaching others enthusiastically. Oliver Gogarty enjoyed the tuition when both were staying with Joyce in Sandycove at the Martello Tower in 1904. Joyce subsequently immortalised the Oxford graduate – whose accent he detested – in *Ulysses,* as the English man, 'Haines'. It was from Dermot that Margot and Cesca had their first Irish lessons about 1907.[14] He taught them the Irish alphabet. He sent them books in Gaelic and information about the London branch of the Gaelic League, which they joined when Cesca was seventeen, and he remained their inspiration and mentor.

Uncle Henry Butcher, urbane, scholarly, politically astute – and a Unionist – was quite the opposite to Cousin Dermot, and his affectionate interest contributed to their development in other ways. Their mother had already given them an excellent start, making sure in July 1906 that they read Dante

11. Reference in S.H. Butcher to Cesca, 4 Nov. 1907.
12. To Margot c. 8 Oct. 1906.
13. See 'Dermot Chenevix Trench and Haines of *Ulysses*', by C.E.F. Trench, *James Joyce Quarterly*, University of Tulsa, Oklahoma, vol. 13 no. 1, Fall 1975, pp. 39–48.
14. Letter from Isabella Trench to Cesca, 5 Jul. 1907.

with Doré's illustrations, and ordering whatever books they wanted; but she felt that he could fill part of the gap their father left. Henry, the eldest son of the Bishop of Meath, had joined the family when he married Father's sister, Aunt Rose Trench. He had been a widower for four years, childless and lonely, Professor of Greek at Edinburgh University (and later a Trustee of the British Museum), and the friendship began about 1906 when he returned to Cambridge and was elected a Parliamentary representative for the University. In November, Mother gave him a classical drawing by Flaxman as a present from Cesca and Margot, and thereafter followed four years of intense correspondence with the girls, or relaxed conversations at 6 Tavistock Square in London and at the family hideout of a century, Danesfort, in Killarney, Co. Kerry.

He was quite unrepentant about his own Unionism and described himself as 'that horrid Uncle Henry with the heart of stone & the spirit of a black orange-man', telling them of a stormy evening in the House of Commons – 'Redmond attacked me with extreme fury & all the Irish members howled.'[15] At the same time he was able to make friends with Tim Healy and O'Brien of the Nationalist Party. Though a staunch Conservative, he mixed socially with the Liberal leader, Mr Asquith,[16] and reported on his lunches with the Prime Minister. Arthur Balfour,[17] then Leader of the Conservative Opposition, was an old friend of Uncle Henry's, and through these connections his nieces were privileged to have an inside view of the current political scene.

Butcher had other interesting friends. They heard how Walter Crane, the celebrated English illustrator, had come to Danesfort to do a sketch from the summerhouse. Cesca herself made her only known watercolour view from a window in Danesfort in similarly misty conditions in August 1908.[18] In January 1908 Butcher told how he had just come back from Ireland. Æ[19] was staying

15. To Margot and Cesca, 4 Nov. 1906.
16. Herbert Henry Asquith (1852–1928), Liberal leader and Prime Minister from April 1908. He introduced the Home Rule Bill of April 1912, which was opposed by Edward Carson and the Ulster Protestants.
17. Arthur James Balfour (1848–1930) was Chief Secretary for Ireland for ten years, and later Prime Minister. Though supporting Home Rule, he would recommend the division of North and South in his book, *Nationality and Home Rule* (1913).
18. C 1131–1, National Library of Ireland, a small atmospheric sketch in wet blues with a little green.
19. George Russell (1867–1935) from Armagh was familiarly known by the pseudonym under which he wrote. Artist, poet, and mystic, he developed the co-operative system for farmers and took an active role in the promotion of Home Rule and in seeking a solution to the Northern problem.

under the same roof at Horace Plunkett's.[20] 'I have never heard such humorous imaginative conversation anywhere. You would have died with laughter over his stories & descriptions.'[21] On another occasion he was there with 'Spanish Gold'[22] and heard him preach the Easter sermon.

But for all his indulgent front, he was concerned about his nieces, warning Margot – 'Seriously, dear girl, don't let politics darken your outlook',[23] and continually counselling Cesca to take a more temperate attitude – 'Why should not Ireland be distinctively herself – as Irish as possible, & yet retain the Union with England in the same way as Scotland has never ceased to be Scotch in her sentiment & all her ways? There was a time – & it lasted a good long while – when Scotland was as hostile to the Union as Ireland has been.'[24]

When Cesca joined the Gaelic League, he warned her about the narrowness of Douglas Hyde[25] and the Gaelic Leaguers, who were insisting on Irish as a required subject for matriculation in the new National University of Ireland, thus putting what some regarded as a peasant's language on an equal status with English and Latin. He himself supported the new Education Bill in an enlightened way, unlike other members of his party, but he was totally against compulsory Irish, a position shared by clerics and the establishment on both sides of the Irish Sea. When the National University Senate resolved the battle in May 1910 – compulsory Irish at entrance or during the degree course – he admitted to one satisfactory element in the outcome: Trinity, he suggested, would be the gainer, 'for many young Catholics will now have a reasonable excuse for going there instead of the Catholic University.'[26] Cesca, however, who was growing more and more irritated with her uncle's bland conservatism, must have delighted in John Devoy's often quoted summing up of the Catholic University's decision in his New York paper, *The Gaelic American,* as – 'the most significant achievement in the history of the Gaelic League' with 'the moral support of the whole country.'[27]

20. Sir Horace Plunkett (1854–1932), though a Unionist, supported the Gaelic League and reformed Irish farming through the Irish Agricultural Organisation Society where he enlisted creative visionaries Æ, Susan Mitchell and Harry Norman to publish *The Irish Homestead* and later *The Irish Statesman.*
21. To Cesca, 18 Jan. 1908.
22. Butcher refers to Canon Hannay (George A. Birmingham) by the name of one of his most popular novels.
23. 13 Sep. 1909.
24. To Cesca, 4 Nov. 1907.
25. Douglas Hyde (1860–1949), poet, linguist, founder and President of Conradh na Gaeilge (the Gaelic League), known widely by his pen name An Craoibhín Aoibhinn ('the little flowering branch'). He would eventually become the first President of Ireland.
26. To Cesca, 12 May 1910.
27. *Gaelic American*, 18 Jun. 1910.

While Uncle Henry's authoritarian mind-set encouraged Cesca to go in the opposite direction, he still admired and encouraged their determination to become fluent in the Irish language. In his letters he praises Cesca's first efforts at writing Gaelic greetings using the traditional script. The two girls visited Aran to speak Irish,[28] and in July 1909 stayed in Achill, at Mr Sheridan's Hotel, attending the Irish Summer School there. 'I thought it noble your doing five hours of Irish two days running . . . after getting your letter I seized a Grammatica Celtica by Zeuss, which I came on in my shelves, & all but dispatched the 2 thick vols. – one for each of you, when I remembered the text is in Latin & that might be a bar – or at least a bore.'[29] But he interpreted their Irish zeal as extreme romanticism, envying them 'even when you are almost lost in a bog!', and deploring the way they courted primitivism, and their 'wild ways and doings.'

A knowledge of Irish was an intellectual asset for the well brought up Protestant young lady that Cesca and Margot accepted was their mould and role when they first left school. They were educated for a round of charitable sales of work, Sunday school conferences, girls' diocesan gatherings and summer camps, suffragette meetings, debating societies, lectures, social calls, relatives, reading of newspapers and keeping abreast with current affairs. But their interest in the Irish tongue wasn't merely academic, they wanted to hear it revived as Ireland's only spoken language. They also read the exciting new Irish literature in English as it appeared – the literature of a nation on the verge of freedom – Yeats, Æ, James Stephens, Joseph Campbell, Lady Gregory and Pádraic Colum: and they copied verses by patriotic nineteenth century poets, such as Ferguson and Davis, into their notebooks. They added *Sinn Féin,* the paper edited by the radical separatist, Arthur Griffith,[30] to their regular reading, also taking *An Claidheamh Soluis,* the publication of the Gaelic League. They introduced Irish legends and historical heroes into the charades in which they participated socially with other young people, and, to their mother's embarrassment, defied the conventions of polite society by deliberately discussing Irish politics and the Home Rule Bill wherever they went.

The girls had wide interests, and sufficient – if limited – income for travel. While in Dublin in 1908, Cesca went to see Hugh Lane's newly opened gallery of modern art in Harcourt Street. That winter, she had a few weeks in Dresden

28. To Cesca, 13 Apr. 1909.
29. To Margot, undated.
30. Arthur Griffith (1871–1922) was dedicated to achieving independence for Ireland. In 1899 he founded the political and literary paper, *The United Irishman*, succeeded some years later by *Sinn Féin*. It was he who originated the Sinn Féin movement for self-reliance, which – despite his abhorrence of aggression – paved the way to the 1916 Rising and subsequent events.

with Margot, where as two 'Celts' they bristled at being called English. Mother rented a house called Abbeylands in Killiney, south of Dublin, for the summer of 1909; and in October eighteen year old Cesca stayed with the cousins at Glenmalyre, murmuring in with the rest at the jumbled family prayers, galloping around on wild mares and being 'chucked off every day',[31] having tea on the bog, listening to seventy year old Cousin Tom explaining the machinery on the farm, or to the local village band who had come up to entertain the big house. After this she spent some time with Uncle Henry in Killarney at Danesfort, glad to bury herself in the library.

Fervour for Home Rule and the new Irish culture was not uncommon among young Protestants in Dublin and London; nor was the genuinely painful rift that this created between them and those parents who were content to remain faithful to Unionism. As long as she kept off politics, Cesca's sending of Gaelic Christmas cards, and insistence on using Irish made writing paper, did not bother her mother and brothers. Though she lamented their inability to share her vision, they at least tolerated her passionate idealism. In July 1910, according to her accounts, she invested in one of Dora French's Irish national costumes. 'It's a Miss Ffrench[32] who invented the costume, a Gaelic Leaguer, & there's a picture called *The Purple Dress* which is a picture of it at the exhibition I'm going to see in Dublin,' she wrote to Margot. The two girls attended a missionary conference that summer, and in September went to the Celtic Congress in Brussels, where they had first hand experience of international concern about the survival of the Celtic cultures. On both occasions Cesca made copious sketches of fellow delegates. Then followed the usual round of Irish relatives, Cesca ending up at Danesfort, whence she commanded Margot impishly not to forget 'the Prionsíos *Ní* Trínseach'[33] when addressing letters to her. It was her last visit there. Despite the cruise to Norway prescribed by his doctor, Uncle Henry, who had been ailing for some time, passed away after Christmas. Twelve months later they learned that his wife's legacy (investments settled on her by the Archbishop), from which he had benefited as tenant for life, had been equally divided among Rose's next of kin, £5,620.16.6 each coming to Cesca, Margot and their three brothers, the small income to be paid twice annually. The sisters immediately began exploring how they might transfer their inheritance into Irish shares.

31. Cesca to Margot, 10 Oct. 1909.
32. Also Deora Frínseach. She was elected to the Executive Committee of Conradh na Gaeilge in September 1915. As a member of Cumann na mBan, she spent some time in prison. Deora Frínseach was to become a member of The Craftworkers' Co-operative who set up workshops at 39 Harcourt Street, Dublin, in 1919.
33. Properly 'Proinséas Ni Trínseach', Irish for 'Frances Trench'.

8 *Figures in National Costume, 1913*

Cesca sketched freely with her pencil wherever she went, but about this time she began writing too, earning a certificate of high commendation for an essay entered in the 1911 Home University Library competition.[34] The first reminiscences about her development as a Nationalist date from now, together with a fierce argument about the nature of the Irish character with her elderly Unionist cousins Tom and Fanny at Glenmalyre, which she recorded in dialogue form on 25 September 1911. She wrote nonsense poems, snatches of historical or contemporary drama, and short stories[35] in the wake of Standish O'Grady.

By now she had been swept up totally into the Irish Renaissance, and alongside her artistic aspirations this was to be her abiding preoccupation. She had taken the name 'Proinséas', soon superseded by the name by which she is generally known now, 'Sadhbh' (anglicised as 'Sive') – the ancient Irish name meaning 'goodness', and often cited as the equivalent of 'Sophia'. While her family continued to call her Cesca, to her nationalist contemporaries and artist friends – and even today – she has always been 'Sadhbh Trínseach'. She rechristened her brothers and her sister, referring to them in her diary as Art, Raghnall, Máighréad and Eiremháin.

34. Home University Library to Miss Cesca C. Trench, 28 Jul. 1911.
35. 'The Planter's Son' was serialised posthumously in *The Gaelic Churchman*, Apr. to Oct. 1922.

9 *Cathleen Ní Houlihan, c. 1911*

In March 1911, she attended the annual St. Patrick's Day concert in London, a rousing evening of entertainment in Irish and English, at which 'all Irishmen and women of all creeds, classes and politics meet in harmony to honour Ireland's Patron Saint', as one observer commented, adding, 'The Queen's Hall concert is a regular occasion upon which the Irish in London take an oath of allegiance to their country.'[36] Douglas Hyde's reminder to Irishmen 'across the water' that 'the next ten years will decide the question of Ireland a Nation or Ireland an English county' did not fall on deaf ears. Cesca found the audience wild with excitement, singing along, greeting each performer personally – all well known from previous occasions – from the floor. 'I have lived my twenty years for nothing,' she wrote afterwards in her notebook, 'if I have not learnt that logic has no traffic, direct or indirect, with Irish political nationalism. I wish to make a distinction between political nationalism & linguistic nationalism. (I suppose it is because I was brought up a Unionist that I never before heard a man sing a song in a public place expressive of his joy at the prospect of someday fighting for his political independence . . . I never heard the words sung in a sweep of enthusiasm by a thousand voices . . .)'

The occasion brought her face to face with the recognition that she was a committed nationalist, and – though she was not yet aware of it – on the brink of joining what the youngest of the Gifford sisters, Sydney Czira, called 'the Movement'.[37]

> It had no other name than that – just 'the Movement' for it was not organised into one body, and it had no recognised leaders. But the Movement did move, slowly at first, and then with tremendous momentum from 1910 to 1916. Many of the men and women in the Movement were very obscure individuals when I first became active in Irish politics in 1908. They had little or no political influence. They belonged to a number of small societies and groups. Some were in Sinn Féin[38]; others in the Irish Republican Brotherhood; others in the Inghinidhe na hÉireann. Still more were in the ranks of the Gaelic League or the G.A.A. Within a few years these scattered groups had coalesced, and an Irish revolutionary force was in being. The obscure men and women of 1908 became the acknowledged leaders of Ireland in 1916 and the years that followed.

---

36. D.Ó Súilleabháin, *Conradh na Gaeilge i Londain 1894–1917* (Dublin, Conradh na Gaeilge, 1989) pp. 108–9.
37. Sydney Gifford Czira (John Brennan), *The Years Flew By: Recollections of Sydney Gifford Czira* (Dublin, Gifford & Craven) 1974, p. 46. Her sisters were deeply involved too. Muriel was the wife of Thomas MacDonagh, while Grace married Joseph Plunkett in his death cell.
38. Then regarded by the authorities as 'a small body of cranks who were thirsting for notoriety', see *The Sinn Féin Rebellion as They Saw It*, ed. K. Jeffery (Dublin, Irish Academic Press, 1999) p. 35.

As a linguistic nationalist, Cesca returned that summer to Achill, this time to the new Irish college opened by Mrs Weddall[39] in Keel, which was enthusiastically supported by the local people. Achill had been predominantly Irish-speaking till the 1890s, but – as elsewhere – decline set in and within a decade half of the children were less than fluent. The new buoyancy that occurred with the promise of Home Rule reversed the mood, and local adults as well as children began attending language classes. 'Scoil Gaedhilge, Acla' offered in its prospectus 'hard work in the morning', bathing, boating and shooting in the afternoon, and singing, dancing and debating in the evening, with lectures in Irish history once a week, and céilís twice a week. Cesca brought her crayons and paints. The sisters were overwhelmingly enthusiastic about Mrs Weddall's venture. Participants were asked to bring their Gaelic dress or kilt, and any musical instrument, and a bicycle. From sketches in her diary of the third Scoil Acla session in 1913, one can see how much the music of the uilleann pipes meant to Cesca.

Cesca's most frustrating tussle with family Unionism came about as a result of her five month visit to India, from December 1911 to the following April. She travelled with Mother via Marseilles and returned through Aden. No doubt it was Aunt Rose's legacy that enabled her to make the visit to see her brother Arthur, who had been stationed there for some years, and to stay with Aunt Edie, one of Father's sisters, married to Reginald Coplestone, the aged Bishop of Calcutta. There were numerous servants in the Bishop's Palace, she reported to Margot – perhaps forty-five – wearing neither shoes nor stockings. She liked the gentle and affectionate Ayah who waited on her in the mornings. But candid as always in conversation, she provoked an atmosphere around her fraught with tension. The Bishop refused to see that Home Rule[40] could work. According to Cesca, his assumptions were clichéd and he was forever making puns. Aunt Edie attempted to smooth things over, describing her niece as 'a great Home Rulist in Ireland, so I think she is on Calcutta's side'.[41] Cesca, she pleaded, was the life and soul of the study circle on China.

Cesca had a trip to Delhi to see her brother, and Art (tired of sightseeing) offered her the use of a flat in Bombay before she went home in April. She wrote to her sister in February 1912, as she travelled in the train from Agra to Calcutta, describing the pinnacle of her experience: 'You know it's true what

39. Emily Weddall (1867–1952), Bean an Uadallach, born Emily Burke, went to England as a nurse, and married a retired sea captain from Yorkshire in 1905. The following year she joined the Gaelic League and went to live in Achill. In 1911, while secretary of the Achill Féis, she founded Scoil Acla.
40. The third Home Rule Bill was to be introduced by Asquith that year.
41. Cesca to Margot, n.d.

10 *Sketches made in India, 1912*

they say that the most beautiful thing in the whole world is the Taj Mahal. It is like a very beautiful glowing dream. It's quite indescribable . . .' But she was immeasurably lonely in Calcutta, totally out of her element, and suffocated by the Bishop's obstinate Unionism. She consoled herself with painting, capturing brilliant colours on her palette, as well as embroidering a national costume from George Coffey's book on Celtic design.[42]

Margot posted *Sinn Féin* and *An Claidheamh Soluis* to her regularly, and made preparations for their return to Achill in the summer. She wrote a long letter with news of the annual Christmas fair held in Dublin by Sinn Féin.[43] Their new Gaelic League friends were all at the *Aonach* – Claud Chevasse, Ella Young, Miss O'Farrelly and the painter Lily Williams – all wondering why Cesca had not contributed to the picture exhibition which was very good, with 'heaps' of Seosamh Mac Cathmhaoil,[44] and some Madame Markievicz and Maud Gonne. A rather handsome smallish man whom they had met at Scoil Acla, named George Irvine, Margot wrote, 'is a prot. & Miss Young was meeting him there to talk about the revision of the Irish hymnal, the new edition to include a number of hymns in Irish.' Both were moving spirits in another venture in which Cesca and Margot were to become involved, the revival of Irish in the Church of Ireland, and Margot told her excitedly à propos of this that if

42. *Royal Irish Academy Guide to Celtic Antiquities*, 1909.

43. To Cesca, n.d. [Dec. 1912].

44. The northern poet and painter Joseph Campbell, who was friendly with the Trench girls.

11 *Sketches made in India, 1912*

Mr Plunkett of St. Anne's were elected to the Bishopric of Killaloe, as seemed likely, at least three of the Bishops would be Gaelic Leaguers.

At the Aonach, she had met a young Home Ruler of increasing interest to Cesca. '. . . Diarmuid [Coffey] & his mother came strolling by . . . his mother is a perfect darling: not very tall & wearing a very old green cloak of no special shape or pattern . . . Diarmuid was peering about, looking immensely tall & giving one such a nice Gaelic hand clasp.' She had gone back to Howth with them, to lunch on bread and cheese and see their pictures. Mrs Coffey, originally a Miss L'Estrange, had told her of the cold reaction when she married, outside her Church of Ireland background, the Catholic George Coffey. Hardly any one – and this included the Trench aunts and uncles – would speak to her because Mr Coffey was such a strong Nationalist, 'but Father was always so sweet & sympathetic . . .'

Back from India, Cesca was in Dublin to attend the Árd Fheis, the annual meeting of the Gaelic League, where she made drawings of the delegates including Mac Giollarnaith, editor of *An Claidheamh Soluis.* Then she and Margot went to Scoil Acla, where again her pencil was busy, sketching the cottages at the foot of the mountain, dancers, musicians and local people at the céilís, Gaelic-speaking friends lying on Croaghaun's peak or on the strand – in national dress

12 *Scoil Acla: Céilí*

as they studied, or ancient costume as they rehearsed dramas about the lofty days of the Celts.[45] It was in Galway and Mayo that she commenced her diary, realising the significance of times that could never be repeated. 'We live on two levels, a fantastic level and a realistic level,' Tennessee Williams wrote at a much later date, and she was determined to live on both, and to record both.

13 *An tÁrd Fheis: Sketches*

45. Notebook 2079TX (National Library of Ireland).

14 *Accordion Player, 1913*

2
Galway and Achill, 1913

The Árd Fheis in 1913 was held in Galway rather than Dublin. Dr Hyde's hitherto uncontested leadership of the Gaelic League was under threat from those who wanted a more political front. Hyde – or, as he was popularly called, An Craoibhín – was a dedicated Church of Ireland nationalist, and showed a particular interest in the gifted granddaughter of the famous Archbishop. He took time to seek her out, but Cesca was ill at ease with him, and – even though he is present at the beginning as well as the end of her diary – she would never be comfortable under his intent gaze. As soon as she arrived in Galway, Cesca went down to the quays in search of visual material for her first commission, to illustrate a book by the Galway writer, Pádraic Ó Conaire, whom she had come to know in the London branch of the Gaelic League.

'Galway is a beautiful old town,' she began in Irish, 'poor, more poverty than beauty, but that wasn't always the case. I was down at the harbour making a sketch for *Tír na nIongantas*[1] by Pádraig Ó Conaire, and I met a man who told me that he remembered when he was a boy there were thirteen mills working in Galway and now there is only one. I had noticed grass growing on all the piers, and the nearly empty harbour. I talked to him about the state of the Irish language, and he told me his father remembered when French, German, Spanish

1. *The Land of Wonders*, a book for children.

15 *Shawlies*

and Italian were spoken in the port, "and there were people there," he said, "who hadn't a word of English." "Was that difficult for them?" I said. "Not at all", said he.'

> Coming back I saluted various women and girls and they greeted me. The streets going down to the harbour are extremely narrow, and it would have been impossible to go past without a friendly word. The girls seem beautiful to me, but Miss Townshend says they are ugly in comparison with the girls of the South. She is a Munster woman, tall, slender, with pale grey hair, and she wears national costume, a green dress with Dun Emer embroidery, a gold brooch, and a gold comb in her hair. I have rarely seen a woman so beautifully attired as her – she was crossing Eyre Square one evening when Máighréad[2] and I were there. Coming up from the harbour I saw two men from Aran. They were fine big strong men, not at all like the Galway men. There is a look of independence

2. Her sister Margot.

in their eyes. One of them was going into the public house and the other was coming out.

Cesca had difficulty getting a ticket for the Árd Fheis, and hung round the premises until Pádraic Ó Conaire appeared.

After a while I saw him beckoning. I followed him through one room into another where Peadar Ó hAnnracháin[3] was sitting. "Sit down," he said briskly, and I sat down. He had a ticket in his hand and was writing something on it.

"Are you going to give me your own ticket?" I asked.

"No," he said. "This is Cathleen Ní Houlihan's ticket".[4] "Oh", I said. He went on writing. "She's a pretty girl," he said, "Nearly as pretty as you."

I was struck silent.

He finished and gave the ticket to me. "Now write your name here," he said.

I did so. "Now, the name Cathleen Ní Houlihan here," he said.

"She should have a pen," said Pádraig Ó Conaire. "Yes indeed," said Peadar Ó hAnnracháin, and he looked around for a pen.

There was none. "This will do," he said producing a purple pencil.

"Now – write in a different way," he said to me.

"Isn't my own writing clear enough?" said I. "Your own writing isn't what's needed," they said together. "It's Caitlín Ní Houlihan's writing we want," said Peadar quietly. "O – I understand – forgery," I said; and I wrote the name "Cathleen" in a different hand. The two of them scrutinised it. "That'll do," they said. "This is your ticket."

So I got into the Árd Fheis. The same night Máighréad and I were welcoming delegates, sitting at one side, when An Craoibhín came over and sat down. Perhaps he thought we were lonely.

"Were you in the Árd Fheis?" he asked . . ."Why did you leave so early?" "I was tired of the Árd Fheis," I said. "That's no excuse," he said. "Wouldn't you be inclined to leave if you could find an excuse," I said, forgetting all my Irish. "I'm angry with you," said An Craoibhín. "What will I do at all," said I, "I'm terrified out of my life". . . . He laughed.

An old blind piper was playing. I didn't like him and asked An Craoibhín his opinion . . . Then –

---

3. Peadar Ó Hannracháin (1873–1965) from Skibbereen, Co. Cork learnt Irish from about 1895, and published poetry, short stories, essays and drama in *An Claidheamh Soluis*.
4. 'Cathleen Ní Houlihan' is one of the traditional names for Ireland.

16 *Band*

> "You look like a Galway woman," he said staring at me. "Really?" I said, "Oh, of course, they have black hair." "And the eyes," he said, looking at me sharply like the old raven looks at Máire Bán in "Tír na nÍongantas." I looked at him intently but I wasn't able to follow his thinking. I am so scared of that man . . .

In the same way as Maud Gonne's commanding presence attracted attention in those heightened times, Cesca's unusual beauty served as an iconic symbol for elated imaginations. But the incident she relates reveals in a touching way the shyness beneath an exterior that appeared supremely confident. Her ever vigilant artist's eye made her self-conscious. Riding on the side car into Galway from the Oireachtas[5] she watched the reflections in the shop windows they were passing, 'Máighréad had a beautiful crocheted dress and a bright green cloak, and I was wearing a black and red dress with a purple cloak around me and a purpley red scarf on my head, and the colours went well together'. She was critical of the pipers they met and followed in Eyre Square. 'It's a great

5 The Gaelic League annual meeting.

pity their kilts aren't more impressive: they're totally disorganised, moving this way and that, with no sense of "style". Their playing is all right, but they're not as good as the Athlone pipers whom we heard last year at Castlebar. At least, in terms of their Gaelic appearance, the latter were much better.'

> We lingered in the Square for a little until it was time to go to the station. It was fair day. An Craoibhín came to say goodbye to us, and he said triumphantly that the Bishop was at the Oireachtas. He had been talking to him about other things before he came over to us. It is a great thing that the Bishop supports us, particularly in a place like Galway.

It was a very hot day, and 'scorching' going through West Connaught where there were no trees. The journey was long with three or four changes. When they reached the station near Gobacurry, hot, grimy and tired, one of the water pipes that filled the engine was dripping, and Cesca had pleasure in recording an example for detractors of Irish of how useful the language could be. The small party for Achill leapt out at once – Eoghan Penn, Siobhán,[6] Máighréad Ní Riordáin, her sister Máighréad and herself huddled together, wiping their hands under the dripping pipe, trying to save a drop to drink and stammering Gaelic among themselves, while Claud Chevasse[7] (remarkable for his height, and for the kilt he wore as everyday dress) spoke confidently with the engine driver and the stoker, both native speakers. The thin trickle of water stopped, whereupon the engine driver got down and started pumping so that the pipe streamed. The stoker found a rusty tin can and offered Máighréad a drink. Though Mrs Weddall was calling out imperiously that the train would be going, and the porter trying to order them back into the carriage, the train driver refused to hurry his new-found friends: he only shook the porter's hand telling him not to be worrying, and continued pumping, giving every one a drink.

When at last they reached Achill, there was still the journey from Gobacurry to Dooagh. It was evening and getting cold: but, for Cesca, the views from the monastery[8] to Keel were enchanting, the mist rising in great waves up

6. Siobhán Betts, Mrs Weddall's niece from Australia, spent vacations in Achill learning Irish and assisting at Scoil Acla.
7. His ancestor Claude Chavasse (son of Claudius Chavasse, owner of vineyards at Dauphiné in France) came to England during the Jacobite Rising of 1715 and settled at Burford in Oxfordshire. Son of an Oxford professor, he heard talk of the Irish movement at home, read Celtic studies at Oxford, and with Scottish students visited the West of Ireland to learn Irish. He wore a kilt, spoke excellent Irish with an educated English accent, and eventually lived at Ross House in Galway, former home of Violet Martin.
8. She may be referring to the settlement of the famous Achill Mission.

17 *At the Summit of Croaghaun*

the side of Croaghaun and the sun throwing an emerald colour on the grass. The air was filled with the scent of turf. 'Oh, it was beautiful!' she wrote. 'The same night, we went out . . . and saw the light still in the sky. My heart burned with a passion for Ireland.'

The two tutors of the summer school, An Paorach[9] and Dónal Ó Riordáin,[10] caused some concern as they were still out sailing in the mist, but they arrived back safely the next morning, and as soon as she heard An Paorach's voice Cesca came out to greet him. '"I heard that you are doing great work in Acaill Beag," I said. "Is the course bilingual? It is, isn't it?" His eyes lit up and he laughed . . ."Every instruction, every lesson except English, is in Irish," said he.' 'An Paorach,' she added, 'was wearing a brown hat with a broad brim, a

9. Francis Hugh Power, generally known as An Paorach. He worked as a civil servant in the London County Council Department of Education. A member of the Gaelic League he performed regularly at the St. Patrick's Day concerts in London, and founded the Irish Pipers' Club there in 1905. He returned to Ireland about 1906 to work for the revival of the Irish language.

10. Dónal Ó Riordáin (1888–1935), born in Limerick and co-founder of Scoil Acla. A piper, singer and dancer, he taught in Pearse's College, edited *Fuaim na Mara*, and translated Synge and Lady Gregory for the Taibhdhearc theatre in Galway. Father of Breandán O Riordáin, former Director of the National Museum of Ireland.

18 *An Paorach (1913)*

jersey and old stained breeches, and the oldest shoes I have ever seen, yet he looked splendid. He's a great little man, no doubt about it.'

The next morning, to mark the start of the course, they raised the flag Cesca had made, shouting, 'Up the Irish Language!' 'Such a ridiculous sight,' Cesca thought, 'Seven women in a line and An Paorach and Dónal at the head.'[11] She was depressed, the weather was bad, there was no news about the painting box she had mislaid at Claremorris, and she couldn't paint. Yet, apart from their enthusiasm for the Irish classes, the group of young aspirants – thrown together from various backgrounds because of their conviction that the native Irish culture was the only future for Ireland – had a really good time. The trip to Keem Bay, an exquisite beach beneath the mass of Croaghaun, was memorable.

> The girls from Granard[12] were wearing "motor-veils", with their hair piled high in a posh way, but we began – all of us – throwing things at their heads and that took the superiority out of them! We waited half-way . . . Dónal sang a song, and Máighréad and I gave a précis of the history of Ireland that Claud had given us the night before. Nóra Ní Chuinneagáin,[13] Bean an Uadallach, Siobhán, Dónal, the girls from Granard and An Paorach were out sailing, and the wind dropped and they were marooned for five hours. They missed the "History of Ireland" because of this. Nóra Ní Chuinneagáin was furious, she hated wasting her time in the boat. We went on then and waited again further up. Maighréad Ní Riordáin had a headache, and I was trying to get rid of it with massage. Everyone had arrived except for An Paorach, who was lame and came on a horse.
>
> When we reached Keem, An Paorach hadn't yet come, but as we started lunch someone spotted him on his white horse ambling up the road . . . Everyone ran on to the sand barefoot – except M. Ní Riordáin who said her headache had come back. We started playing Connacht and Munster and after three or four minutes M. Ní R. arrived barefoot – once more it was a wonderful cure! She has enormous feet, unlike

11. A photograph of Sadhbh Trínseach with her companions raising the banner she designed accompanies an article on Scoil Acla in *An Claidheamh Soluis* (20 Dec. 1913) p. 11.
12. In Co. Longford.
13. Nóra Cunningham, a minister's daughter. From 1907–8, Seán O'Casey had urged the Conradh to start a 'Gaelic League Mission to Protestants' to spread the nationalist gospel to all the Irish people and he was supported by Ernest Blythe, George Irvine, Nóra Ní Chuinneagáin, Sybil Tuckey and Séamus Deakin (who was later one of the leaders of the Irish Republican Brotherhood). The group pressed for Church of Ireland services in Irish, and persuaded the Grand Master of the Orange Lodge to send a memorandum to the Dean of St. Patrick's asking that services in Irish be introduced.

Maighréad and myself or the girls from Granard. Claud was leader of Connacht and Eoghan of our side, but they beat us although Dónal was with us, and he is a great runner . . .

A port and harbour official came down the meadow and watched our goings on. Shortly afterwards An Paorach went to talk to him, [he was] seated on a boat. On his return I said, "You had a nice talk with your English friend, didn't you?" "It's possible to learn from enemies", he said seriously!

It rained that evening but, what harm if it did, we had a wonderful view from the harbour. The sea was a dark turquoise under the rocks, and like opal further out. The hills on the other side were blue wraiths and the clouds huge and round, changing every moment in the gleaming blue sky. While we ate our tea, Dónal went out to play his pipes, walking up and down on the white strand. Siobhán was walking in the sea at the same time, holding her clothes up above her knees, her plump white feet looking good against the blue of the water. "Look! a seal!" called An Paorach. We saw something black coming close into the strand towards Siobhán and Dónal. They turned at the same time as the "seal" did and then we saw a wing shape like an ugly knife. "It's a shark! It's a shark!" shouted An Paorach, jumping up. "Get stones! We'll kill him, the blaggard!" Claud cried, and he and Eoghan and the other men leapt up, and they all ran down the strand and we followed them with stones. But when they reached the strand the shark had taken a dislike to them, not surprisingly, and disappeared in the twinkling of an eye. He dived not far away from me, and so we lost him.

We prayed down on the sand, standing in a line looking out on the sea. An Paorach put up the tent, and Dónal was soon blowing his pipes, inviting people to come to the céilidh. The children came running, and the older people more gradually, and we then started, songs and recitation and pipes and fiddle.

As we were waiting, some one said, "Hé, the moon should be in the sky, where is it?" Others began remarking on it and at that moment (An Paorach was playing the pipes in front of us) Máighréad took hold of my hand and said, "Look!" I looked. A golden shield was rising smoothly, right on the back of Croagh Patrick. It wasn't long before she was fully out, beautiful, noble, yellow. The tide was going out, it was the most stunning night I have ever seen. Sitting down was fairly chilly. Claud came over to us when there was a pause, and said "You'll get cold", and dropped his cloak over us. Then we went down to the part of the strand

19 *Máire and Treise Sleeping*

near the water, shining under the yellow moon, and we danced, black figures against the silver water, an enchanting scene.[14]

At half past nine we went up to the house again, and had supper. Claud sat down in the kitchen with a large slice of bread and jam on each knee, a slab of bread and sardines and "tongue" in each hand, and a cup of tea at his feet! We had to stop at last because supplies came to an end, only a small piece of cheese and oatcake left. We'd been saying it would be nice to go for a walk because it was still early, but we didn't in the end. The women headed for the tent and An Paorach and Seán Joyce to the boat. Mrs Weddall said to Máighréad, with a worldly wisdom which astonished her, that it would never do to have it said that the students spent the night walking about together. The women all lay down in the tent. M. and I let our hair down around us, that is to say north/southwards because we had it in two plaits. My cloak which is capacious, thank God, covered us, we had a mantle under us, and as we lay we were comfortable and warm from the walking. The moon shone in under the flap of the tent which was raised a little by Mrs Weddall who was lying next to me. I made a pillow for myself from the sand. Poor Nóra Ní Chuinneagáin complained of a headache and earache but I think she was warm enough.

But what a night! After a while suffering from pins and needles in my feet, Mrs W. advised me to go out for a walk. M. and I slipped out and saw Claud coming down with something white on his shoulders. He saw us going over to the water. "You're not going swimming at this hour!" said M. and myself, and "Are you going in to swim?" he said at the same time, and we answered the questions together. "Have you seen my cloak up there?" asked M . . ."Are you cold?" said Claud, "Here – put this on,"

14. The following year, in the Paris atelier, Cesca did her composition *Dance*, inspired by this experience.

20 *Siobhán Sleeping*

and he put his brat[15] round her. . . ."I'll get the cloak – wait here," and he went off.

M. and I strolled up and down on the sand. The golden moon was riding high and it was bitterly cold. We saw An Paorach's boat lying peacefully on the water in the shelter of the cliff, the sail arranged like a tent over her. Claud came back with Máighréad's cloak. She put it on and gave Claud's brat to me . . ."I've found a nice hole among the rocks for a bed", said Claud. "Come and see it." We ran there. The sand felt hard without shoes. It was nice. "I was told that it was a place the pigs frequent," said Claud. "But I'll be grand and warm – and dry, the sea won't come as high as this, please God," . . . and he indicated the shelter the island gave – apart from his brat and some other covering.

I was sorry to have to relinquish the brat when we went back, it was so nice and warm, and I had reservations about our own quarters . . . "Did you know Chevasse would be out there?" Mrs Weddall asked sleepily in English. "No," said Máighréad. I didn't take much notice of the question, neither did M., I think, but what cheek. We'd have been furious if we had. The other girls were walking about outside, and we called them in severely!

So the night passed, cold and uncomfortable, but happy. M says that every time the girls from Granard moved they pulled some of the cover from her. I know every time I myself moved, my head was squashed on my sand pillow. Everyone woke early. Mrs W. enquired how we had passed the night. We were fit to laugh at everything. Each described her experience. "You've got a nice way of behaving, Máighréad Ní Riordáin", I said, "Didn't anyone hear her, she shouted out just as I was trying to get to sleep,

15. The short Irish cloak or mantle, worn with kilt or Gaelic dress, served a variety of purposes.

21 *Cottage in Achill*

> 'What'll I do at all now?'" . . . "On the contrary", said my Máighréad, "She said, 'What'll I do at all now, lads?" whereupon you said severely, 'Don't do that, anyway'". "And," said I, "*you* added firmly, 'There are no lads here'".
>
> Everyone tried to go to sleep again for a little. I went out [to see] the rising sun. In the West great amber and topaz clouds tipped with red were coming up in the opal sky and I couldn't distinguish where the sea began. Deep brown knotted rocks were sticking out of the sea, garbed in smooth gleaming green seaweed. The hollow between the two islands shone under the blue veil of morning dew. With M's cloak thrown over my shoulders I soon found it too warm. I went to get washed, but it was difficult to find any water. M. and I prowled about together with bars of soap in our hands. Then I went back carrying my purple cloak which M. had brought out with her, and her blue cloak. I put the purple cloak on the ground, lay on it, and put the blue one over part of me. Considering the blouse I was wearing was red, the whole colour combination was rather fine. Lying there I wished I could see myself . . .

Cesca wrote glowingly about the visit to Achillbeg Island where An Paorach lived in a cottage. She brought drawing book, knife, pencil and rubber, to make sketches. 'I wore my red skirt, with a red linen blouse, and brought my purple cloak and my big deep blue brat. Máighréad had another brat and her blue cloak, and her blouse crocheted from fine wool and a crocheted skirt. That was plenty. My satchel would act as a pillow for me, and the same for Máighréad.' The women travelled on the side-car and the men in An Paorach's boat.

> It was a fine sunny day when we reached the harbour above Achill Beag. The fresh blue water was clear and quiet enough, but there were strong currents and they made stripes the colour of violets across it. There is a little opening between the island and the mainland where there are big rocks, and the waves were swelling over them, luminous and soaring, with the wind above them.
>
> We weren't there long when we saw the bright sail of An Paorach's boat going by, but we had to wait for an hour or so before he came up to us. The boat had to go round past the island, and when she was between the land and the island it was hard work to cross the waves. Mac uí Ceó[16] had a telescope and lent it to us, and when Mrs. Weddall looked she swore she could see the sail, the blue of the sail, even though the boat was so small that you could scarcely see the mast . . .

16. This may be the Keogh who was a celebrated professional photographer in Dublin at the time.

22 *An Paorach Sitting*

They eventually arrived at Achillbeg harbour, and climbed the cliff path to the little house where An Paorach had a room.

> M. and I went in and out getting tea for ourselves and the other people, white bread for cutting, butter to put on it, sardines and jam – we were very busy. Claud came in once and said, "Ach, you're not getting a bit for yourselves", but we drove him out saying that there wasn't enough room for a person so huge.
>
> The room was small enough. On the wall was a notice saying that "the undersigned" promised the Sacred Heart that he wouldn't drink at all during his life or something like that, in language of the most hysterical emotion – a promise no better than a lie. An Paorach has the odd book and a bed etc, and a fire, as if we weren't warm enough from our walk down to the house! The others sat out on the stones in the sun. When the girls came back (they had gone to the top of the hill on the island), M. Ní R. and Seán Joyce sat in a corner in the room and ate everything they were given.
>
> The island is really a double island. There's a little harbour on the east side with rough black rocks at the entrance which are covered with short – incredibly green – sweet grass. We all wanted to go to the top of the eastern hill,[17] and Máighréad and I went saying to ourselves that we would

17. Knockmore.

23 *The Trench Family at Home*

> cross the shoulder of the island and find some way of going up the east side. We came down a meadow between the two hills, and up again on a bright green grassy place on the opposite side, but it wasn't much good for the sort of climb we had promised ourselves. When we reached the cliff a great gaping chasm opened up before us, with sea water pounding away below. Myself and Nóra Ní Chuinneagán made the summit however . . .

Cesca's romantic response to landscape in the wake of writers like Synge and Loti led her to resort to superlatives from Gaelic poetry as she expressed the emotion the West of Ireland coast aroused in her:

> there was a wonderful view from that spot towards Ireland and Gobacurry, everything bright blue, mauve and green, shining with the sun – Oh Ireland, love of my heart, my soul, my delight, my treasure, my darling! . . .

Regrettably for her and Margot, because of the way political events were shaping, it was their last visit to Achill and the carefree fun they enjoyed there. When the Summer School came to an end on 31 August, they went home to 'the people . . . common and vulgar and Folkestone dressed',[18] back to intelligent debates about communism and theosophy, back to repetitive arguments with Unionists of the immediate family and despairing confrontations about the Irish Question with the rigid Trench cousins and their circle. Cesca's annoyance was relieved by high points such as a visit to the exhibition of Velasquez and the seventeenth century Spanish masters in London in October, or the excitement on September 19 – 'Yesterday we all ran out before breakfast to see an airship. It was moving very quickly, high up, and making a harsh sound. Herbert was

18. Cesca's comment in an undated letter to Máighréad.

the first to hear it, and told us it was there. We didn't see it at first because it was over the house. "Did you know it was an airship from the sound?" I asked Herbert. "I'd know that sound anywhere," he said, his eyes flaming.'

Cesca would have much more opportunity to experience the thrill of this modern innovative science when she reached Paris,[19] where on 22 November they went to the cinema. 'There was a drama about "Seventy", very good, but the Pathé Gazette was wonderful, Chevillard and Hucks, the Englishman,[20] making circles in the air: and it said that another man today did something terrible, coming down head first to within five metres of the ground and then turning and going straight. It said that people are going wild too. Another day there was a great wind at Içy [sic], and the airmen didn't want to go up and people were so angry that they threw stones and shouted at them. It's as bad as the Romans.' They went to an exhibition of airships with her brother Reggie (Raghnal) on St. Stephen's night, 'I didn't know that they could be so interesting. They are a passion. There was every kind there and R. knew some of them and explained them to us. There was a Cinema Pathé "spectacle" in the same hall of every contest big or small of airships that happened recently. This Swiss man, B—(I don't remember his name), was in it and he was flying through the Alps. A story came yesterday about a man who flew three hundred miles in five hours, and he was higher than six miles up in the clouds all the time and he knew where he was. He saw the top of the Jungfrau[21] sticking up into the clouds.'

Cesca's main preoccupation before she left Folkestone for the atelier in Paris was making greetings cards for the Gaelic League. 'We're doing our best on the cards,' she wrote on 16 October. 'Goodness me it's hard work. We're absolutely exhausted, the horrid little things. We got an order for 84 *Nodlaig na nGaedheal* [Irish Christmas], 12 *Dia do Bheatha* [God Bless You], and 36 *Céad Míle Fáilte* [A hundred thousand welcomes], from Mrs Weddall today.[22] I sent her a card saying, "The order will be sent to you during the week," – very "business-like" altogether! *Cumann Gaedhealach na gCártaí* [The Irish Guild of Cards] is "hectographed" on the covers and we have to do everything properly,

19. International aviation had advanced immeasurably through half a decade due to the enthusiasm of competing pioneers, and had now reached a high degree of sophistication. Some of the most successful experiments took place at the French flying ground at Issy, and at Buc aerodrome near Versailles where the loop-the-loop was first performed.
20. Hucks was the first Englishman to fly upside-down, in September 1913, two months after French pilot Pegoud.
21. One of the highest peaks in the Berner Alpen, Switzerland.
22. In Notebook 2077TX (National Library of Ireland) there is a sketch of Mary and the Child with a young man in brat and file, and other sketches, ideas for further Christmas cards.

24 *Gaelic League Christmas Cards*

and write down in the book everything we have paid out. We have a little black book that belonged to my father, and my mother put it into a rummage sale at St. Saviour's because it was nearly empty, but I retrieved it and am using it now.' The design of her cards was affected by Jack B. Yeats's strong outline, adopted by young artists like Beatrice Glenavy who designed for his sister at Cuala, and which later as a recognised national style would influence the productions of the Cluna Press. Cesca's version reflected her own personality, with a raw, rather than sweet, element that was natural to her way of expression.

> Miss Every was here this afternoon. I met her going past the park. When she came near, I called out to her reproaching her for going away before I had come back. "I know you're going to give your life for your country", she said when she came up to me. "Why, do you think people are going to rise up and kill me?" I said laughing. "Yes I know you are", she said, "You're such a patriot, you'll be a martyr to the cause and one day

we shall see in the paper" – she shook her head. "But they don't make martyrs for the cause now", said I. "I wish they did, the cause'd be much more flourishing. What's going to happen to make a martyr of me?"

"Ah what is going to happen in Ireland", said she, "I'm sure I wish I knew," sadly. "It'll be very interesting to see," I said guardedly.

PART TWO

'The Paris Atelier'

AN CLAIDEAMH — Aibreán 4, 1914

Éadaige Bán

Now that the season of Feiseanna and reachtas is at hand, it is the duty of every shwoman to supply herself with a National stume. This is a patriotic duty which volves no sacrifice, for the dress is artistilly beautiful, delightfully comfortable to ar, and equally becoming to young and old

designed dresses to wear, felt cheap and commonplace when walking about with the men in their gay fileadh-beags, a feeling which no self-respecting Cailini like to have. Two drawings of the dress were given recently in an Claidheamh, one of which shows it simplified and adapted to children. We give

However, other Irish materials sug themselves, and for those who can affor a brat of Irish poplin is very beaut The price of the paper pattern of the ro 6d. and embroidery designs ready for iro on the material, cost 1s. 6d. Both of t can be had from Deora Frinseach, Se

25 *National Costume designed by Deóra Frínseach, published in An Claidheamh Soluis, 1914*

3
Cesca the Artist

A large portion of the diary was written while Cesca was at art school in Paris. Being an artist was not unusual for a Trench. A cousin of the le Poer branch, Eileen le Poer Trench had had her work accepted by the Academy, exhibiting for a few years running, and there were other Trenches before and after her exhibiting there, or with the Watercolour Society, and various British institutions.[1] None became famous, but there was a strong vein of artistry in the family, and Cesca certainly merited the good grounding in drawing she was fortunate to acquire at school in Malvern. She began using a perpendicular board when she went there, doing a study of Dante's head from a cast at fifteen, and she was continually encouraged by her tutor, a Miss Farmer. Despite this, she didn't go immediately to art school, and when at last she did at the age of twenty-two, she was conscious of how extremely young some of her fellow students were and how enviably talented.

Descriptions of views that excited her while in Achill and Clare may be ecstatic and often poetic – like most creative people she found the Irish countryside a heady inspiration – yet she was not interested in painting traditional Irish landscapes. Her artistic leaning was towards the figurative and the symbolic. She wanted to paint portraits and thematic pictures, and took her training

1. See A. Stewart, *Royal Hibernian Academy of Arts: Index of Exhibitors and their Works*, 1826–1979, vol. 3 (Dublin, Manton, 1987); Theo Snoddy, *Dictionary of Irish Artists: 20th Century* (Dublin, Wolfhound Press, 1996).

seriously, eager to learn as much as she could. While Irish art students before her headed for Colarossi's – known, as Julian Campbell has recorded,[2] as the 'ladylike studio near the Étoile' – and she did draw from the nude there from time to time – her background, with prolonged periods in Switzerland, Italy and India as a girl, had given her a different experience. She decided to work in the studio of Émile-René Ménard,[3] a Barbizon-trained painter. He and her other tutor, Lucien Simon,[4] had been members of the Bande Noir, followers of Cottet, the Breton realist and symbolist, in Paris of the 1890s. Known as the 'Nubians', as opposed to the more radical 'Nabis' who grouped around the 'prophets' Bonnard and Vuillard, they admired Courbet, and the monumental classicism of Puvis de Chavannes, and in their small scale *intimiste* subjects emphasised drawing and warm colour.

The political situation in Ireland remained very much on Cesca's mind, and she kept in touch with what was happening by letter and newspaper, eager to be back in Dublin as soon as the Home Rule question came to a head. Her love for Ireland was obsessive, and she peopled her view of history with images of Celtic heroes of the past or those who resisted the foreigner invader in seventeenth century Ireland. 'One thing I can be certain about,' she told Margot after a few months in Paris, 'There is something great in store for the Celts. I see this in a way I never did before I came to France, they look on Éire as a mother, the personification of inspiration for the Celtic race.'[5]

Convinced that her future was to be in a new Irish-Ireland, the commission to illustrate *Tír na nIongantas*[6] by Pádraic Ó Conaire had been most welcome. She had worked at the project, sending her illustrations to the writer for approval – but to her disappointment, after much delay, it came to nothing. The book was eventually published in 1916 with a cover design by Jack Morrow, and without the images which she had been trying unsuccessfully to retrieve from Ó Conaire. According to his biographer, Andrias Ó Cathasaigh, it was difficult enough then to publish in Irish since there was little profit, and publishers were reluctant to include illustration. Ó Conaire did however ask

2. 'Art students and lady travellers: Irish women artists in France, 1870–1930', in *Irish Women Artists from the 18th Century to the Present Day* (Dublin, National Gallery of Ireland and Douglas Hyde Gallery, 1987) p. 18.
3. (1862–1930) pupil of Theodore Rousseau and Troyon, and friendly with Corot, Millet and Diaz. He encouraged mythology and symbolism, and preferred inspiration to representation.
4. (1861–1945), a pupil of Bouguereau, he painted popular scenes of Brittany and decorative panels inspired by Pierre Loti's novel of Breton life, *Pêcheur d'Islande*.
5. Cesca to Margot, c 1914.
6. *Tír na nIongantas* had been serialised in *An Claidheamh Soluis* (8 Mar.–27 Sept. 1913).

26 *Sketch for Gaelic League Poster, 1913*

Cesca to do the cover for his volume of short stories, *An Chéad Chloch,*[7] and it was to appear in August 1914 with her stylised Salome, that might almost be a self-portrait, a strong black outline dancing languidly across the centre of the rose coloured linen, head thrown back.

There may be nothing particularly nationalistic about the Salome, but the striking Éire/West Britain poster[8] she made for the Gaelic League's Seachtmhain na Gaeilge language collection, another early commission, carries a strong political message. A preliminary sketch in an early notebook dates to July 1913,[9] and she completed the poster – executed on two sheets of cartridge paper – some months later while in Paris. She wrote on 22 November, 'Today I was making a propaganda poster, Gaelic Ireland and West Britain. A dark black-haired girl was posing for me and she held an umbrella like a spear and two young men in front of her [were] trying to make her laugh but after a while they hadn't succeeded.' Éire-Ireland, unlike mendicant West Britain, is elegantly artistic. Dressed in a rose red Celtic robe, a filet binding her braided hair, she commands the map of Ireland, controlling all the shipping with one hand and holding a spear in the other. Poor West Britain, with a Union Jack for clothes, crouches on the east coast, looking towards England with outstretched palm. She sees the merchant ships all issuing from the British ports.

7. See p. 105. Cesca saw Ó Conaire in London in June 1914, and began to design the book cover on her return to Dublin shortly afterwards.
8. National Museum no. 2671, see col. plate 1.
9. The sketch for the two figures in the poster appears in Notebook 2078TX in the National Library of Ireland, among sketches of Scoil Acla, July 1913. See fig. 26.

Cesca is asserting Sinn Féin's confidence in unilateralism, asking 'On which side are you?' and urging support for the national language. The gold sunburst on a blue ground between the two figures is drawn from the new Gaelic League flag,[10] and she signs her initials 'S.T.' in Gaelic characters, as she did on her Gaelic League Christmas cards.

These early images were a promising start. She arrived in Paris confidently. She had already been to art classes there during the winter of 1912/13 – the undocumented experience is referred to in passing in the *Malvern Newsheet* published at Christmas 1913: 'Chesca Chenevix Trench . . . Studied painting in Paris last winter . . .' The diary, subsequently commenced, as a whole contains little information about her work as an artist, other than noting people of arresting appearance, colours she caught sight of, possibilities for subject matter and the names of some compositions, so the account of her second period of study embarked on in October 1913 (a rare enough document in art history) is particularly interesting.

She was returning to the apartment in the rue d'Assas, near the Sorbonne, which she had occupied with her mother during her first sojourn. Her life, according to her French friend, Gab Genoud,[11] who owned the Left Bank apartment, was 'so full of disruption, undertakings, ideas, that one is never sure whether you are using your time as is best for you . . .' Nothing could daunt Cesca:

> 68 Rue d'Assas Paris VIième. 26th October 1913. Máire[12] and I came here last night. It's amazing how short the time seems since we were here before. The woman who had Máire's apartment went off suddenly and she didn't leave the key with the concierge. Because of this Máire had to sleep here last night. She came back with me, and the Mademoiselles Genoud[13] gave us a great welcome. They were very affectionate with us.
>
> Yesterday morning we went to mass and after breakfast to Máire's concierge. "Would you mind," we said, "if we climbed up on the roof with the ladder that's there; and then we'll open the window in the appartement and, once in, the key is there". But she wasn't interested. She didn't like

10. The Conradh's original flag was blue and orange. In 1912 a competition for a new design was won by The O'Rahilly's yellow sunburst with 17 rays, alternately long or short, on a field of blue.
11. To Cesca, from Paris, 29 Sep. 1913.
12. Cesca tended to give her friends Irish names: Marie, a fellow student during her first period at art school in Paris and now a close friend, for the duration of her studency was dubbed 'Máire'.
13. Gabrielle and her sister Ferdinande, propriétaires of the apartment.

27 *The Atelier, Sketch of an Art Class*

> the idea. The roof was at a steep angle. If anything happened she would have the responsibility, and certainly we mustn't do it. It's such a nuisance going up with "himself" to see if the lock can be forced from outside.
>
> We went up, then there was the ladder and after that the window. One can always have a look. I climbed up quickly, and – believe me – once up, I didn't go down. I took my shoes off, and I found the right window. Máire climbed up to confirm it. I hit my hand on the glass and broke it. I opened the window. Máire kept it open and I lowered my shoes and the umbrella and myself down seven feet or so. Then there was the key to find. But it wasn't there. All I could do was to struggle with the lock. I did this, but still it wouldn't open. The lock continued to stick on the other side. In the end, Máire and the concierge put their full weight on the door on their side, and I pulled, levering it as wide as I could from my side, and it opened. My word, it was a great victory.

'The real work begins tomorrow,' she continued rather precociously, 'skill in our hands rather than "strength". Inspiration in our hearts & truth in our mouths are the tools a painter needs.'

Under Ménard, Cesca was to develop her strong dark outline and controlled pictorial energy, together with a relaxed expertise in charcoal and pastel. Two scenes done in Paris[14] – an Irish class at Scoil Acla being conducted by Claud Chevasse, and a critique in the atelier – are vivacious, and confident in the art of composition. Of course the students concentrated on life drawing, a daily discipline. Cesca always made sure she arrived early, noting on her first day of attendance, 'I went to the atelier early in the morning to get a good place. I got number eight . . . The poor model was very pale, and she had to rest frequently. It was a difficult pose but she was rather ill as well.' The models, who worked in poor conditions and were often in poor health, troubled her. Sometimes they fell asleep, sometimes they were late – the male students occupied the time playing football in the studio as they waited. Another 'was sitting down, her head in her hands, on the "throne". I went to talk to her. She said she had a heavy cold and she felt shivery even though the room was very warm. She had a fever, and she was as white as the wall. I gave her a half box of Bromoquine.' One girl who was late was wearing rouge, 'but looked very sick and the rouge couldn't hide it . . . She looked so white the first hour that I thought that she was going into decline. She told me that she was posing repetitively the day before yesterday from one o'clock to seven and after that till midnight, and the

14. Both in the National Gallery collection, NGI 3812–3821.

same thing yesterday. She gets up everyday at half past six. The nice dark girl said to me, "look how she is painted. God knows where she is come from." But I told her as much as I knew about her.' She changed her opinion about an English girl because of the latter's sympathy for the sitter:

> We had a very lovable lad for a model tonight, seven or eight years of age with a head of long brown hair and he seemed frightened of us but had courage at the same time. I gave him a couple of sweets and he sat down resting and washing himself and he had a little shirt on and he was looking over his shoulder. When I came in after buying them I waited at the door so that no one would see me except for the boy and I showed him the sweets. A very small smile came onto his face. We gave him a pose that was very tiring, his foot up and him doing his shoe. There was a plump English girl there, a girl we didn't respect very much. After 15 minutes she said in her anglicized French, "Shouldn't he have a rest?" I have great respect for her now, nobody else would say so although it was quite clear that the pose was bothering him greatly.

The adult male models adopted the classical poses, holding or defending themselves with a stool. Cesca had special praise for another 'smashing model, fundamentally, I like her – she is half-draped. My word she is difficult. I am doing it 'saleté'[15] as I usually do.' A fragment of one of Cesca's life sketches – a pair of legs – is preserved in the National Gallery of Ireland collection.

Cesca told her fellow students that she was at art school to learn to compose pictures of the history of Ireland. One day she started a composition of a céilí in Achill – after a visit to Versailles. 'I went to the school the same night, but I didn't draw well at all, I was much too tired. Though I got a good enough "crit" from Simon! He said my thing was "perfect", but he only stayed a couple of minutes. I started on a composition of a céilidh in Achill. Seán mac Piotáin is in it, and Ceaim Síoda, and Máirín Ruadh and her son, and Claud ruling the fields, and many others whose names I have forgotten. It's a pity that, as I was working on it that night, I put in a Tipperary man, with head long, round and black, chin and mouth pointed: and now he has a sorrowful lonely air, even though he is watching the dance, I imagine because he is among strangers. Certainly he looks out of place. Perhaps it's because I am a Tipperary woman that he came in, but he will have to go.'[16]

---

15. 'Darkly' or 'murkily'.
16. Her pastel landscape of Achill (or Connemara), Cat. 22, may have been made about the same time.

28 *Claud Chevasse Teaching an Irish Class on Achill Island*

29 *Models in the Atelier*

Cesca was overwhelmed by Versailles. 'It was the first sunny day,' she wrote on 3 November regarding the trip a few days earlier, 'and the last it seems, for there's been no sun since. It's very obvious to posterity that Louis XIV was enormously arrogant, because it was his arrogance that told him that nothing less magnificent than Versailles was good enough for him. When you stand on the terrace, you could say that you are seeing to the edge of the world. The clear blue water stretches into the distance, with the "green carpet", as it is called, to each side, and the wood on each side of the carpet, yellow and gold and red and brown like a grove in a fairy story.' She went to Amboise and Touraine in the spring, had a quick trip to Boulogne to see the Lenten procession, and, in February, visited Moret sur Loing (haunt of Sisley and Monet) to paint, dressed as a rustic in the tradition of the original Barbizon artists.

> Moret, 8 February 1914. I am writing this in the café of this hotel, Hotel de la Palette, the walls covered with pictures made by artists who have been here. Yesterday Maud and I reached this place, and left our baggage and went immediately into the Forest, and we didn't come back

until 12.15. Then we ate lunch with three country people and the woman of the house, who started when we were all satisfied, and we went out again to the Forest. I took off my shoes and it was beautiful to walk barefooted on the dead leaves and the green moss and the black clay. We reached a soft moss bank and lay down in the sunlight and looked at the slender firs swaying and creaking in front of the blue sky. I almost fell asleep.

Next we did a little "exploration" and then went back a small part of the way and came on the Route de Vidossang. We followed it and came to a place where a man and woman were burning wood. When the woman saw us she called, "Come and warm yourselves at this fine fire and welcome." "It would do us good," I said, and we leapt across the leaves to them. I helped them burn the wood and they were astonished that I was barefoot. The woman said to me that I had a country person's instincts, that I looked no more than sixteen, and that ouillade boeuf was the best thing to make the hair grow. In the twilight, we came back together to their house. She told me her age and showed me her thick long hair. She showed me her garden with vines, and every kind of rose and strawberries, and finally she gave us a long narrow cup of wine she had made herself. She said I was as pretty as the Virgin, and one would never tire of being with me, and she put us on the right road. We came back in starlight and reached our hotel at six or so.

I bought the colours I needed and had a brief look about the town. At seven we ate a large supper and by half past eight I was in bed. This morning, Sunday, I woke at half past five, and went out to make a picture of the sunrise. Alas that the light comes so quickly. At eight we went to Mass in a beautiful old church with dreadful windows and we ate breakfast. Then we explored the town. My word it is stunning. At ten we went out to the Forest and we are there since. To the viewing point, over to the Long Rocher, and now we are at the Pleine de Rozoir. At the Carrefour du Croix de la Grand Maître, a gentleman asked me the way to Marlotte. He thought that I was a peasant, I was without shoes or hat, and had a bright red silk scarf on my head . . .

We came back, and on the way we went past a place where the elms were growing straight and bare and grey on yellow-brown earth with dead leaves, and the bright gold sky and green foliage behind them. Oh they were beautiful! I made a picture of them and as we were walking Maud threw it on the ground. (Not deliberately.) When we came to the railway it was dark and the moon was up. We met three country people

> and they asked had we lost our way. We said we hadn't. "You know the convict is lost for the second time, so be careful."

Cesca occupied her time fully, going to concerts and picture galleries, attending a session in the Parlement, and she heard mass regularly in the great Parisian churches. The Sainte Chapelle impressed her. 'I've never seen anything as beautiful as its windows, tall, rich, dark, glowing with colour. But the colour! It seemed to me that if I should stay there long enough everything would be decided for me.' A constant inspiration for her eyes, when she passed through the Place in front of the Invalides, was the Celt in the garden.[17] When she and Máire came out from Mass at the Benedictines, they went into the little public garden in front of the hostel. 'There was a statue there, a fine young strong slender Gael looking at his sword. "Now the roman eagle should be under his foot," said I. "But look," said Máire, "it is". I looked and it was sure enough. There was a sign there; I didn't recognise it at the time.'

She went to lectures on a wide range of subjects, and bought Bergson's *L'Evolution Créatrice*, the central philosophical concept of which – 'je suis une chose qui dure' – was much discussed among Parisian intellectuals at the time and reaffirmed her own feelings about reincarnation. After a lengthy lecture at the Vieux Colombier Theatre, which as an interior she admired, she denounced Rimbaud, 'a man who was not very likeable . . . and hated the human condition', and she dismissed Laforgue for his 'sympathie de femmes' – 'my impression is that it was decadent poetry although it had a lot of beauty.'

> The same night to the Salle Gaveau.[18] It was the worst day since we came here but it was the greatest day of them all! Oh if I should live to be a hundred I would never hear anything as glorious as *Bonnets à Poils*. It isn't right to play this kind of thing in a public place, it arouses every kind of hidden sentiment. I could hardly sit still.[19]

In March 1914 Cesca and Róisín bought tickets to see Sara Bernhardt on stage, and had a mixed reaction. 'She has a wonderful voice but she was playing *Phèdre,* and it is a drama of destruction, and in the second act where she is in love with Hippolyte she was screeching. There was an awful delay at the beginning of the act.' About the same time, the Abbey Players came from Dublin, presenting *Riders to the Sea, How he Lied to her Husband* and

17. This copy of a Roman statue which so fascinated Cesca is no longer in situ.
18. Musical salon situated between Bd. Haussman and Faubourg St. Honoré.
19. The military melody, 'Fur Bonnets', arr. J. Furgeot, popular for parades. A sketch (fig. 30) of two girls singing in NL notebook 2074TX refers to this.

30 *Bonnets à Poil*

The Shadow of the Glen with the actors Máire O'Neill and W.G. Fay. 'She was only middling but he was good,' Cesca thought.

Another notable performer had an accident.

> Monday 9th March 1914. Yesterday I was painting Mr. Louis, and Mme Acley [?Ackerly] said that Mr. Debussy had broken his thumb and he wouldn't be able to play tomorrow. We were all commiserating about him when Mr. Louis said, "Well it's about time something happened to him." We were all asking why, and he said, "Did you hear about the woman who killed herself for him?" "Well, don't tell me anything horrid about him for I just adore his music," said Donna. "Maybe it wasn't his fault," I said. "It was his fault," said Mr. L. gloomily.

Cesca's friendship with 'the brown man from Alsace' was ambiguous, partly a flirtation – though he professed to be in love with some one else – and partly stemming from of a genuine interest in each other's work. They shared an interest in reincarnation and Celtic culture. Georges Cornélius always sat near Cesca at the atelier – in a letter of January 1914, she described him to Margot as an 'iasg ait' – 'a queer fish'.

15th November . . . Yesterday I was teaching Irish to Róisín Blaud and the brown-haired man was near her. "What's that tongue," he said. "It's from the Celtic," said Róisín. He leapt up from his stool and he came nearer. We continued for a moment and translated for him. He said, "I know the five circles, isn't it, of Armron and Abred." I didn't understand, although I heard the sound as being familiar. "What are you saying?" said I, and he was still explaining when the model began posing and we had to shut up. Today he came in when I was getting my things from my locker. "Good morning mademoiselle," said he in his slightly German French, and he went in. When I went in, I found the *Revue d'Nations* on his stool. I began drawing, and he came after a while and showed the essay about *The Book of the Bards* to me. There is a lot there about reincarnation, and the Cercles and such things.

"Oh! You take this?" I said. "Yes," said he. "I also," said I. "What country do you come from?" "Alsace," he said. "Then you are a Celt?" said I. "Yes indeed I am," he said cheerfully. After that we talked about the essay. He is a Lutheran but says that he hates Christianity and that he believes this (nodding at the *Review*) "and is this not a thousand times better than the Jewish inventions about Purgatory et cetera." "But it's the same thing under different names," I said . . . He agreed with me about that. Later he said that he read the Gospel three times and that he hated it . . . "And why, we Celts, must we have a Jewish God?" . . . "I have much more respect for people since I have believed in reincarnation." "Me too," he said. "Give me your hand!" I did.

16th November 1913. Today I was late at the studio after *The Three Musketeers* last night. I didn't like it this time half as much as the last time. It's a great pity that none of them had any morals, either man or woman. After one of the breaks, going back to my place the brown man from Alsace said, "Mademoiselle, help me", in a voice that was very melancholy. He was "tied up" with the head, which wasn't very like, but I was surprised that he would ask me for help. I didn't help him, I'm no good at that. You can understand that he didn't want to show me his canvas yesterday because he said it was so bad! He said that he made a "composition" of Cuchulain, and that he would show it to me if I liked. He said it was good certainly. I would hope so because he has much talent for compositions.

19th November

I went to see the pictures of M. Cornélius, the Alsacien, today. He asked me to go on Monday, and we arranged for today. He and his

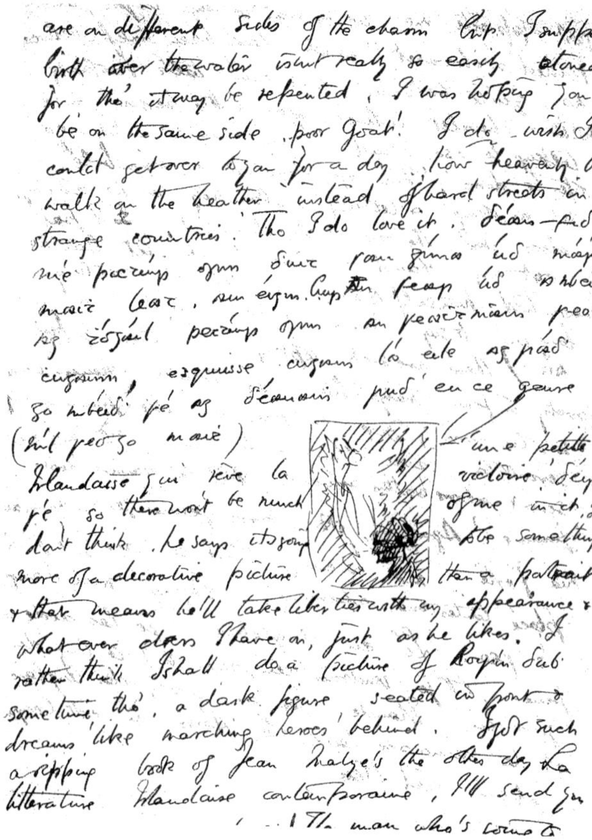
are on different sides of the channel tho. I suppose birth over the water isn't really so easily atoned for tho' it may be repented. I was hoping you'd be on the same side, poor goat! I do wish I could get over to you for a day, how heavenly to walk on the heather instead of hard streets in strange countries. Tho I do love it. [illegible] esquisse [illegible] en ce genre ([illegible]) une petite Irlandaise qui rêve la victoire [illegible] there won't be much of me in it, I don't think. He says it's going to be something more of a decorative picture than a portrait & that means he'll take liberties with my appearance & whatever dress I have on, just as he likes. I rather think I shall do a picture of Roisin Dubh sometime tho', a dark figure seated in front & dreams like marching heroes behind. I got such a ripping book of Jean Malye's the other day La littérature irlandaise contemporaine, I'll send you [illegible] the man who's coming to

31 *Letter to Margot mentioning Georges Cornélius, 1914*

mother have an apartment in the Boulevard Raspail.[20] I went up in a lift. I rang the bell a little fearfully. An old woman came and showed me into a salon with a lot of pictures arranged on the wall. After a couple of minutes waiting, M. Cornélius came in and welcomed me. We went into his studio and then I found out that he didn't know my name!

He has a big divan on one side of the room and a nice large window at the top. We talked and he showed me his pictures and compositions. One of them tells the story of the birth of Cuchulain, that some god made himself into a tree and caught a nymph whom he loved. They are strong pieces, but seemed morbid to me and weird. One of the pictures was of an old woman and a girl, and I said something about age and youth. "No, Mlle," he said, "it's worse than that," and he told a story of how he had seen that old woman with the girl, and it was the old woman who accosted the man and offered him her granddaughter, and she was painted – . It was a strange thing for the man to be telling a story like that to me but

20. Not far from where Cesca was living. The boulevard cuts across the end of the rue d'Assas.

he did it in a very simple way, "that's what I saw," he said in a melancholy voice.

His mother came in while he was showing me his compositions, a middle-aged woman, very fat with an old brown skirt and black blouse, and she sat beside me on a stool that her son gave her. Some of the pictures were of women who had given themselves up to vice, or who dance after the god of gold. I said they were all "of very weak women." "Yes, he always chooses weak-willed women, doesn't he?" she said. When she came inside she said to me that she had heard a lot about me from her son. I wonder what he said?

After a little while she went off again and he showed me some more of his pictures . . . He sat down then and began talking about the things people say to him about his "symbolism", "but M'sieu, it isn't art, it is literature," and such like; and he said that he was very discouraged now that he knew that there was nothing there but a premonition of a step into the future. At the beginning of this conversation, he said, "So M'elle, do you think that I've been wasting my time?" "Wasting your time," I said, completely surprised. "Yes, you don't think I would be better to be a mason or something?" he said this in all seriousness, I do believe. Mme Cornélius came in and told us to come to tea. I followed her to the salon through another room where M. Cornélius was waiting to wet the tea. A lady and a man, a couple, were there, and Mme. C. said introducing me, "Here is our young Celte". Then the man started talking to me about the Celts, giving me his chair, and he went on talking till we went into tea having been told that the son had it ready for us.

Then German words started coming into the talk here and there, and at every moment "Alscace" . . . The lady asked would the Home Rule Bill be going through. I said I thought it would. "And the Irish won't be satisfied then," said the man. "This isn't true enfranchisement?" "I very much hope that we will not be satisfied," said I. "I know well that it's not true enfranchisement, it is a little move and we'll let it go on turning (with a gesture) until we have our complete liberty." "Ah, I like that sentiment," said the man (he is a sculptor), and when I was going he said, "Vive les Celts." "Vive l'Alsace," I said, and they were delighted. M.C. gave me my cloak in the studio and said that it was a great pleasure to see me, and I went off. He has the most extraordinarily small hands and feet (with sandals on them) and he shows it because he is not too tall; but he has a big head and broad shoulders

> and a lot of brown hair on his head and his nose! – goodness, he has a big nose! . . .

Cesca and Cornélius began to discuss each other's work, making what they tactfully called 'suggestions'.

> I asked for advice from M. Cornélius today. "Certainly," he said, looking pleased, and he gave me a critique readily. While we were going through it, he said, "It's like that with those ones," gesturing at his canvases, and pretending he was fighting. "It's a battle." "You are going to win this battle," I said. He shook his head. "I am at the bottom of a hole," he said. " . . . all, all that I do, except painting alone, fails. Ah, I am at the bottom of a huge hole. It seems to me that I paint like a child, dirty, feeble, horrible, and I am so ambitious."

Despite her confidence as a draughtsman or as a nationalist, Cesca too had misgivings when it came to painting.

> 20 Feb . . . Simon said to me today, "Are you going to show in the Salon." I would have liked to have exclaimed, "Me!" but I said quietly, "No, M'sieu." "Have you ever tried to exhibit there?" he said, and I said again, "No, M'sieu." Then he said that I had time to do things for myself and so on. That kind of talk doesn't raise my heart since I know how incompetent I am. I am working on *The Black Abbot* and it is wretched. I argued with Y. Jéquier afterwards about what is "Art" and was it right for an artist to have a definite theme or was it right for him to work with a vague model of – I don't really know what – to represent perhaps some emotion. She was angry with me because I said I was learning to make pictures of the history of Ireland. She says that it is not right to do it for "any object that might be called useful." But I think that the cause of Irish Nationalism is a cause for Art itself. We weren't far from the English woman, my enemy at that moment!

Cesca's lack of confidence made her very self-critical, and is one explanation for her longing for understanding from her mother and brothers and for a greater flexibility in their views. It suggests too why, despite her extreme and vociferous political opinions, this charismatic character could be so attractive to and loved by those who did not share her passionate beliefs. An over confident Cesca would have been unbearable. She describes a visit to a Mme Ackerly with Yvonne Jéquier, 'and I had no hope of enjoying myself, and I was discourteous and standoffish and selfish when we were there. She was kind and gentle and pleasant and polite to me. Today I am saying to myself that it's not right to be among nice people when I am so sure of myself and so full of contempt for others, and I am so direct and so foolish in my judgements.' Her self-doubt expressed itself in dreams.

> . . . I had a dream that we were playing some game, and it got more serious than I would like, and we did something bad and two of us had to die as a result. I was one of them. Well I know now what it feels like. I was angry and fearful, but I knew I had chosen it and, when I was speaking with my mother, Raghnal or someone else called me, "Will you be going over, Sadhbh?" (in English), and I had to say that I was going to die because of the shame I would feel if I refused. And I said, "Will you give me ten minutes to write a couple of letters or are you in a hurry?" and they gave me time, and I was starting the letters when I woke up. But I was crying for ten minutes or so from cowardice and fear. It was bad, much worse than anything I have ever felt.
>
> They were ready to shoot me outside in the garden when I was called, and I was torn between fear that I would show my terror and my desire to have another moment in the dear world for the thousands of things I had to say and to do before leaving. My mother said to me that I would be in Paradise. I am happy that I did not let myself say the thing that was in my heart, that I would prefer the common life of this world to the eternity of Paradise. I said, "Well, however it may be, nobody will remember me at all as an old woman." (I was getting comfort from this when I remembered the pictures of me so alive and strong and I regretted, believe me, that this girl should be expelled from this life so suddenly, in the flowering of her youth. This isn't a dream but a reflection of my feelings on that subject. I love this life. I love the things of this world. I don't think that I have a drop of disinterested love in me.)

Being spiritual by nature, Cesca was attracted to the studio of Georges Désvallières, a deeply religious painter who had been a pupil of Moreau, and, after Cesca's time, would start an atelier d'art sacré with his friend Maurice Denis. Désvallières, a devotee of Italian art, taught classical drawing, and she worked with him for a while. 'It is good,' she notes, 'me in my corner there, and work in the very air.' Désvallières' critique was 'tough', which at first pleased, but later depressed her. She did feel that Ménard's atelier was more friendly. Though Ménard might tell her that her sketch was 'as ingenious as the composition of a buffoon', or that her *Life* and *Death* were too symbolist, M. Simon was positive and inspiring, and kept encouraging her to send work to the Salon.

32 *Christ and Mary Magdalene, 1914*

'Modern' art for Cesca developed slowly through an instinct for colour, based on strong figurative drawing. When her friend Róisín Blaud,[21] who greeted her on arrival, told her that a fellow student now went to the Academie Moderne 'and that she thinks that there is nothing now but Art Moderne,' she commented, 'She had good ideas about colours, it's true.' But Matisse and the innovators were beyond her comprehension. The Sale from the Peau d'Ours Association collection at the Hôtel Drouot on 28 February 1914 was in the news because for the first time works by Fauves and Cubistes were up for auction, alongside older, revered artists. Cesca describes the Sale as 'pictures by Matisse and his friends', ignoring the many Picassos, but she had probably gone specifically to see the Matisses. However, 'Matisse is wonderfully beautiful for M. Louis', she writes. 'I find him pitifully ugly.' His flouting of perspective and his flat, decorative manner would have grated, yet the hypnotic *Danse* by the 'wild beast' of Fauvism would surely have appealed to her at some time, had she seen it (and there was the opportunity when it was exhibited by Roger Fry in London), as would the spirit of his *Luxe* paintings. She had been working on her own *Dance*[22] while she was in the atelier, a composition inspired by that exhilarating moment

21. The Swiss girl is probably correctly 'Rosa Blaud'.
22. Exh. *Irish Women Artists from the 18th Century to the Present Day* (Dublin, National Gallery of Ireland, 1987) p. 65.

33 *Dance (Nymphs and Satyrs), 1914*

in Achill during the summer, when she and her companions went down to the part of the strand near the water shining under the yellow moon, 'and we danced, black figures against the silver water, an enchanting scene.' The experience is recast in charcoal as a feral dance of modern day nymphs and satyrs, accompanied in the preliminary study by an uilleann piper.

Máire's fiancé Alfred Palmer,[23] an English opera singer turned artist, whom she met first in November 1913, was to be a great friend and influence. She still pursued Irish subjects, noting, '6th January I am working on *Dance* and *The Death of Cuchulain*', and later she expressed her intention of doing *Cuchulain* in oil. But before long she was working in the Palmers' studio, getting advice from 'Mr P.' with *The Pipers* – 'a great help'. When it was too dark to work he sang a song, and another and another, and "Die Beiden Grenadiers" at the end, and afterwards we were so moved that he had to sing '"The Sweetest Flower that Blows"! Sugary, sugary, úch! but it has an aura of tranquillity.' She made one of her Celtic sketches, *Fergus,* in the Palmer's studio, and when in the atelier used two of the American students as models for *Cuchulain* and *Maeve.*

The Palmers' studio was a refuge from the constant presence of her mother at home. 'I am almost certain that I paint better if She isn't there. She is like "cottonwool" surrounding me and in my mouth.'

> 26th February 1914. I was at the Palmers' again yesterday, and then to Colarossi, and back here, and I drew *Cain and Abel* badly, half-heartedly, while Mother was reading in a loud voice. I hate that, I hate everything that comes between me and drawing, and "family life" does definitely.

She also liked the American artists – 'Donna Leonora, Julia Stohr, Mr Peters and "the Boy"' (probably Charles, as she dubbed him 'Cathal') – and she posed for them. 'I like Americans very much . . . They were commenting about everything but always had something intelligent to say, and more often than not something "amusant". Tonight I came in from Colarossi singing a song, "Casadh an tSugáin",[24] loudly, and going up the stairs I heard Mother say, "Sh sh darling, you mustn't make such a noise in a public place," and then a man's voice, "Oh, it's jolly, she's got a lovely voice", and when I reached the top of the stairs who was there but Mr. Palmer . . .'

She and the Palmers made a friend in common, Welsh singer, Megan Jones, studying with Jean de Reské, and his favourite pupil. Cesca's description of

23. Alfred Field Palmer (1877–1951), Máire's English husband. After training initially as an opera singer, he studied with Raphael Colin in Paris, and exhibited with the Salon des Artistes.

24. 'The Twisting of the Rope', a traditional song on which Douglas Hyde based his one-act play.

34 *Portrait of Cesca in Orange by Alfred Palmer, 1914*

her when she first visited herself and her mother was fervent.' 1 December 1913. Megan Jones came to tea with us today. This is what she is like, fair hair over a broad shining forehead, a delicate nose and long enough, pleasant red lips and grey eyes. She wore a black hat with a red rose on it and a red ornament at her neck, and her quiet beauty was like a day of summer rain. I will do a picture of her.' She and Mr Palmer drew her together in her national dress, 'red cloak and big hat. Mr. P was mad with the hat. "I'm drawing it now. Can you draw it, I bet you can't," he said. "What?" said Megan. "I was just asking (pause while I exploded with laughter) Mademoiselle – whether she could draw your hat?" "Who?" said Megan. "Draw my hat?" "The – the rival," said Mr. P. He hadn't the courage to call me "Cesca".'

Palmer made a series of portraits of Cesca in pastel.

> 22 Feb 1914 . . . This afternoon Mr. Palmer began the fifth picture of me. I am standing hands on hips, wearing a black hat, and looking round and laughing.[25] Mr. Palmer is delighted with it for the "silhouette" and the colour. They are very happy, truly artistic people, I think. I gave yellow flowers to Máire who put them in a blue pot and danced around them! Then we sat on the divan without shoes and we drank tea.

Her friend Bosca Uí Névolé had had a solo exhibition – 'Some of the things were good, two or three pastels were very pleasing' – and though she was only twenty she planned to send a canvas to the Salon. Bosca took the canvas to Ménard for an opinion when Palmer was visiting the master, and Palmer's view was that he was overpraising her and not giving advice. 'It's a great shame if this is true. She has a true-talent and she is so young that it can only be ruined if this goes on.'

If Cesca tended to have negative feelings about her own work there were others who were even less confident.

> 12th January, 1914. Friday. The fair haired Russian girl came to me and put her head on my shoulder and said, "I'm going to drown myself." "Why darling," I said. "You don't understand –," she said. "Oh, that's not quite true," I said; and I did my best to comfort her. Another student began to dissuade her. "Hanging is so banal," he said. "Everyone does that", and his advice to her was to go to the Pont Neuf to drown herself so that we could go as a body to save her. She said that she would tell us the day and the hour. Yesterday I saw her beautiful gold head and her rosy cheeks all well alive, and she said she had postponed the drowning until it was warmer.
>
> After that I went to school in a great mood. I began a picture of Loie Fuller[26] and everyone came and asked me what was going on until I was mad. I saw some one I knew on the other side and decided to go there, although M. Cornélius was near her, and I put my canvas back to front so that no one would see it. The following week was the occasion of the arts ball – I have never flirted so much before. The English are too heavy and the Irish serious when they speak "gaily", but the French are "parfaits" . . .

25. Cat. no. 93. In an undated letter to Margot, she wrote, 'Mr Palmer started a picture of me this afternoon with the black pointed hat & the purple cloak & me looking around over my shoulder like that man in the great cloak by Velasquez. The greatest contrast to M. Cornélius's one you can imagine.' This portrait has not yet been traced.
26. The American dancer (1862–1928), famed internationally for her serpentine and Chinese dances with special effects, portrayed by Toulouse Lautrec, and a poetic symbol for W.B.Yeats.

> We were talking a lot in the costume room which was decked with red lights and hangings that looked like purple and were really blue, and the White Russian girl was there wearing a pink dress, her hair powdered, and a dark haired boy at her side, and M. Simon came and when he saw her he took out a book and made a sketch.'

Cesca's life as an art student continued to be full of contrasts, as she commented, 'I feel sometimes as if I was in the middle of a hundred under-currents more or less connected with me, and many more than I'm conscious of. As when Donna L says I'm like wind . . . and Cathal says it's known thro' the atelier that I have golden eyes (!!!) and Róisín says "they" were talking about me (to the effect that I might do something some time), and M. Cornélius says Mlle Hearn hates me, and so on.'

> Sunday 15 March 1914. On Friday evening, I was depressed. I went to see Mrs Beaufort to give her tickets for the Petit Theâtre Anglais, and then on to the atelier. I couldn't work. I was raging with everyone, heavy hearted, lonely, melancholy. I'm stupid and didn't let on what was wrong, but Désvallière's "crit" went badly for me. It wasn't what he said, but the way he said it. I went to the Luxembourg Gardens and brooded bitterly on Life and on myself, the little worth that is in me, and the difficulties Mother and I have trying to understand each other.

Back from Amboise in mid-April 1914, she went to the atelier, 'and the first thing Róisín said to me was that I was exquisite. The second thing, I went into atelier Simon, where he was giving "critiques", and I saw M. Cornélius looking at me with a pleased smile. "Do you know that you look absolutely superb?" he said. "It's because I've been in the country," I said smirking . . . Then he stopped and looked at me keenly, and went back to his pipe. ("I'm going to smoke a pipe to celebrate your return," he said as he began. "This is a great compliment," said I. "It certainly is," he said. "Particularly because you do it so rarely", said I [sarcastically], "It is very *very* flattering." He laughed.) . . .'

> Eiremháin was here when I reached Paris on Saturday and he went back last night. When I returned this morning the Mother had just refused to sit for Palmer. Something that Eiremháin said yesterday had caused this, and it made me angry and I went to my room and wept and tore at my clothes in a fit of rage; and then I went out to get food – some bread and apples – and ate it in the Luxembourg Gardens on a bench.

4
Pan-Celts in Paris

Ménard's Barbizon subjects, drawing on the natural harmony of Rousseau, and Simon's landscapes of Brittany, filled the Paris studio on the eve of the First World War with art students from the small repressed countries of Europe. Czech, Alsatian, Hungarian, Baltic and Breton nationalists, in an era of pan-Celtic and Pan-Germanic ferment, they had a common sympathy in their love of land and liberty, and were encouraged to study one another's languages and cultures at the Sorbonne. Cesca had a natural flair for languages as well as a fascination for other races.

> This evening the Pole was telling the Spaniard, a small, broadly built boy with a weighty forehead, about some of the tortures the Mexicans inflict on each other, such as peeling the skin from a person's feet and making him walk! He didn't want to tell me what he had been saying. He said it was "too impressionistic"! The Spaniard said he didn't mind and told me this, and was ready to tell me some more, but I stopped him. When the pose began again, the Pole was at the Spaniard quickly. He told him a far worse story, going completely "impressionistic!" He made me drop all my charcoal! He said that he would go to help us in our "great revolution", he said that the English would be skinning their own feet if they made a prisoner of him. Then he said that he would have a ring with poison in it, and if he were to become a prisoner he would drink from it. "You mightn't have time," I said. "You'd have to drink it before you went," said the Spaniard.

> . . . That Pole said tonight that he thought I was like Iseult, it made me blush a little! . . ."You hate all the English, mademoiselle," he said. "Yes, I detest them," said I. "But it is not just detesting one person," he said. "I hate nobody," I said, "I hate a nation. You, do you not detest those who have oppressed your country?" "Ah no," he said. "You can't say that I detest them, I despise them" – "Well, that's what I do also," said I. "To hate them is too strong, it is more like despising, but my word it is difficult to despise when they are stronger than us." He started to laugh, "You have the future," he said. "We all have the future." –

Having tea with Máire one evening, Cesca met a very nice young woman, Sean[1] from Armorica, who was hardly there before she was asked to give a Breton lesson. 'It is very like Welsh,' Cesca wrote in her diary, 'and sometimes Irish, for example "dec" and "oin-ec" ("déag" and "aon-déag").[2] Only eight hours in the train from Gare Mont Parnasse, and you are in Guengain,[3] Sean's native place. I must go there sometime and stay with Sean's mother.' Madame Popoff and a friend gave her a Russian lesson, which she found 'great fun – Máire came in looking for me and we went to the Spanish class. There are so many tongues with delightful sounds to learn and I have only one life now.' Besides the Spanish class, which was taught in a local school, she had found out that the 'Spaniard' was South American and ready to speak Spanish with her every day. Her next venture was Old Irish at the Sorbonne, under the tutorship of M. Gaidoz. 'There is one other student there, an old grey-haired kindly man sitting on the chair sideways, his elbow on the back of the chair and the rest of him bent over the table. We are reading a German grammar of old Irish.'

M. Maillidhe – as she sometimes called him, but correctly 'Malye' – a teacher and Breton nationalist, talked with her about the possibility of getting together a group to practise spoken Irish. 'He thought there were many French "braves" who would say, "Right, we'll go, vive l'Irlande", and they would be there for a couple of classes and after that they would fade away realising that it was too hard. But if there were a few true and serious students so that Lord Ashbourne[4]

1. Jeanne.
2. The numbers ten and eleven.
3. Guingamp.
4. (1868–1942) He made history as the first person to address the English House of Lords in the Irish language. Born William Gibson, son of the first Baron Ashbourne, Lord Chancellor of Ireland, he succeeded to the title in May 1913, after which he took the name Liam Mac Giolla Bhríghde. He was President of the London branch of the Gaelic League until 1914, when he resigned because of the growing political bias. He married a French Protestant in 1896, who converted to Catholicism as he had done, and lived for the most part in Paris, where he was recognisable for his wearing of the kilt.

would teach a class,' wrote Cesca, 'He himself would be one of them he said, and myself another, look there's two,' I said. 'Róisín would come, and he hopes that he could get another girl. He heard talk about a girl who was involved in an incident with an English woman about nationalism and we thought that she was favourable material. He doesn't know her name and he says that he can't visit her without it, but I thought that this might be an introduction!' Cesca approached Lord Ashbourne (who liked to be known by his Irish name, Liam Mac Giolla Bhríghde), and the classes were arranged almost at once at the Cumann Ceilteach in the Sorbonne. After an evening speaking Irish there with Mac Giolla Bhríghde, she wrote, 'A shiver of delight went through me while I was doing it, it seemed so strong and noble after French or English . . . I am amazed at the number of similar words there are in French and Irish, "Dia do bheatha", "Dieu ta vie", and many more.'

Cesca kept up her interest in Breton.

> 25th January 1914. Sunday. On Friday I had the best night since I came here. I went to the Sorbonne School Social with the card M. Cornélius gave me and M. Goblet[5] spoke on "The present political and religious situation in Brittany". He is a Breton, with head broad above and narrow below like a *sean-Ghaedheal*.[6] He began with "theories" about the Celts, then went on to prove them with examples from Celtic nations of our time. He thinks if Christianity had not come from the Eastern world that the Celts would have invented it . . .
>
> 26th January. I feel there is a great future for the Celts. The world is developing ideas that suit them well. It is becoming more adapted to qualities one would regard as feminine than to those regarded as masculine. This means a resurrection for the Celts and a great change.

On 1 March 1914, M. Goblet spoke about 'Gaul, wild and pure,' 'and this is the role of Brittany in France, he believes. What Gaul was should be an example to the French.' Goblet was one of many French intellectuals who regarded Brittany and the West of Ireland as relics of an ancient civilisation which would vanish within a generation, and he went to Ireland to meet those in the Movement who recognised the value of the Celtic culture and worked for its

5. Y-M. Goblet (1881–1955), geographer and journalist, had an active interest in Pan-Celticism and wrote widely under various pseudonyms on Brittany and on the situation in Ireland.
6. An Irishman of olden times.

preservation.[7] Cesca herself was so involved in French Celticism that as a member of the Cumann Ceilteach she felt obliged to go to a banquet on St. David's Day, and to teach a four-hand reel to three Breton girls and an Albanian to perform on the occasion. 'After they had learned the dance,' she wrote, 'we sat down on the floor, and they sang songs from Ireland, Scotland and Brittany. The Breton music is wonderful.'

But there were more sombre aspects to the pan-national fervour. A Roumanian, Mme Cantacuzene, had to go away unexpectedly, telling Cesca she was with the Red Cross. 'I was reading that brochure, *La Verité sur la Bulgarie*, and she saw me and said, *La V. sur la B.*, ah it is terrible, the truth about Bulgaria." "Well," I said, "it appears that we have done them a great wrong." "No," she said, "Truly, they are not civilised, I have seen terrible things. The Turks at least have a civilisation, but the Bulgarians haven't any, they are children."

> "What do you expect," I said, "They have been slaves for so long, isn't it one of their proverbs, 'The sword doesn't touch the bowed head'? And they cannot become a nation of men immediately after being less than children." "No", said she, "and they have done marvels, but you notice that they are immature, after the war they reclothed themselves in new uniforms, with new arms, so that when they passed before the allied armies they wouldn't appear like a vanquished army. That cost millions." "Well, I like it as a gesture," I said. "It's immature, perhaps, but it's a fine gesture, oh that pleases me greatly." "Yes," she said, "It's natural to go to extremes at the beginning, and when they are completely free they won't be patriots any more, like us in Roumania, we aren't any more: but the people of Transylvania are all patriots as long as they are without the Hungarians, like the Alsace Lorraines." She says that she will send me postcards with costumes of the Roumanian peasants when she is at home. "I must go there to see them", I said. "Yes, and come to my home

7. In a letter to Margot (15 April 1914), Cesca describes how M. Goblet visited Arthur Griffith, editor of *Sinn Féin*, in Dublin at his office, 'up a little dirty street & into a small tumbledown slummy court & up some stairs so uneven & irregular that you often had to take one step where two should have been & there was only a hole instead, till you got into a long very narrow room (the glass of the door was broken & *Sinn Féin* pasted over instead) with shelves on one wall from top to bottom, three of them & two packing cases. The top shelf was covered with old *United Irishmen* [the *United Irishman* was predecessor to *Sinn Féin*] & string, the second was the editor's table & the third with odds & ends. The editor sat on a packing-case, surrounded by & covered with ink, the other was for visitors.'

> in the country," she said. That would be really great, and I will learn Roumanian.

Malye used to tell her stories about the grand times he had with his friends in Ireland. 'Once they took down a British flag that was up in some Orange house and substituted an Irish flag on the pole, two of them keeping "Cave" in the corners of the street. And then the Orangemen had a big job taking the green flag from the pole, because they were scared to tear it in daylight and that was the only way it could be done. At night the boys, like Seán Ó Ceallaigh and S. Malye, would be shouting and thwarting them.'

Cesca was interested in Malye, whose articles on Bergson and the Celtic ideal were published in the *Irish Review*,[8] but she found him loud voiced, it was impossible to get a word in edgeways, and he had an inflated ego. Expecting to go soon to Ireland, he had decided that 'he himself will be a breath of fresh air, and will teach us many things we should know. He will be working to simplify the language, he says. I hope that he will learn it properly first.' She helped him translate some 'nonsense' from the Franco-Irish Society for St. Patrick's Day, '"congratulations to John Redmond for the definitive triumph of the great Irish cause, and our calm in the face of ridicule and odious provocation from Ulster". I translated a little of it, I put "cuid chúige Ulaidh"[9] and I left out "definitive".'

When she went to Máire's apartment with Bosca and Róisín, to arrange the visit to Moret, they didn't do much about the arrangements, but instead listened to Bosca who was singing and telling stories about Bohemia.

> Three years ago the people were trying to establish a Republic so that they would be free from the Germans. For a fortnight there were demonstrations, and many of them in front of their house because it is on the Square in the old town in Prague. One day she and her brother went out without her mother's permission and they came upon four German students who were speaking German. Bosca burst out, "How can you dare to speak your vile language here, dirty foreigners that's what you are," and so on, and they mocked her, because she was very young and slim, until she was so angry (and they wouldn't let her and her brother get past) that she hit one of them on the nose and it bled.
>
> Then they started fighting with her brother, and they wanted to take them to the police, but at that moment ten Czech students reached

8. 'Le mouvement philosophique en France' and 'Le culte de l'Idéal', March, April 1914.
9. 'Part of the province of Ulster'. Ulster consists of nine counties of which six rejected Home Rule.

> the place and it was down with the Germans, and up with Bosca, and she went back to her house victorious! The next day there was a demonstration in the Square, people, students, going and coming from every direction without saying a word, and lining the Square until there were thousands there, all the time without a sound. Then they formed a procession with a fine big good-looking boy at its head with a sword in his hand and they clapped together as they went, "Bí do bhí, Tec u bhai", it's the national song.
>
> They were shouting in front of her house too, and it was when they were at it, more or less, that she was so excited by it that she fainted. She sang a lot of Czech songs as she sat on the divan smoking tobacco. One of them is, "We will die, We will all die, but the blood of our hearts will be like a shield around our native country". I was trembling and shaking when she stopped. I have never heard a voice ever that moved me so much. If only I had a voice like that!

Cesca enjoyed the social life of the studio. At the same time the many newspapers she read in several languages kept her thoroughly informed about the gravity of the political crisis building up on the Continent. As she recounted in her diary on 3 December, 'Every day there is something new happening in Saverne.[10] Yesterday it was a lame shoemaker who was wounded by a German officer because he mocked him and his soldiers when they were going on a manoeuvre. Thirty put in a damp cellar for twenty hours, and that's not the half of it at all.' She refers to an article in the *Éclair* on 7 January discussing the antagonism in civil and military affairs. 'There is war between the Crown Prince of Germany and his father. When the Crown Prince comes to the throne, I think myself there will be a great change in Germany. The armies are strong.'

In conversation with M. Cornélius, he asked her what 'Home Rule' was. 'I explained to him. "It's a species of little parochial council which the English want to give us in the hope of making us satisfied," and we discussed this for a few minutes. "How sad you are all of a sudden," he said. "Well Ireland isn't a very jolly subject, you aren't very gay when talking about Alsace," I said. "Yes," said he, – "It is sad not to have your own place. – Alsace will become uninhabitable." "Because of them?" I said. "Yes", said he, "Those people, who have all the rights over you."' He told Cesca's mother, 'You know they are not

10. On the Zorn and Marne-Rhine canal. The 'Saverne Incident' between civilians and the Prussian garrison in the autumn of 1913 prompted a domestic crisis in Germany, leading up to the subsequent outbreak of war.

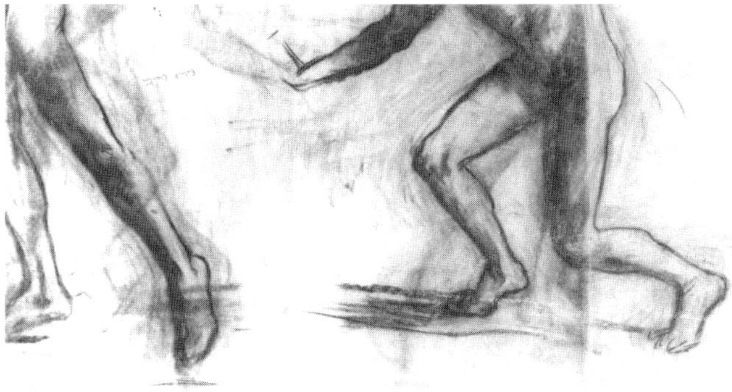

35 *Life drawing (a fragment), 1914*

at all as they seem, the Alsaciens, outwardly they are calm, but deep inside they are on fire.'

> 4th December 1913. I went today to the Cornélius' house. It was pleasant. M. Cornélius gave me a composition that he had done and showed his *Chanson de Roland* to me. It is well done indeed, he has a lot of talent. Another Alsacien came in and they were talking about a conference that the Judiciary of Colmar had yesterday about PanGermanism. The room was packed. He says that the conference man has an astonishing knowledge of politics in Germany, and his opinion is that there is anarchy there. There was a riot in the Reichstag yesterday, similar to the one at which they attacked the emperor for forty-eight hours two years ago. The socialists and other honest people have used very strong language on the events in Alsace-Lorraine (Saverne) . . .
>
> Today the model was very late. While we were waiting, me sitting reading *La Légende de La Mort,* M. Cornélius came and he nearly threw his newspaper at me. "Look at that," he said nodding at one section. I read about the new incidents at Saverne. German soldiers (officers), drunk going down the street, and the Savernois laughed at them and they were arrested. "Won't it be war if this goes on?" I asked. I was angry. "It must be." "No," he said, shrugging his shoulders. "In this case, there is indifference, it's frightening how indifferent people are. There won't be war". "You are angry?" I asked. "Yes," he said, "if there is war I will also go". He made a gesture again as if fighting. He can't be serious.
>
> I asked him later on if he had done his military service in France. "I came, I had left Alsace to come to do my military service in France, but I have a left eye which doesn't see very well, they didn't want to take me so I haven't done my military service". "And if the Germans take you

> they will treat you as a traitor?" I said. "Yes," he said, chuckling. "But you could shoot also, you would go all the same?" "Have no fear", he said. "Oh that's splendid," I said. "If only I were a man to do it, that would be magnificent". "Yes, but—," he said. "Yes, but—?" I said. He took a stool and sat down. "If you think that, if you are of that mind, why are you so, – so – gentle when it comes to closing the door?" (Yesterday I was trying to close the door, and I couldn't, and M. Cornelius slammed it noisily. "That's not the way a door should be closed," I said. "It is," he said, "that's the best way." "No, one must close it discreetly, tranquilly". "No," – he said, but the nice dark girl came to talk with me and off he went.) "But when it's a question of the country it's different," I said. "Also it's the violence, and when one is strong it's not necessary to be violent. But for the country it is necessary." (While I am writing these things down, my remarks always appear much less intelligent and less well-expressed than they were, but I only remember the tenor of the conversations and a phrase here or there which have struck me).
>
> After this we were talking about the Celts. I said that the next generation would be less indifferent on the subject of Alsace as a result of the nationalist movement which is making itself felt. He said that it was very clerical. I said it was more than that and perhaps the "Celticists" could get control without letting it be too clerical. He agreed with me. We were talking about the place of women among the Celts, a good place. He said that he hated seeing women all painted up. "The Celts like always what is pure", he said. "That's lovely", I agreed with him. "And that's what our enemies said to our faces, isn't that true, the rogues". "You are the only woman that I know," he said, "who gives me this feeling," – and something else that I don't remember, and he finished chuckling. "I salute you," making a gesture as if he was raising his hat. I blushed. That kind of talk embarrasses me.

Despite all the serious discussion and premonition of future events, the students were still young, and a little mad. Cesca describes how Yvonne and she were walking quietly on the road outside the Academy one day when Róisín, Donna L. and Julie, 'and the Baltic Province itself caught up with us and explained breathlessly at the tops of their voices how they'd been having coffee and rolls at a café and hadn't paid for them, and how the garçon had said if they didn't come back he'd come after them, and then we all raced down to the end of the street and danced in the sun. Mother was just coming along

36 *Letter to Margot describing Costumes for Eoghan Ruadh and a Messenger*

and saw a group of wild looking girls and hoped she didn't know any of them until they all rushed up and introduced themselves to her! and we divided her two petits fours and each had a 3rd. Then we went off up again and paid the money and the garçon rubbed it off the pavement where he'd written it in white chalk . . . The sun was shining, the wind was blowing after the rain, the oldest of us was 25, what d'you expect? Boulevard Raspail and Mont Parnasse bestowed on us amused laughter!'

Romance too was in the air, and very close where Cesca was concerned.

> 14th November 1913. We are reading the *Coryston Family*[11] and there is a lot of "love" there. I read that it only took from April to July for Arthur to fall so deeply in love with Enid Glenwilliam, and I said "no longer than that?" with surprise. "Yes, that's the way these things happen," said Mother. "Oh is it?" said I vaguely. "Darling Pet," she said looking at me lovingly and laughingly, and saying to herself that I would know about it someday without a doubt. "Well, I'm sure you ought to know," said I. "There's no one whose opinion I'd sooner take than yours". She blushed then! It's very queer for me to be pretending that I don't know about such things, and I'm sure that she thinks that I don't. I wonder has she any suspicion indeed. I said to her once, when I was sure she would be

11. By the popular novelist Mrs Humphry Ward (1851–1920), who was Matthew Arnold's niece, Aldous Huxley's aunt, and an active opponent of women's suffrage.

37 *Diarmid Coffey, c. 1914*

> "worrying" unless I said something, that she shouldn't be afraid that I would fall in love with Diarmuid because I knew that I could never be anything but friends, but "please don't ask me anymore", and I don't know what she gathered from that. I'm sorry about Diarmuid naturally, but I don't feel for him in the same way that I do about Claud. Diarmuid will fall in love with somebody again and he will marry, and he'll be happy, but I'm afraid that with Claud it's the real thing. It worries me rather. His people won't ever like me when they find out. But that's not the thing that is worrying me most. Je ne puis supporter de lui donner de la peine.
>
> It'd really be awfully jolly to marry Diarmuid, I wish I was in love with him, wouldn't Mrs Coffey be a topping mother to have. But then I think that it'd be awfully jolly to marry Claud too, his people would think I was just good eno', 'specially his mother, who rather liked us I think, and they'd be so happy that he should have got someone so much in sympathy with all his ideas and yet of good family! I'm a fool to be writing this and in English! . . .
>
> I am getting apprehensive about whether it's right to let Claud and Diarmuid write to me. Well, I'm not sure that there's any danger with Diarmuid, but Claud . . . it is he who said can't we be friends always . . . But his poetry, he is deliberately "declaring love to me" in it, even if his letters are more or less "innocuous". And when I wrote saying that he mustn't express endearments and so on to me he said that poetry was different . . .

Cesca was relieved that she could keep all this to herself. 'My mother is very good about asking no questions, because naturally she wants people to be making love to her daughters like any other daughters.' There already were two romances in the family anyway, which made Cesca feel more kindly to her brothers, or at least she thought it had the effect of mellowing them, and she approved of their choices. Art was married in London in December, and she and Máighréad were there.

> I see I have written nothing about Art's wedding . . . she is nice, but, looking at them together, I have no doubt which of them is the more beautiful being. Art has a voice very like Diarmuid's voice, and in the photograph is very like a young king. Oh if only he were a Gael. Don't I remember well the way Mother said to me, "I must tell you it's *so delightful* dear Reggie hopes soon to be engaged to Clare Howard", and how happy I was, and it explained the long letters that were going to Mother

from Raghnal for a long time. And one should see Art's heart filled with happiness too, he is so overjoyed and kind.

Hurst House. 12th December 1913. We have a full house here, Art looking happy, and Raghnal looking blissful with his Clare, and Eiremháin looking pleased and kindly in what he says, and Madeleine and Mother and myself, not to speak of Auntie Blanche and Uncle Johnny. We had a bad journey but we came third class for the whole voyage . . . But there's a great change between there and here. It's difficult to be energetic here, either intellectually or physically. Everything is so quiet, and "taken for granted". Today I went to London to see the dressmaker. The dress is nice, white with a light red rosy belt . . . Raghnal and Clare met me on the platform here, they came on the same train.

Sunday 1913 [14] December. They have done it now, bless them. There were a lot of relatives there, and Art and Deora were white-faced throughout, until we went into the sacristies, and then everyone started kissing each other and their colour came back and M. says that they went down the aisle shining with joy . . . M. and I went to the church from Auntie Francie's house – it was there that we changed our dresses. M. had a blue-green one made from blue silk, with Dun Emer embroidery,[12] and a black hat. She looked nice. Uncle Raghnal didn't do a reading for them because they left out part of the service and he said he wouldn't read if they left out the bit about the reasons for marrying, and they did. That is so English, the eejits.

And then the surprising thing is that I don't like my relatives! How long can a person love people when she can't talk about the things that are nearest to her, or has to be defending them the whole time? Is it that I am narrow minded? Well, I can talk with them in an understanding way about the things they like, but they can't do the same with me. – One day I will marry and have a large family and they will be sympathetic to me, and there will be understanding between them and my husband and myself, and my work will have its reward . . . Were it not for Máighréad, I don't know what I would do. There isn't one, not *one,* among them that I can talk with as a friend. When the newspaper comes in the morning what is a cause of pride for me is the cause of sorrow to

12. The Dun Emer Guild, run by Evelyn Gleeson in Dublin, made dresses and cloaks with Celtic embroidery.

> them, and what is a cause of pride to them is a matter of disinterest to me. It is surprising that my love continues as long as it does.

Cesca was working in the studio from seven-thirty till ten on Christmas Eve. Raghnal arrived even later that night, and, she was pleased to see, received four letters from his fiancée while he was in Paris. He and Mother called on Cesca at the atelier – 'very interesting sight,' he wrote to Clare, 'there are a lot of studios in the same building. All the rooms so hot for the models' sake: they apparently are able to control the atmosphere.' Conditions had obviously improved since Cesca first arrived. Then Art came through Paris, seven years her senior and always remote; but she found herself feeling more warmly towards him. 'We were talking, himself and myself, about German politics, and he was talking to me as if I was some intelligent person rather than a sister. Deora is obviously doing him good – or perhaps it's his true nature, the dear creature, and I have been misjudging him.'

She felt she was no nearer to solving the mystery of Cornélius' secret passion.

> Two out of three days I feel much older. Today I went to the Cornéliuses' place so that he could do a picture of me. Mme was out. He showed me a stone to play with when he was drawing me, from Vércingetorix's fortress near Clermont. I said if I had money I would put Vércingetorix on in the cinema. He was scandalised. "Vércingetorix at the cinema!" "Certainly, so that people might know something about their ancestors." But he wasn't happy. That's because the Celts are like a sacred memory to him while for me they are a living inspiration. "No", he said, "we are finished, there won't be any more of us, we have suffered too much, we are destroyed. All these wars; all these words" – to which I replied that we are not finished when we haven't yet overcome, that it isn't suffering that destroys races, and that we haven't had so many glorious deaths and wars that we can perish now before accomplishing our task.
>
> 20th February. Yesterday I saw the Palmers' pictures with Róisín, and we talked. It's wonderful the temperament and the talents she has. She was telling me about her life in Switzerland and tonight she was talking too. I must seem a very uninteresting person beside her. I am almost certain that Cornélius is not the one. She says that "Himself" is a friend of his, and that he knows well about the matter and teases her about it. Unless this is all a tissue of lies – I don't think it can be, she can't be such a consummate actress and cheat! We were discussing M. Cornélius, and she said, "He ought to be married, why don't you marry him, Saive?"

38 *Sketch Study: Bearded Man*

and if it hadn't been that it would have been stupid I would have said at once, "I thought he was in love with you".

Then I went out to buy coffee and going up the rue Vaugirard the sun shone on me and on the wet street and I took off my hat and the soft wind blew through my hair. I prepared the tea, honey on the gingerbread and rolls, and it was nearly ready when Marie and M. Cornélius arrived. After a couple of minutes "Monsieur" came, but it was a great pity that M. Cornélius didn't bring the picture of me with him. He said he was shy because he thought that perhaps we wouldn't be alone, "And so. . . ."

He brought it this afternoon. Mother is reasonably pleased with it but not altogether. She says there isn't enough spirit in it. And she doesn't like me to look so sad. She asked what did the panther mean and he said that it represented hatred and he would have gone on, had I not warned him against saying anything about hatred of England. He gave me some advice about the *Black Abbot,* but when he was gone I saw someone very like him standing in front of my window on the street. I only saw him for a moment or two, because I looked straight across the street so that I wouldn't reveal that I had seen him. But it couldn't have been him. I am almost certain that it was him all the same, but I don't understand the ass . . . Yesterday Róisín said to me that he was not in love with her and that she thought she had "nipped it in the bud", if he ever had been. So one of them must be lying largely. She, of course . . .

Cesca outlines the love story of Cornélius and Róisín with a certain amount of frustration at their refusal to make up their minds about each other – this though she herself was quite undecided about her own suitors. But she confided only in her own diary. She had become very fond of Georges Cornélius and the Swiss girl, and after she left Paris often speculated how they might have fared during the War.

Meanwhile she looked forward to Máighréad's visit to Paris.

> 20th April 1914. The Goat has changed her sailing, she won't go till May now, and we were expecting her this week. I was very sad on Saturday, and when Róisín and the Alsacien came to visit me, I told them why I was so sad. "That doesn't matter", said the Alsacien, "we are all your brothers and sisters." "I have no wish for you as brothers and sisters", said I forcibly. They laughed. "You see," said the A. to R., "She doesn't want us, she doesn't want me for a brother! Naughty! (gesturing at us!) Naughty!" (Róisín lets him make love to her tho' she's in love with the other, I suppose, and anyway doesn't intend to marry this one. It's an open secret thro' the atelier, M. de Gothard made some laughing reference to it the other day, as they were sitting together talking and everyone chuckled or exploded inwardly and looked at the unconscious ones) . . .

27 April 1914. I will continue with Róisín and Georges another day . . . Megan, Cathal, Róisín, Frère Georges [Cornélius] and myself to tea in Máire's appartment this afternoon. They were so nice and happy. They went up on the roof and were behaving like two children. The concierge came to say there were complaints about us, too much noise, but I got her to quieten down. Megan had a headache, but she took three aspirin. Another day, she and myself were singing Celtic drinking songs, myself in brown, she in a white dress. Mostly Breton airs, very beautiful. When I came in what was there but a packet of the *Irish Volunteer* from the beginning and a copy of *Irish Freedom*. . . , a cause of great joy, and I spent half the night reading. It's true I am passionate about the affairs of Róisín and Georges, and I truly wish them a happy ending, but nothing matters for me but news from Ireland.

39 *Diombáidh*

5
Home Rule

Besides being supplied with Irish newsprint as long as she was in Paris, Cesca was in constant correspondence with Margot, who now worked in Belfast with Rosamund Stephen,[1] and could report first hand on the irrational dark thoughts and fearsome ructions Carson was arousing among his followers. She heard what was happening in Dublin from Diarmid Coffey, who was working in the administration of the newly formed Volunteers, and few days went past without her noting down developments as they were happening, copying extracts from their letters into her diary.

> 5 November 1913. This is a strange world. I read a story in the new *Claidheamh*[2] about "Arms in the middle of Ireland" being prepared for the

1. (1868–1951), an English lay missionary in working class Belfast at the time of the Great War. She established the Guild of Witness and opened Sunday Schools for the impoverished, but her pursuit of ecumenicism ended in disillusionment. Her account of her life there has been edited by Una Walsh as *An Englishwoman in Belfast* (Irish Narrative Series, Cork University Press, 2000).
2. *An Claidheamh Soluis*, the only Irish language paper at the time, was published by the Gaelic League to encourage people to the language movement. Under its new manager, the O'Rahilly (described by Stephen McKenna as 'an honourable and gallant gentleman if ever one walked the earth', see Sydney Czira, *The Years Flew By*, pp. 58–63). *An Claidheamh Soluis* was flourishing. He changed its image, illustrating news reports with photographs, and asking Irish artists for cartoons, so as to reduce the number imported from English and other foreign papers. He was also responsible for the sword image bursting through the print of the title. See *The O'Rahilly* by Marcus Bourke (Tralee, Anvil Books, 1967).

40 *'Ceist Hóm Rúil Mar Atá Sé' (An Claidheamh Soluis, 20 December 1913)*

fight against Éamon Carson[3] who is promising loyalty to the King of England.

9th November. It's great to be alive at this time. The new *Claidheamh* is sparkling with strength and the leading articles are very good. Two of them are from Eoin Mac Neill and Pádraig Mac Piarais, but they startled me so that I couldn't think of anything but the new Éire we will have, and what I will do there. I mustn't lose a minute here. I love Pádraig Mac Piarais's writings. He isn't afraid to talk about fighting or battle or even war. He sees further than the [Gaelic] League, and he isn't afraid to say what he sees. He says they must have a "forward policy" after "an Essential Irish" fight: and that much will be lost unless this is done, and they should have it now. And the *Claidheamh* has it. Claud told me not to falter in my resolve but, upon my word, I don't think anything will prevent me from helping with the cause in Ireland. It will be the most entertaining[4] thing in the world.

3. Edward Carson (1854–1935), born in Dublin, he led the Unionist move against Home Rule in Belfast. In January 1913, he founded the Ulster Volunteers and succeeded in bringing in arms for them at Larne on 24 April 1914.
4. Not finding what she feels an appropriate expression in Irish, she inserts the word 'amusant', which conveys the languid air of a French aristocrat.

Her Sadhbh Trínseach persona had accompanied Cesca to Paris, and she continued to regard herself as one of the initiators of the new culture for Ireland. Her closest friends in the atelier, to whom she taught Irish, called her 'Sadhbh'. They appreciated the conspicuous image she created for herself in her various national dresses, which also inspired Alfred Palmer to paint the series of colourful pastels that best describe her. With all her self conscious artistry, however, she was simply following the current trend in Dublin.

About the time that Cesca first decided to devote herself to the nationalist cause, Irish Nationalists had realised that it was essential to declare themselves visually as well as verbally, committed men donning kilt and brat, the women wearing a modern version of ancient Irish dress decorated with Celtic embroidery.[5] So strong was the feeling for this as a cultural necessity that the *Irish Homestead* announced on 29 July 1911 that within the annual art exhibition of the Oireachtas held at the Rotunda Rink the Gaelic League would include a costume display, comprising examples of ancient and modern Irish dress, 'to give impetus to the national dress movement'. Susan Mitchell of course quickly saw it as a subject for satire, suggesting humorously in the 'Peeler's Song' chanted in her one-act play *Leaguers and Peelers*,[6] that it could lead to the reintroduction of penal laws:

So let us draw our batons
And batter down all those
Who speak the Irish language
Or wear the Irish clothes . . .

An Claidheamh Soluis had been in no hurry to pick up on this development in its fashion column, and, infuriated by the anglicised designs it was publishing, Diarmid wrote to Sadhbh encouraging her to send drawings for New Ireland fashion to the paper from Paris. Her concepts were more practical than the Deora Frínseach dresses which were intended for social and formal occasions. Her own ideas catered for everyday wear, and were readily accepted by the editor.

> 11th November [1913]. I am "fashion correspondent" for the *Claidheamh!* What fun! I sent a card to them with little pictures and my opinion regarding fashion, and I sent them a fashionable Gaelic design that I had

5. See M. Dunlevy, *Dress in Ireland* (London, Batsford,1989) pp. 175ff.
6. *Irish Review*, October 1911, pp. 390–406.

41 *Fashion Sketches from a Sketchbook, 1914*

> done also.[7] Yesterday I got a letter from them saying "Thank you. The fashions we had weren't very good. It would help us greatly to get fashions from you regularly," etc. They'll get them as long as I'm in Paris.

Her distinctively artistic designs were published during the winter of 1913/14,[8] no doubt unwelcomed by the reigning fashion correspondent, Cáit Ní Dhonnchadha, who soon began like others to make her own renderings of Irish fashion. The O'Rahilly next asked Sadhbh for political cartoons (cartoons at the time were being reprinted from *Punch, Le Patriot Illustre,* or Polish, Australian and other sources), and, as well as taking suggestions from him, using her own initiative she made simple stylish images picking up on current affairs such as the Home Rule question.

> A week or two ago, they put a cartoon from a Polish paper in the *Claidheamh* showing a beggar, and England like a rich young woman giving Home Rule freely to us. I made one changing the story, a robust young

7. There are some preliminary fashion sketches in Notebook 2077TX (National Library of Ireland).
8. *Cultacha Gaedhealacha* I-V, 22 Nov., 29 Nov., 13 Dec., 27 Dec. 1913, 10 Jan. 1914; other examples 17 Jan., 24 Jan., 28 Feb., 14 Mar. 1914 may be from her hand.

42 *Designs for An Claidheamh Soluis, 1913*

man taking Home Rule from a rich ugly old woman, who was screaming. I sent it in this week.[9]

She was optimistic about Home Rule, writing confidently, 'We will win in the end.' And her optimism was justified. The generally held belief was that a friendly Ireland was essential to England if the German menace was to be faced. Already in America a combination of Irish with German influence had succeeded in weakening that nation's support for Britain: so, however unwillingly, to secure Ireland as an ally England was bound to pass the Home Rule Bill. What nationalists were asking was, under what terms? The more Ireland valued her own worth, the more other countries were likely to respect her. Unfortunately, despite the fact that there were Unionists who believed that the Orangeman and the Nationalist had a single aim, to resist Imperialism – the Orangemen decried the dominance of Rome, while the Nationalists wanted to free themselves from

9. 20 Dec. 1913, 'Ceist Hóm Rúil mar atá sé'. The caption may be translated, 'The Home Rule Question as it is. We published a picture not long ago by 'Múca' Warsaw showing how the Poles understand the question. Our artist shows here how it is in reality.' Some other unsigned cartoons may be by her. 'An Dochtúir Séan Buidhe', 2 May 1914, was published with her name in print beneath it. It deals with the question of partition, the cowardly doctor suggesting that a clear cut now may result in reunification six years hence.

43 *'An Dochtúir Séan Buidhe' (An Claidheamh Soluis, 2 May 1914)*

the British Empire[10] – and this might have been a useful starting point – affairs had taken a darker turn. Soon after the Ulster Volunteers had been formed as a civic force, Eoin MacNeill[11] published an article on national defence in *An Claidheamh Soluis* (1 Nov 1913), which led to him being asked to found and head a corresponding body in the South. 'The Orangemen say that they know we will be doing something to oppose their Volunteers,' wrote Cesca in her diary, 'but if they have the sense to read our papers they'll know what our sentiments are on that question.' She had been having trouble with the French authorities asserting her nationalism, being told by the police when she was looking for an identity card that she must go to the British Consulate because she was a British subject. 'That made me think "Will I have to submit to this and the shame of it?" But I've been able to arrange it without having to put up with that.'

10. 'On history repeating itself–or the Orangemen and the Pope', by an Ulster Imperialist, *Irish Review* Sep. 1912, pp. 337–342.
11. Eoin MacNeill (1867–1945), from Glenarm, Co. Antrim, founded the Gaelic League with Hyde in 1893. A follower of Griffith and Sinn Féin, he became Professor of Contemporary Irish History in the new University in 1908.

Máighréad, back for Art's wedding, had news about everything in Ireland.

16th day [of December] . . . The Volunteers are doing well, Diarmuid is one of them, good boy,[12] and they were talking about women volunteers, but they won't be starting until the spring[13] and it's unlikely that we will learn how to use guns, only ambulance work. I hope we won't, whatever happens, even though I would like it the other way, but I'm a coward. I'm fearful and I would be afraid to try to wound anyone at all. M. has a calendar from the [Irish] Decorative Art Association[14] with "It isn't *What about the night,* but *What about the morning and the day ahead.*" She showed me a letter from Mrs. Weddall about a controversy in Achill. A meeting of schoolmasters opposing Irish, and a meeting of the people in its favour, and the latter won, and the people are more supportive of it now than ever. Praise God if it is true, and the same news came from Claud, but he wasn't there and so it's likely that she is his source as well. M. says that Captain White[15] is all right, but "a bit of an ass" . . .

Today, when we were drinking coffee and talking about Raghnal coming here, I said, "I wish *one* of my brothers was Irish." Mother didn't say a word. I'm a right fool to think that she would feel the same as me. When we were at Hurst, Auntie White said, "I suppose they like and admire us a good deal in France, don't they?" Mother started saying this was true! and I shook my head and made a grimace. She saw this and questioned me. I told her what M. Maillidhe said, "An alliance with England is all very well, but there is no security in it." I was delighted to say this. She didn't like it at all.

22 December 1913. Máighréad says that Eoin Mac Neill got applause for Carson at a meeting of the Volunteers in Galway the other day. He tried to do the same thing in Cork, but they didn't like him, and some of them broke up the meeting. But 700 men joined the Volunteers. Colonel Moore[16] wrote from Galway to say that he would come to help them.

12. In fact Máighréad was mistaken, Diarmid didn't join until later.
13. Known as Cumann na mBan. Cesca joined when she returned to Dublin.
14. The IDAA held an all-Ireland exhibition of Arts and Crafts annually from 1894 till 1921.
15. Captain Jack White (1879–1940) of Whitehall, Ballymena, had served in the Boer War and was one of the founders of the Irish Citizen Army in 1913. He published his autobiography *Misfit* in 1930.
16. Colonel Maurice Moore, brother of the novelist George Moore, joined the Connaught Rangers in 1875 and served in the Kaffir, Zulu and Boer wars. He was a major figure in the organisation of the Irish Volunteers and a member of the Provisional Committee. After the 1914 split he continued in prominence in the Irish National Volunteers (as those who followed Redmond were named) writing his own account of the force, *Tús agus Fás, Óglach na hÉireann 1913–1917*, published in 1936.

That was the 18th in Galway, and the meeting in Cork had been Sunday the 14th. Mr. Walsh[17] was injured with the blow of a stick.

M. has two swords in Belfast. I hope they won't take them from her when she goes home. They are very stringent searching out arms after the Proclamation.

Some of the Volunteers are depressed, and Mrs Weddall says, "We got arms before they were prohibited, and we will get them again." I don't know how. An Paorach's boat, that might be useful. I went out very early today, at dawn, and reached the atelier at 7.15, and I was the first there. It was misty, and hardly anyone in the streets, half-dark – and cold! The cold is beastly, I hope it goes away soon.

Máighréad, 'working like a horse, and she says that the officials looked as if they didn't know what guns were,' wrote to her about the arms prohibition soon after Christmas,

> "Canon Hannay[18] describes how Ireland's three armies, the National Volunteer Force, the Ulster Volunteer Force and Mr. Larkin's Citizen Army, are cheering each other and looking for any enemy to fight. No doubt, the Government has an enemy somewhere waiting for us. I think' we may trust the G. in this matter. It has shown extraordinary wisdom and fairness in its treatment of the difficult matter of letting us arm ourselves. It has not allowed one army to gain an advantage over the other two at the start. It will produce a satisfactory enemy in due time."

'The [Canon's] article,' Cesca added, 'goes on to say that we will be "Rebels", and that the Government has the right "to confiscate property of rebels." So they say, "we will let them fight, then we will take their property as punition." The Sasanach is always the Sasanach.'

6th January 1914 . . . A letter came from the Goat tonight. This is part of it:

"The Dean (Grierson) came here on Tuesday, he is such a dear, a tremendous Orangeman but all for freedom of thought and said that at all costs we must try to be friendly to those who we know to be in the wrong. I went to a service this afternoon for the Ulster Volunteers at

17. J.J. Walsh, later Postmaster General, who wrote a memoir of the Rising.
18. Canon James Owen Hannay (1865–1950) from Belfast, who wrote under the pseudonym George A. Birmingham, had recently published *Irishmen All*, a discourse on contemporary Ireland. From 1916–17 he was to serve as a chaplain with the British army in France.

which he preached. The enormous majority of them are extremely young, many of them can be barely 18 and so small and thin and stooping and undergrown. I expect the drill will do them a lot of good.

"A woman was at T at the same time as the Dean, a Miss Ferguson, and she talked and talked about a big unionist meeting she had been to and told me all I wanted to know about the provisional government and what a scurrilous set the nationalists were and finally asked me to go and work with her, "us" she called it. I said what would they want me to do, so she said go to England and tell them what Home Rule really would be like etc: or if I wanted to stay in Ireland there was plenty of speaking I could do here for the sacred cause of liberty. I asked her if she knew any Nationalists and she said, "Know a nationalist? Certainly not. I wouldn't". When I told her if I spoke at all it would be on the other side, she refused to believe me and said, "I'm afraid I can't believe you, you're far too nice and speak far too well (this was when I had dished her over 2 or 3 bad mistakes she had made), and your grandfather's[19] granddaughter couldn't possibly see any good in Nationalists."

So you see how very mild I must have been! She went off entreating me to go down to the office to see her and to go to T next Sunday! Such a Sinn Féiner[20] I never met! no mere Nationalist could equal her dislike of England!"

8th January 1914. This is part of a letter that came from M. yesterday. About the [Home Rule] Bill:

"Everyone here nearly is praying like mad that it won't (pass), only they put it thus "that we may be delivered from evil war". Maybe the prayer will be answered & the bill will still pass. Everyone thinks it will, only they look for a divine interference at the last moment. The Prots: I visit say William of Germany is coming, that these 2 visits Carson is reputed to have been paying to the waters at Hamburg have really been conferences with the Kaiser, that directly the bill passes he will come with his soldiers & make war on England with Ulster supporting him & maybe after all, as the Rector says, we'll be better off under a foreign government & a foreign king. We couldn't be worse off anyway & we'll get rid of the English forever & their bloody soldiers. The Rector hadn't quite

19. She refers to Archbishop Trench.
20. 'Sinn Féin' (ourselves), being the equivalent of 'our own', a very Protestant sentiment (Máighréad was given to sarcasm like this while she lived in Belfast).

said that! A perfectly lovely woman, with raven hair & grey eyes, a regular Galway woman, said this to me, she had got it from her husband, a covenanter, & a v. well off couple with a v. nice little house & a gun.

"All the Prots. harp on the same string; the Kaiser's coming & their intense dislike of George V because of the coronation oath, they say. Miss Stephen says it's because he didn't come to Belfast, probably that's it too: they won't recognise any part of Ireland at all & think no other city has any sort of right to prosperity of any sort. The Dublin strike interests them not at all; they don't know of it. The R.Cs & Prots. all live in different streets which makes visiting very easy; all I do is to look on the wall & if I see "Damn the Pope", "Remember 1690", "Dolly's Brae", "Confound their papish tricks", & skulls & crossbones about, then I know I'm in a Prot: street. In the Papist streets, the walls are covered with "God bless our Pope", "Remember '98", "Ireland a nation", etc. Most of the self-respecting houses have "No Pope here" (as if the Pope wanted to go to Bray st.), "Kick the Pope", "No King here", "Down with the King" on their doorposts. All quite simple. No one cares a straw for the Union Jack or for England except as a weapon against the Pope."

11th January 1914. "They are frightfully pleased at the idea of being able to overthrow the British Empire & of getting notorious somehow, it doesn't matter how; that they should actually be having services in St. Paul's [Cathedral] about Belfast is really too exciting & they think they will have to do something to justify it . . . The anti-nationalists here are sending people to Eng: to convert the electors; Miss Stephen met one the other day who'd been speaking in Bucks: & she said, "Well what did they say in Eng: when you told them about Belfast." The speaker said, "They said they didn't believe me." I think Carson will die soon & that'll help matters . . .

"Miss Stephen wants to develop this into a *national* settlement, in time; national church first – she doesn't see the Gaelic civilisation the same way we do, but wants someone like us to keep that atmosphere in the place, it would be entirely a Sinn Féin ideal, not the least like a settlement really, wholly independent & national in every way. She is really a doat [sic]; she sits on the floor cleaning the grate, breaking off now & then to hug her knees & talk ecstatically about the national church of the future: fairly amenable about Irish manufacture & bought single width Irish linen for a counterpane, instead of double width foreign, quite off her own bat, saying to herself in protest, "Well that fanatic will have to sew it up anyway!" She now says she must get some new slides for the

44 *Diarmid Coffey*

magic lantern & they must be "instructive" by which she means our use of the word."

Máighréad, despite an extreme nationalism which nearly surpassed that of Cesca, had a genuine rapport with Miss Stephen, a passionate Anglican, who wrote to Cesca, 'mentioning "her zeal" and, "what is not very common at her time of life, so tempered & mixed with generosity."' I think she appreciates Máighréad. She says, "I often think of you with gratitude for having lent Margaret to me."'

Diarmid's letter at the beginning of March told about the current very delicate state of Irish politics:

> Unless the Bill goes through, "we shall have to make a demonstration & it will certainly be a failure & that means another dose of coercion & extra police & searchers for arms. Those who had gone out would be lucky if they escaped out of the country & can live as free men in a foreign one." Then a piece that I won't write down because I won't forget it. Then, "The last bit of this letter seems highly melodramatic & serious & high-minded – Besides one might be killed which'd be rather heroic!" (Yes, great fun for you I daresay, my son. You'd jolly better not be. S.T.) "Anyway I am sure you will keep me up to the mark!" He thinks Eoin MacNeill is not strong at all, and neither The O'Rahilly – nor the leaders – are at all plausible. I am referring to Pearse and Arthur Griffith.

9 March . . . I read a lecture that Canon Hannay gave a couple of days ago about the Stage Irishman. I hate people explaining Ireland to England . . . If there is a Rising in Ireland, and I'm here without lifting a finger, I'll be ashamed for ever. To go back when everything has been resolved, and perhaps Ireland is under even greater oppression from the English. What good would I be to Ireland?

11th March 1914. I must go back on a visit, whatever happens. And what is happening to my grand plans not to go to Ireland so that they will forget me?[21]

On St. Patrick's Day, to the delight of the Mlles Genoud, she went walking to the barricades – symbolic of French liberty – instead of working at the atelier. Knowing how fragile the situation was she could think only about her return to Ireland. 'I must go . . . after Easter. I got a letter from Máighréad yesterday saying, Come as late as you like so that you will be nearer to the "crisis." I'll go to Belfast. Miss Stephen too would like me to come later. I'd like to do shooting or signalling or something effective.'

There was an article about us in the *Daily Mail* the other day, I never heard such rubbish, saying that we in the [Gaelic] League were against Ulster. "Irish-Ireland is their motto, that is to say, anti-Ulster, anti-Protestant Ireland!!!!!" The cheek of an Englishman like that to think Ulster wasn't Irish! I was going to reply and say as much, but the next day I couldn't find the paper and I think Mother destroyed it of her own free will!! I can laugh about that, but, God! if we are deceived again – . . .

Máighréad says in her letter, "I had fearful bothers because my piper refused to play 'God Save the King' & had conscientious scruples against standing up for it – so I had to arrange that he should leave before it. Also he said that he would probably be mobbed in the Shankill & that, if I didn't mind that, he didn't, as he was used to rows with the police, but that if anyone hit him he'd hit back. And I can quite imagine that he would. However the policeman on that beat was told to look after him & my '98 man (a man who has a pistol that his grandfather had in the War) was there & a private detective: so we got thro' alright & it has been the talk of the parish "Irish night" for weeks before & ever since (2 nights)."

21. She must be referring here to her two suitors, Claud Chevasse and Diarmid Coffey.

Another piece . . .

"The night before last we were awfully thrilled about hearing Asquith's speech &, when I got in at 9 P.M. after the Band of Hope,[22] Miss Stephen came out & called over the banisters, "He says exclusion by counties according to votes." So I came in & we talked over the fire for about an hour & drank cocoa, & tried to pretend we weren't listening for newsboys, & then presently we heard one coming & he was calling out something very long. So Miss S said "that means there's nothing important." Then I said, "I believe he mentioned Home Rule," & went to the window & looked out & tried to hear thro' the wind & storm what he was saying, & faintly I heard an echo down the street about H.R., or thought I did, &, as I drew my head in, simultaneously Miss S. said, with the deliberation of intense excitement, "Yes, go & get a paper." So I went out & pursued the boy thro' the rain & got it, & it was the 8th edition & nothing new."

25th March . They say "warrants" were issued for the arrest of the Ulster leaders, without Asquith's knowledge, by order of Churchill and Lloyd George. It's oppressive to be so much loved.

29th. I've been putting off writing this from day to day, like the fool I am. The latest is that French and Ewart have resigned because they thought the Government'd been so lamentably weak in asking the [Volunteer] officers if they'd fight. The Gov: have now sent for Gough to give up the paper F. and E. signed promising them they'd not have to. It's great news. Yesterday I was recounting it at the Cumann Ceilteach in the Sorbonne. It is said that there will be a General Election, and the Liberals will go back, but because of dissention about arms chiefly, because the English are terrified of military autocracy.

M. Goblet has cut off his beard and he doesn't look nearly so handsome. He is like any one else now. On Friday night M. Pfeiffer came, under the wing of M. Meuris and Seán Maillidhe and Róisín and Dr. Warner, to the discussion about Ireland (M. Pfeiffer has just come back from Ireland and has written an article about Home Rule, coming out against it, in favour of the "Ulstermen"). He doesn't think there will be a Rising without the Bill, and he thinks there will with it, so –. Dr. Warner is a splendid woman, with a wild free face, and courage and light in her eyes and sensitiveness in her nose and purity in her chin and tenderness in her mouth. She was raised as a Unionist, as were her

22. An organisation attached to many Protestant parishes in Ulster, having a rather narrow, missionary outlook in tackling the problem of drink.

> sisters and her brothers, and now they are all Nationalists. She says all the girls who were at school with her are the same . . .
>
> Róisín did her bit saying she knew nothing about the subject but, and then a lot of absurdities about religion and the hatred between Catholics and Protestants. She got them from Mother. Why wouldn't I be angry to hear that kind of talk from her when it was from my mother's mouth? It's strange. Everyone remained of the same opinion in the end, not surprisingly. I heard that Mr. Pfeiffer said he preferred discussions with the English than with the Irish because they didn't get so "excited". He should discuss with the English whether the Germans should rule them and he would see were they "excited". He said also that I was an "Irish type" and Róisín wasn't, something that annoyed R., and she said it was quite the opposite. He had a strange voice, very high and hard in sound.

Cesca had been making illustrations for Lamartine's 'Le Lac',[23] a much quoted romantic poem reflecting on love and the passing of time, when Raghnal arrived in Rue d'Assas on an unwelcome mission.

> 6 April Monday 1914. Raghnal came to Paris, and Eiremháin went to Belfast, to persuade us not to go to live in Ireland. R didn't succeed. "It's strange", he said. "Well, do think over what I've said, Cesca", and I said, "And you think over what I've said," but he didn't say he would! Why? Aren't I as right as he is? Must I give in entirely, and shouldn't he give way a little?
>
> This is what caused our conversation, there will be regrettable "friction" if we are in Ireland, and Mother will be depressed. And here is his alternative. Us to live near London in England and to "go over to Ireland" for some months in the year, and if we have Irish papers and correspondents [who are] Irish, isn't that enough?!!!!!! He is a fool, a complete fool, to be talking to me about "duty"! He said that Mother told him that she would prefer to live near London in England but when I asked her why she hadn't told us that she said it wasn't true at all, but she is afraid that we will be mixed up in political things.

Diarmid's letter at Easter was much more to her taste, and she entered part of it into her diary.

---

23. Alphonse de Lamartine (1790–1869) published 'Le Lac' in *Méditations Poétiques* (1820). Cesca mentions working on 'Oh Time, delay your flight', etc. Her illustrations do not appear to have survived.

Easter 1914. This is part of a letter I had from Diarmuid about the Ulster Volunteers:

"I didn't think much of them. There were three or four men in a big field "drilling". It was awfully well stage managed up to a point, you see. I went to Belfast hoping to see them & found that they were very difficult to see, I was staying with Mr. Bigger[24] . . . & of course he could not get me in. However, by chance I met a friend who is up there as special correspondent for an English paper & he said he would try to get me in if I didn't "let on" I was a Nationalist.

It was at about 8.30 PM we came to a great courtyard door in Sandy Row. There a crack of the door was opened & my friend's pass examined by the light of a small lantern – I slipped in behind him & we were escorted by an "orderly" into a large courtyard lit by three bright orange electric lamps. The orderly saluted the commanding officer who as soon as he heard what paper "we" represented was as civil as possible & took us over the building, a disused brewery. In the yard were what seemed an incredible number of men standing grim & determined, in serried ranks & looking extra fierce under the orange light. Well we were shown over the building, 1st a miniature rifle range but only half of it was working. Then a room where men were getting ambulance lessons & then above this the drill hall.

While we were in the drill hall up came some of the men from the yard. They seemed an endless stream. I was awfully impressed while the "commanding officer" told me that there were about 1200 men in the battalion. However I gathered my scattered wits & began to count. There were about 100 men in the room when one looked at them in cold blood, certainly not more. These were the "special service" men & about half of them had khaki uniforms. Then we went down to see the drill. The men in the yard also began to diminish in numbers when I started counting them. I found that there were exactly 303 men there. Therefore the total who turned up was at most 420 allowing for the ambulance men. They had no arms except 5 miniature rifles. This was rather a shock to me & made me think I was too easily impressed. Then they began to drill. "Company A left wheel," shouted the commander. 40 men turned to obey but alas they right-wheeled. "I said left," said the officer & I think he was

24. Francis Joseph Bigger, a Presbyterian lawyer devoid of bigotry, was a nationalist, antiquarian and patron of the arts. He had converted an Elizabethan tower house, 'Castle Sean', on Strangford Lough where Mrs Stopford Green, Sir Roger Casement and Liam Mac Giolla Bhríghde used to visit him.

45 *Boyne Cartoon, 1914*

going to say more. Then he remembered us two Daniels,[25] so said "it does not matter". Then they did some very simple marching with only a couple of mistakes & then we went home.

While in the courtyard I met a horrid little English cavalry officer who told me he had no connection with Ireland at all but that he had come over to join "Trimble's horse"[26] to defeat "the Bill" & because the Nats: had fought for the Boers . . . The political affairs are very serious, I really think now that the Bill will be passed into law. Then we must see that it is put into force. I have a great hope that this army business will mean that the Liberals will come back after the election probably in July. Much as I hate the Libs, I think they are more likely to put the Bill into force at once than the Unionists & it would be a great thing to get it in without fighting if possible. I don't believe that 20% of the Ulstermen mean to fight.

Despite Diarmid's poor opinion of the battalion he saw, Cesca was impressed when she heard that Carson had succeeded in procuring arms for the Ulster Volunteers. Like the leaders of the Irish Volunteers she believed that, armed

25. 'Daniel' for 'Domhnall' – another version of the derogatory term 'Taigue', applied to Catholics presumed Nationalists.
26. William Trimble was a member of the Royal Irish Constabulary.

and trained, the two bodies could act as a common defence force for the Ireland of the future, if necessary against the British.

> 27 April 1914. The Ulstermen have landed 25,000 guns in the North. Bravo! Neither the peelers nor the soldiers, nor the harbour officials, could prevent it. Besides they didn't know what they were up to. (And Máighréad is in the middle of this, how happy she must be!) Friday and Saturday night, according to the Gaelic reckoning, they were doing it. The Government afterwards ordered three regiments of English soldiers into Belfast. According to a statement from the Unionist Cumann of Ulster, the Government is planning *a rising to occur* in Cork, unless the soldiers agree to fire on the people of Ulster. So that they would have an excuse to kill people whatever side they were on. They are bloody devils of murderers if it is true.
>
> But it's a long time until July. Why am I not in the middle of what is happening? Is it more useful for Ireland for me to be here or there? I made a picture tonight of Ireland clapping hands for Ulster in grief, and sent it to *An Claidheamh,* but I'm afraid it will be too late. Another day I made one of Ulster and the guns there, saying, "Is it for me you're preparing that, you scoundrel?" and the Volunteers cleaning their guns and replying, "No it's for that rogue, if he makes a plan again to murder you or me!" If the picture "Bravo" isn't there in time, I will send it in because it won't have any meaning after a week.[27]
>
> 21 May 1914. This is the position now. The Bill will go through, after that the G[overnment] will put another bill forward, it's called the Amending Bill. The main thing in that bill will be "the indefinite exclusion of Ulster." The Nationalists of Ireland won't take to that and the G. will have to withdraw it or they'll be at war with Redmond. They will be afraid to withdraw it because they will expect war in Ulster because of that. So Redmond will declare war and the G. will be put out at the General Election. The Unionists will go in and then God knows what will happen. Will the Unionists seek to rescind the Bill? There'll be an uprising then for sure, God between us and it. And when will this happen? That's the most important question.

Cesca went to England in May to fetch Máighréad, who was staying with their Uncle Bernie – 'she was thin and tired . . . She gave me a fright'. The following

27. Neither was published.

46 *Margot*

month they went on their long awaited 'tour' together. But the strain of events, the waiting for news, came between them and their enjoyment.

> 11 June 1914. Longemer. The holidays go slowly by since we came here. It's raining, yesterday was dry with wind from Alsace, and we planned to go to Colmar walking from Slucke to Münster, and then in the train, and we would have to go early in the morning on the first tramway, and not surprisingly it is raining today again. We are living for the post now, full of hope before it comes, full of resignation when it has gone and gathering hope for the next day. Every night nearly the eternal boredom of this place overcomes me, and Máighréad, I think, though she doesn't say much about it.

PART THREE

'Upon my Word, It's a Great Time to Be Alive'

47 *Ulster Volunteer and Irish National Volunteer, 1914*

6
The Howth Gunrunning

On her return to Ireland at the end of June, Cesca stayed with her elderly Unionist cousins Maria, an authoress of some repute, and the twins Fanny and Jane, who were known, and particularly Fanny, for their charitable generosity. But 'Unionists are like ostriches. Disregard the fact of the Irish nation and it will cease to exist – that's their hope and their belief,' the equally caring but passionate Cesca was to expostulate in her diary. Life with the cousins at Lisaniskea was not easy for one nearly fifty years younger than they.

> Lios an Uisge, Blackrock. 27 June 1914. I reached Ireland the day before yesterday. The guard on the train to Blackrock was a Volunteer. It's a while since I have written about what has been happening lately. Redmond says that he wants twenty-five delegates, nominated by the Irish Party, on the Provisional Committee,[1] because only Dublin was represented on it. The P.C. said that they would prefer to have delegates from the counties chosen by the Volunteers. Redmond heard this as a threat, and said that unless they put the delegates he chose on to the Committee that he would make separate Committees in the counties and that he would ask the Volunteers who were faithful to the Home Rule cause to take orders from them. That would certainly make a split,

1. The Provisional Committee of the Irish Volunteers.

48 *Lios an Uisce, Blackrock*

Lios-an-Uisce by Karl Uhlemann, 1945. Called Lisaniskea from 1828 to 1935, the house was originally known as Peafield Cliff.

and the P.C. decided to agree to him. They promised. Nine of them weren't happy about it, but they stayed, because three of them, Éamonn Ceannt and O'Rahilly and Pádraic mac Phiarais, did.[2]

So Redmond has a hold on the Volunteers, and they are trying to provoke them against the Ulster Volunteers: "You're giving Carson's boys the power, men, and we will show them what we're made of if the good people of the North try anything on, or anything worse." If that thought can be lodged in their heads, it will be possible to disperse them when the Bill is through, because the Tories will disband the Ulster Volunteers quickly, or ask him to do it. Then R. will say there's no need for the Irish Volunteers any more because their raison d'être has gone. Another thing, the Volunteers can't continue in Ireland under Clause Two of the Bill, which makes it illegal. This is a summing-up of Sinn Féin's thoughts on the matter.

Yesterday I was at Howth with Mrs. Coffey. I can't write down here what they told me but it is great news. Upon my word it's a great time to be alive. This young man is much stronger than he was, believe me, or maybe I am becoming more aware of it. Whatever happens, he has made up his mind that I will marry him some day. We went up the hill without going back for supper and he explained his point of view to me. "I know you'll change your mind sometime," he began, staying where he was, lower down than me, looking up at me laughing. – "Oh you *do,* do you?" I shouted out loud. "Well I know I shan't. I'm just as determined as you are, Diarmuid." "It isn't a question of determination," he said. "Of course I'm not a good match, but I think I could make you happy." (I'm not certain that he didn't say, "I'm sure".)

2. When the split came, those who followed Redmond became Irish National Volunteers, while the others kept the name Irish Volunteers.

I told him the reason I can't love anyone at all, in my opinion. Then we were nearly home. "I don't believe I ought to have sent that telegram," I said. "Why did you make me, Diarmuid, it was your fault, you always get your way." "When I'm Prime Minister," said Diarmuid—"You'd be rather a good match then," said I.—"Yes, wouldn't I," he said, "or President of the first Irish Republic"—"Oh don't do that, are you a republican?" said I – "Or Dictator better still." "You shan't be that", I said, "I'll vote against you for one." "Oh, but then you'd be a Dictatoress," he said. I stopped. "How many times more have I got to tell you *I won't?*' I said. He was laughing as he followed me. "I mean to get my way," he said. "I daresay you will get your way," said I, "not about me but with the other things." "I'm not really so very gentle," he said. "No, you're not," me. "You're hard, for all your gentlemanness." With this we had reached the house.

Monday. The day before yesterday I was in Glasáin's shop, there was a sample of the Irish Volunteer Cloth in the window and a small blue-eyed man looking at it and enquiring about it. There will be a kilted "corps" in Dublin, Colm Ó Lochlainn[3] and Mac Giolla Bhríde are starting it. The members of a hunt in some place are founding a mounted infantry. I saw Pádraic Ó Conaire in London and he said when the Volunteers have guns they'd get rid of Redmond. Pádraig Ó Glasáin said that they weren't at all concerned about the dispute and it didn't cause "disunion" or political rifts and that they were only asking for one thing: guns.

I have to send the first draft of the book cover to Pádraic Ó Conaire,[4] I promised he would have it within a week, and it isn't finished yet. Yesterday I went to Rathfarnham to see the Dublin Battalion National Boy Scouts. I lost my way, but that happens to me in Dublin and I reached the place at last. Then I drew them for as long as I liked, and went off in the end. I saw Pádraig mac Phiarais looking at us intensely as we were going out. It's said that Mary Spring-Rice has given £200 to the Volunteers, and that milord doesn't want everyone to know about the deed.[5]

---

3. Colm Ó Lochlainn (1892–1972), founder of the Three Candles Press. He was deeply involved in the Volunteers. While printing a document for Plunkett in 1916, he learned of the unauthorised plan for the Rising, and alerted MacNeill. Later, he became disillusioned and devoted himself to printing and research, publishing two important collections, *Irish Street Ballads* (1939) and *More Irish Street Ballads* (1965).
4. Book cover for Pádraic Ó Conaire's *An Chéad Cloch,* see Ill. 49.
5. The Hon. Mary Spring-Rice, daughter of Lord Monteagle and cousin of Nelly O'Brien, was an active member of the Gaelic League in Foynes, Co. Limerick, and prepared to take extreme action in the struggle for freedom.

49 *Salome: Cover for An Chéad Chloch, 1914*

50 *George Coffey, July 1914*

Howth. 9 July 1914. This place is beautiful, there's no two ways about it. Ireland is more beautiful than any place on earth. There's a crisis vis-a-vis de nous in Dún Laoghaire harbour, she came in days ago, and occupied herself with larking round. The day before yesterday she came back in under full steam and she has lain outside the harbour since. It is said that she is searching the fishing boats for guns.

The Irish Times had a story yesterday that they succeeded in landing 1,000 guns in Inishylyne in Mayo the day before yesterday from a boat from Scotland. There wasn't a word in the *Freeman,* and this could be caution or lack of knowledge, I don't know which. I was sitting writing this when Mrs. Coffey came in to tell me that the master[6] had a rumour to tell me about something to do with the Volunteers, and I went into his room and she read the piece about the 1,000 guns. He was absolutely delighted, as was I. He is pleased that this kind of thing makes me happy, she says . . .

Of course she is a darling, so affectionate to me. I have never seen such patience. Last night . . . after supper we found that the master was cold and we rubbed him, I rubbed his hands, and she his feet, in front of the fire, and she said, laughing ruefully, "If only he hadn't invented this

6. George Coffey (1857–1916) was Keeper of Antiquities in the National Museum and a member of the Dublin Contemporary Club (which promoted Home Rule) with J.B. Yeats, who painted his portrait in oil. When Cesca knew him he was retired and a permanent invalid.

ridiculous game of being ill, how rich and grand we'd be, he'd be Director now, very little work and lots of travelling, all his expenses paid", and the poor man in the chair laughed futilely, so handsome with his noble head and blue eyes, and so tall and broad, a much finer-looking man than Diarmuid. She told me how once he had been able to do everything, sing, dance, skate, and every other sport, a scholar who could draw with his shapely clever hands, - and, naturally, his archaeology, a true nationalist, and so determined and courageous. And when he was strong and vigorous he worked in politics from time to time, and he would suggest things, and everyone else would get the praise. She would say that it was disgraceful that he was never given any recognition and "It doesn't matter if the work is done," he would say. But if only they were rich – without having to worry about the wherewithal.

Three days ago a letter came from Diarmuid saying he had seen the list of civil list pensions and that the name of his father wasn't on it, and he was furious and upset and said that he would come home, and he was sure that T.P. Gill[7] would get something for him. And this made Mrs. C. very distressed, and she asked Gill could this be true and the secretary said it must be last year's list and "don't worry". But all the same she did worry, because, if it were true, Diarmuid would not be able to remain at the bar. But some people have written to her since on the matter and they were all certain that it was last year's list, and it's true that TP asked Redmond to talk to Asquith about it, and that he promised to.

So I hope he is secure, but even if he is they will be poor enough until Diarmuid is bringing in some money, and that's not yet. Mrs. C says she would like me to marry some one rich, but she wouldn't mind if I married Diarmuid all the same. She says, "What I should like would be for you to be good chums for several years and then if you meantime had not found someone rich and very nice who you fell in love with and if you did fall in love with Diarmuid – I'm sure he won't have changed his mind, he's terribly faithful." She is a jewel . . .

They have a lot of reviews of Diarmuid's book[8] now, and I read a good many of them to the master, and they are almost all good and appreciative. I hope they will sell the book. He was right, according to the reviews.

---

7. Thomas Patrick Gill, Secretary of the Department of Agriculture and Technical Instruction, uncle of Tomás Mac Giolla of the Workers' Party.
8. *O'Neill & Ormond, a Chapter in Irish History*, published by Maunsel in 1914.

10th July 1914. Lios an Uisce – Why am I so happy? I am, great waves of joy sweep thro' me every now and then as I lie here on the grass in the sun with a half-finished blue shirt beside me. It can't be because I'm unselfish because I'm not, or because I don't know enough sad things to make me sad, or really because I'm so indifferent to other peoples' sorrows, because I'm not on the whole. Or because Ireland is so happy and prosperous, for it's not and I do care about that, or because I'm with Nationalists, now, tho' that might have been it at Howth. No more can it be entirely because others have pleasure for their eyes in me, tho' that does delight me. It can't be because of D. or I should have felt that last year, it did please me certainly but nothing like this. I believe it's really partly because these people here like me and think well of me, but I wish I could be indifferent to that.

It's not because of D's succeeding in his enterprise either. Mrs. Coffey sent me a letter from him saying that there was some uncertainty and he didn't know would they remain there or would they return to Ireland, and if there were no progress he would come back without delay. That he was very cross because it wasn't their fault but people had muddled the whole affair, and, whatever about it, it was desperate to feel he had been wasting all his time there. She said in her letter that she got a curt message from him yesterday, saying "sailing tomorrow", and so she hoped that things were panning out better. But I hope to God they are . . .

Yesterday I came back here, and the folk were at a Garden Fête at Linden, it's a Convalescent Home, and the Aberdeens[9] were there. And when they were going, some one tried to rouse a cheer for them, and there wasn't a sound.

14 July 1914. Carson said yesterday, "Let them make a clean cut or come and fight us." At moments I feel black misfortune is coming, and at other times the Kingdom of Glory. If there is a battle while I am in England, God help me. Aren't I the great patriot, knowing nothing about the art of shooting, or medical matters, or anything at all. If there is a fight coming, I won't go to England, I can't . . . The Government will pass exclusion over Redmond's head, the Northern Irish Unionists are pledged never to accept Home Rule. They'll fight, the others will help them. What will the Orangemen do? This is a bad quarter of an hour. I can't go back in August.

9. Lord and Lady Aberdeen, the very popular Lord Lieutenant and his wife.

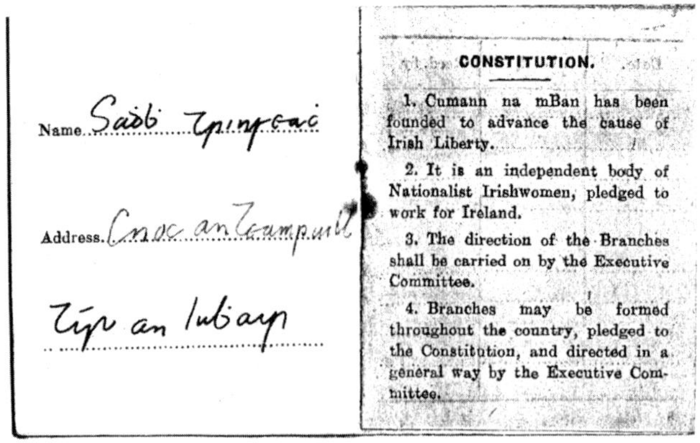

Name. Saḋḃ Trinseaċ

Address. Cnoc an Teampuill

Tír an Iuḃair

CONSTITUTION.

1. Cumann na mBan has been founded to advance the cause of Irish Liberty.

2. It is an independent body of Nationalist Irishwomen, pledged to work for Ireland.

3. The direction of the Branches shall be carried on by the Executive Committee.

4. Branches may be formed throughout the country, pledged to the Constitution, and directed in a general way by the Executive Committee.

51 *Cesca's Cumann na mBan Membership Card*

I saw the "Liams" on Sunday. I drank tea with them and they were telling me stories about Ella Young's[10] house, the little annexes to the big rooms, and the doors, and how you could conceal a person there . . . Miss Young, from the Rest Home, is a Volunteer Nurse. The "Liams" were telling me of the great success of Cumann Gaedhealach na hEaglaise,[11] numerous letters from people who you wouldn't think liked anything Irish, and at the last meeting Alec Wilson in his kilt and the Dean of St. Patrick's were sitting together, and the Dean was telling him something about the Hymn Book they were going to publish, without his name or the name of the printers, so that Catholics as well as Protestants would be able to buy it, especially for the Gaeltachts. And Colonel Moore came in with Roger Casement.[12] The Colonel stood up. "Why aren't the hymns in Irish?" he said, listening. "They are in Irish, Colonel Moore," said the Dean mildly, concealing a smile. Mark you, no dread of proselytism from the keen R.C., only an enthusiasm for the language shared by the Protestant Dean!

Cesca had joined Cumann na mBan as soon as she arrived in Dublin, and began to give instruction – no doubt passing on something of what she had learned from her military brothers, even in her ability to lead – at her first drill in Fairview Park.

10. Ella Young, writer and poet, author of *Celtic Wonder-Tales*, illustrated by Maud Gonne, (Dublin, Maunsel, 1910), actively supported Sinn Féin and the Volunteers.

11. The Irish Guild of the Church, inaugurated in April 1914 to promote the Irish language and the spirit of the original Celtic Church in the Church of Ireland.

12. Roger Casement (1864–1916), born in Dublin and educated Ballycastle, Co. Antrim. He joined the colonial service and while in the Congo and Peru uncovered atrocities, for which he was knighted in 1911. A keen supporter of the Irish language, he used the Irish form of his name, 'Ruaidhrí mac Easmuin'. He came to Dublin in 1914 to assist Pearse and MacDonagh organising countrywide branches of the Volunteers. War broke out when he was in America collecting money for guns.

> That was an awful farce. Cousin Henry C-B[13] came to see me, and brought me on to it from Amiens St. Station on a car,[14] and we drove for about 20 minutes before we could find it. When we got there, there were a man and a woman in the park who smiled and said there was supposed to be drilling there, when I asked. By and by B. Cassidy turned up, and we talked for a bit walking up and down. Then [joined by] another woman with lots of teeth and a blue woollen cap.
>
> I started teaching them semaphore drill. There were six in the end and me. Three girls sat on a bench and looked on. I asked them would they like to join and they each said that they'd join next week when the others did. Óinsigh![15] Tomás MacDonagh[16] was watching some of the time with his wife and child. Just as we were going out the men came marching in. It was rather thrilling – we watched them a bit and then went back . . . I found a letter from Mrs. Coffey saying she'd had a card from Diarmuid from Ruytingen reporting a good sail and they hoped to be starting home "soon, so he may be back early next week", she said.

Cesca packed that night for County Wicklow, where she was to stay at Lough Dan; and she puzzled without success over the Browning automatic pistol she had purchased which awaited her when she got back from drill. She put it in her bag. In the morning she cycled out in the direction of Whitechurch, passing men milking, and a few people walking on the still rural roads near Sandyford. A cyclist who passed her stopped.

> . . ."Is this the right road for Glenduff?"[17] I said. "What part of Glenduff?" said he with a north of Ireland accent. We got into chat, as we went up the same long hill, and we walked on side by side. He was Maunsel & Co, a friend of Synge's, and knew the roads well, and told me I'd not be at Roundwood till eight tonight. "Why how many miles is it?" said I, "We're near half way, and walking it's four miles an hour, so five for a bike ought

13. Henry Cole-Bowen, married in 1890 to a third cousin of Cesca's, Florence Isabelle Pomeroy.
14. i.e. on a side-car. She has crossed out 'in a cab'.
15. Fools.
16. (1878–1916). Poet, and lecturer at National University, he helped Pearse to found St. Enda's School. He was a member of the Gaelic League, on the Military Council of the IRB, and one of the leaders of the Easter Rising. His wife was Muriel Gifford, sister of artist Grace Gifford. MacDonagh published an account of the Howth gunrunning – in its title 'Clontarf 1914' recalling the significance of Brian Boru's victory there – in the *Irish Review Supplement* July–August 1914.
17. Gleanndubh, or Glendoo, the 'black glen', above Rockbrook.

> to be ample and it's only three now. Will it take me five hours? Three should be lots." He looked doubtful. "The roads are very bad," he said, "it depends on what sort of cyclist you are . . . it's a sort of cart-track." We talked about plays and actors and books and maps. He turned off on the road to Glencullen, and said I'd be very welcome anytime in Middle Abbey Street.

The road climbed up through the woods and out on to a windswept hill. Motors passed her and nodded and smiled encouragingly – 'regarding me obviously as a picturesque peasant girl.' 'One full of young men invited me by gestures to join them.' It was 'dangerous hot', she was dying with thirst, and she turned in at a house called 'Cyclists' Rest' for a drink of buttermilk. The woman of the house gave her further instructions as to the way, and said Roundwood would be about an hour from the top of the Sally Gap.

> This cheered me. I rattled down a hill and plodded up another, a long one, till I got to the top of the Gap. It was grey with occasional gleams of sunlight. I considered the possibility of having to sleep out and the notion did not attract me. But I was getting awfully tired, and my bicycle difficult to balance as time went on. At last I struck a road with a signpost on it and "To Roundwood" written there. I was thankful for this, for only for it and meeting a motor just before I'd have thought I'd lost my way. The road was awful, worse and worse as it went on. Steep and rough in the extreme. At the end it went up steeply. That was a struggle, getting myself and the bike up it. However it was done in the end and, just as I got to a fairly steep but slightly superior road down, I got a puncture.
>
> Holding a bike back is almost as tiring as pushing it up. I was reeling down when I saw a woman who came out of a bohereen. I saw the house at the end and wondered whether I would ask them to put me up, or mend my bike, or anything, and finally decided to ask the woman the way to Roundwood . . . She came on with me in the dark and rain to show me the way to Mrs. Doyle's. Good woman, my heart warms to think of her. That last stage was really awful, I could hardly walk straight, or keep the bicycle straight, and it was 3 miles or so. As we were coming along we saw a light low down, glowing. – "A fire," said she, then in a whisper, "them's tinkers." We dimly discerned a tent in the dark. "Good night to you," I said as a corner of it lifted. "Good night," they said back.

She spent the night at Mrs Doyle's and eventually arrived at Mrs Farmer's, to find that – despite her having received only kindness from Mrs Doyle – there was a feud between these two families.

52 *Loch Dan, July 1914*

> There was a boy here last night cutting hay, and as it was raining he sat down inside in the accustomed way . . . And he told me stories about Billy Byrne of Ballymanus, and Michael Dwyer,[18] and the people who "informed" on them. "Ah," he said, "if it was to come to that again now, there'd be plenty of informers to find." The farmer stopped, he was looking for his knife. "There could," he said, emphatically, "and you'd find one without moving far from where you sit." I stared at him, I was making brown bread. "I don't mean you, miss," he said. "Is it yourself then," I said laughing. "No, it's not, nor any of us." Patrick Byrne, the fellow who had been cutting hay, made a gesture. "Ah, down there is it?" I said, pointing to the Doyles' house. "It is," he said, and P.B. nodded too. I'm sure they are right, and I hope they won't give him much mercy. He has a shifty look.

Cesca remained in Wicklow sketching for about a week – 'it was as hot as Africa,' she complained, 'I was tormented with the heat' – when she heard from Diarmuid to say he wouldn't be home until the 26th, and, 'if I was near Dublin that Mrs. C and I could go to Howth harbour at one on the 26th, but "don't say a word to anyone else"'.

---

18. Renowned Wicklow insurgent of 1798.

Sunday 26th July 1914. A great, soaring day, a glorious day. The best day I've ever had.

Mrs. Coffey was waiting for Diarmuid last night, really worried about him. He had told us to go to Howth pier at 1 P.M. I went to church, and out of it at 12.35 as I was to meet Mrs. Coffey at 12.45 at the head of the pier, which was 10 minutes or so from the church. As I came down on the road, I saw carts of mineral waters go by, with men on them in bandoliers and pouches, more men in front and behind them, and a corps of cyclists standing in a row near the station just the other side of the railway bridge, the side nearest the pier. I quickened my pace and came up with more Volunteers, and I saw lots more ahead. They broke into a run on getting near the pier, and ran onto it and down to the furthest end. Then they proceeded to keep all outsiders off it by forming double cordons across the end and on top.

I stood there a bit, then I thought I'd see better on top, so I went to a company commander. "Am I allowed to go past?" I said. He was a small man with keen blue eyes and clean cut face, rather red. "You're an Irish speaker!" he said in Irish, "but don't go over now, we don't know for certain what we are going to do." "I know," I said. "I hope to God that a boat is coming in," he said. "Oh it is, it is," said I. I might have told him I'd seen it, for I had, Erskine Childers's yacht,[19] only I didn't know it was his or that it had the guns, but I had seen it as I came along, anchored at the end of the pier.[20] "I hope to God it is," said he, pale with anxiety. "I'll wait," I said, and I went back to the knoll.

We waited. Some boys behind me began complaining to a policeman that they hadn't been allowed onto the pier. About twenty people had collected by this. "We tried to go on," they said, "and a whole lot of those fellows came on us and wouldn't let us past." The policeman made some

---

19. *Asgard*. Robert Erskine Childers (1870–1922), served in the Boer War, and then as Clerk in the House of Commons until 1910. His mother was a Barton of Glendalough House, where he spent much of his boyhood. When War was declared he joined the British Navy and was awarded a DSO, but he was drawn into the 1917 Convention, became director of publicity for the Irish Provisional Government 1919–21, and Chief Secretary of the Irish Peace Delegation in 1921. He opposed the Treaty, and later was executed for carrying a pistol, which had been given to him by Michael Collins.
20. Encouraged by Sir Roger Casement, who was determined to challenge the Larne gun-running which had provided the Ulster Volunteers with arms, Erskine Childers and Alice Stopford Green initiated the buying of muskets and ammunition for the Irish Volunteers. Childers and Darrel Figgis were despatched to Germany to make a deal. Childers' yacht and that of Sir Thomas Myles (Ó Maolmuire) were used to bring the guns secretly to Ireland.

non-committal remarks. "And when we asked why, they said it was by order of the Provisional Government of the Irish Volunteers," finished the aggrieved youth. The policeman didn't seem very much distressed.

I tried to conceal my thrills. The white yacht was there, and the large detachment of the INVs were there, but it was too far off to see well what they were doing. At last they began to march towards us. Some policemen had previously tried to pierce the lines, and had failed and been brought out again. There were about five of them there but only two tried. "Right about face," said a commander. The Volunteers right about faced and saw the others coming. There was a sort of shadow aglint above them and they all had the left arm at a small angle to their bodies. I thought they had the guns but wasn't sure. They came nearer and we saw.

Then we cheered and cheered and cheered, and waved anything we had, and cheered again. Mrs. Coffey came in the middle and waved her hat and I my cloak. To see and hear that was the best thing that ever happened to me in my life. We went to some policemen who were standing there and said, "Isn't that grand?" "It is," they said, "it's great," and broad smiles all over their faces. We were looking for a good place to see them from, so we went up on top to a place further than which we weren't allowed to go. I saw St. John Ervine[21] there with a gun. The armed Volunteers were lined up guarding by this time and another detachment had gone down. "Are we allowed to go past?" I said. "Yes," he said without a moment's hesitation, and they opened out to let us thro', and smiled at us and showed us their guns.

We stood there and a squall of rain came on, so fierce that we went down again. Another armed detachment were standing just below us, they smiled up at us and we at them. "Do these people know you?" Mrs. C said. They didn't of course but how could I help smiling at them. I could have done more than that. The Volunteers opened out, and some motors went thro' racing. They cheered them.

The crowd had by now swelled very considerably – every one was laughing and saying hurray. One of the Volunteers said to us we'd better not be going there, as a warship had been signalled for and they had to get the ammunition landed elsewhere as it was. "Will they try to take the guns from you, the warship people?" we said. "They won't take mine," he said, and gave it to us to feel. We went to speak to Lawrence

21. Belfast playwright (1883–1971), who became manager of the Abbey Theatre in 1915. After the 1916 Rising he became disillusioned and returned to his Unionist roots.

[sic] Kettle.[22] We didn't know him, but Mrs. Coffey said Diarmuid was down helping, and that was introduction enough. Fancy being able to say your son was down helping – any relation, if I'd been able to say I had a brother! – We asked him how many. "Nine hundred", he said. "It'll be five thousand on the papers tomorrow". (He was a nice handsome man with a beard.) "Have they got the ammunition off?" we said, "where's it going to be landed, I hope the warship won't catch it." He smiled, "It was landed ten minutes ago", he said, "Five taxi-cabs".

They were going off by this time, marching lightly and smiling and whistling all together. We thought of the reception they'd get in Dublin. We waited for Diarmuid a bit, and missed him somehow, so we went in to get some warm milk in an hotel nearby. In there we saw the yacht going out, so we ran out with the glasses, and I made a sketch of it on the back of my Defence of Ireland Fund collecting card. The skipper was very anxious not to appear in the matter so we weren't allowed to go down and see them on board.

We saw Pádraic Colum[23] looking very happy. Then we went into the tram and spoke of it to the conductor. He said he didn't take any interest in those Volunteers, very contemptuously, and that he was a northerner. Even one of the loyal and oppressed minority might have been pleased tho', I should have thought, at a daring thing like that, broad daylight under the nose of the helpless coastguards, and so well carried out that no one was prepared against them and no reporters on the spot. Diarmuid says the Volunteers themselves didn't know what was up as they all do route marching on Sunday, and he was among them this morning. It knocks Larne, winked at by the English, into smithereens.[24]

22. Brother of Professor Tom Kettle the MP, poet, and Volunteer, who chose to join the British Army when war broke out, believing like others that such an action would hasten independence for Ireland. Colonel Laurence Kettle was a founder member of the Volunteers, and was in charge of arms.

23. (1881–1972) distinguished poet and playwright of the Irish literary renaissance, he was a member of the Gaelic League, and staying in a cottage on Howth at the time.

24. Some members of the British establishment were concerned about the situation. Mary Louisa Hamilton Norway wrote in her account of the Rising, 'about eighteen months ago a large number broke away from Redmond's National Volunteers and formed a volunteer force which they called the Irish Volunteers. They are frankly and openly revolutionary, and when it became known some months ago that they were obtaining large quantities of arms and ammunition various persons did all they could to open the eyes of the authorities to the dangerous situation that was growing up. But as the explanation was always given that the force was for national defence only, the Government failed to take any steps to put down the movement.' *The Sinn Féin Rebellion as They Saw It*, ed. K. Jeffery (Dublin, Irish Academic Press, 1999) pp. 35–6.

We met Diarmuid, and Mary Spring-Rice and a man called Gordon,[25] who were all on the yacht with the exception of the first-named, at one of the minor stations on the line up. They came to lunch. Mary Spring-Rice had on a red skirt, which had been the signal to the others. All last night they were going up and down in the bay wishing to put in to Dunleary Harbour, and afraid to and didn't in the end. They weren't sure the cruiser wasn't there, and if it had failed.

– After lunch, which happened about 3, we sat and talked about it, at least they did and I listened, and my respect for Diarmuid has increased about 200%. This evening he lay on the sofa looking picturesque and tired, and about twelve years old, apparently they didn't any of them have enough sleep for weeks. His cargo is yet to be landed. Martha came in, as we were sitting round the fire after Mr. Coffey had gone to bed, and said, "Would ye like to see the Stop Press news. There's war in Dublin." We read about it. The King's Own Scottish Borderers were sent out against the INVs who were coming from Howth. Also the Dublin Metropolitan Police all armed. Shots were exchanged, tho' the INVs tried to avoid a fight. Apparently the soldiers had to get out of the way, tho' they wounded some INVs. I hope the latter wounded some of them.

On their way back they fired on the citizens on Bachelors Walk. Twenty people, mostly women and young girls, were hurt. It's like an Englishman to fire on women. One has since died at Jervis Street Hospital, where they were all taken. I hope the soldiers will be identified and hung. D says any Dublin jury would convict them if it got half a chance. They say some of the D.M.P's refused to attack the I.N.Vs, which is the best thing ever heard of them if it's true. Anything more criminally foolish than to send them out to interfere like that I never heard – even of Dublin Castle. They must have wanted to provoke a riot . . .

31 July 1914. The King's Own Scottish Murderers is how the K.O.S.B[26] are known now. On the *National Volunteer* this week: "The Right to Murder. England's Claim." The *Evening Herald* calls it "The Military Pogrom."

Three people have died since. There was a great funeral procession through the streets of Dublin, thousands of people, and who was keeping them in order? – the Volunteers. The Pro-Cathedral was full of

25. Probably Major Gordon Casserley, ex-Indian army, who trained officer Volunteers.

26. King's Own Scottish Borderers.

friends of the dead, and Volunteers, and there were hundreds of people outside who weren't able to get in. When the service was over, they were afraid if they opened the doors suddenly that the people would run inside. So some Volunteers came out and made a cordon this way,[27] hand to hand, and made the congregation go out quietly in a line. Some boys started whistling. They said, "No whistling, please", and they stopped. In the evening, which was getting dark, nothing was seen but a great host in the dying light, and nothing was heard but weeping, and Chopin's funeral march, as the coffins went past.

2nd August 1914. Germany is mobilising to balance Russia. France is bound to be in it. England can't keep out if it means France'd be beaten. "Not merely honour but interest", as the *Irish Times* puts it, forces her in. How absolutely horrible. I wonder if Jean Malye will be killed, or will Frère Georges go and volunteer. And Reggie or Herbert have to fight, and the Howard girls make use of their first-aid knowledge. Meanwhile we are so peaceful here, you'd think such a thing as war didn't exist.

Yesterday there was a storm, and in the evening Diarmuid and I went down to Sutton to get the paper. There wasn't one left. But we had a fine walk – a strong wind from the sea, without the rain wetting the air. The number of places D and I both have always wanted to go to! Carcassone is another discovered yesterday, and Nîmes, besides Spain and the Loire castles, and a lot of other places. This morning we went to Howth to buy things, and we were discussing religion going and coming. The Atonement is the major dilemma, and confuses us both. But he says he was elevated almost by the 14th chapter of St John, "Let not your heart be troubled", etc. In the evening he read me a good bit of *The King of the Dark Room* by Rabindranath Tagore. I like that play . . . We went out to light a fire on the strand. We saw Mr Orpen[28] then. We made our fire with pieces of wood which we found on the ground there so that I would have a notion of how a flame looks for Pádraic Ó Conaire's picture . . .

This evening I was lying on the sofa, because I was tired, when he and his mother went to put Mr Coffey to bed. He came back after two or three minutes and sat down in front of me looking extraordinarily graceful and picturesque, his shapely dark head and shoulders against

27. She draws a diagram of a square with one open side.
28. William Orpen (1878–1931), brilliant portrait and subject painter of his generation, had a house on Howth Head. Beatrice Glenavy, whose work Cesca admired, was his pupil, as were Grace Gifford, Seán Keating, etc.

the light background of the creamy distemper, and one thin brown hand holding a long stemmed pipe, and the other on his cocked up knee. I'd liked to have drawn him then and there. Tomorrow night perhaps.

4th August 1914. Things go too fast here. Yesterday Redmond said in the British House of Commons, "You can withdraw your armies and we will hold Ireland against foreign invasion, the National and Ulster Volunteers united". Not in those words. This is '82[29] over again, or the beginning of it. May God give us the same sense of purpose. *The Irish Times*, which I will quote later, in a really remarkable leader says Irish Volunteers of both kinds ought to keep the food in the country. We are all right if they do, certainly. Is this the dawn of that long sought unity?

Conor O'Brien,[30] his wife, and Robert Hanna were here on Sunday, all slanging Creed Meredith[31] for having taken all the fun of the landing of the guns at Greystones, and without telling them, who wanted to have some of it. "Diarmuid's guns" – there were 600 of them and 20,000 cartridges. They brought them in Sir Thomas Myles's boat, and then motorboats to land, where Volunteers all nipped into the water and got them. Diarmuid was in Dublin this morning and saw the Secretary, who said he'd been in up to his shoulders for two hours. The papers said 10,000, I wish it had been. I'm glad he brought them while it was risky, because it was, and now anybody at all can bring them in. He thinks himself that the Government will be giving them to us now. The Unionists were so delighted at John Redmond's speech. They were very much afraid, it seems . . . However, it's really rather a humorous situation, as they don't any of them seem to see that we may have double reasons for urging so keenly on them to withdraw their troops! Once we got them out in the name of the Empire we can keep them out in the name of Ireland.

Rumours of Provisional Government to be set up in Dublin by Redmond and Carson. Do they really think we shall go back to our Home Rule farce after that! D says Amiens St. was guarded by 20 soldiers and little encampments all along the line. I saw them the other day, Thursday,

29. 1782, when legislative freedom was obtained for the Irish Parliament by Henry Grattan and the original Volunteers.
30. Conor O'Brien used his boat, the *Kelpie* (in which Diarmid Coffey sailed, the companion boat to the *Asgard*), to transport some of the guns, which he landed in Kilcoole on 1 August, three days before war was declared. See Pádhraic de Bhaldraithe, *Loingseoir na Saoirse–Scéal Conor O'Brien* (Baile Átha Cliath, Coiscéim, 1996).
31. While a barrister, James Creed Meredith, took an active part in the Irish Volunteers. A philosopher, and author of literary works, he was to serve both Ireland and the League of Nations as judge in the Republican Courts and the Supreme Court.

the encampments I mean, coming back from Dublin. If we got rid of them we could take all their depots in the name of the Empire and keep them in the name of Ireland. We'll guard Ireland against foreigners, any kind . . .

5 August 1914. – Lios. The little cousins had a letter from Ivan Kirkpatrick,[32] who is very busy arranging for the embarkment of troops from Ireland and the disembarkment of troops for service in Ireland. Oh yes, I forgot, England has declared war on Germany. We shan't get rid of them all so easily, well one might have forseen that.

6 August 1914 . . . Nothing in the world is good enough to say about the National Volunteers now that the English think they will get us to help them. The attitude of the papers must be explained, the *Freeman* is fulsomely loyal and anti-German. It prints a chorus of approval of John Redmond's speech from public bodies. Lots of them are sickeningly loyal, and others appear to think it means what it doesn't.

But the Athlone Meeting, it's worth putting this down. "Last night a very representative meeting of the Protestants of Athlone was held in St. Mary's Rectory grounds for the purpose of considering their position, and the proceedings were most enthusiastic and harmonious." (Just now I interrupted myself half undressed, flung on my saffron dress and I ran out thinking that the Volunteers were going past. I heard a horn, but it was only one of them practising.) "Mr. Thomas Chapman, Managing Director, Athlone Printing Works Co., acted as Hon. Sec. to the meeting. The Chairman said they got a good lead in that morning's papers to direct them, in the letters from Captain Bryan Cooper, Lord Monteagle, the Earl of Bessborough and other prominent Unionists, but the principal lead they got, the lead that struck home, was the great speech made by that great and noble Irishman Mr. John Redmond (loud cheers).

"No matter how much they differed from him, and some of them were as opposite from him as the poles, they all recognised Mr Redmond as a great man and great leader (renewed cheers). His speech moved the House of Commons, which was not easily moved; but it moved their Irish loyalty too, and it became them to respond with all generosity of heart to the suggestion and patriotic sentiments of Mr. R. They would show their sympathy in this way. Athlone was distinguished as being the first to move in the National Volunteer movement,[33] and they could now make

32. A Dublin Castle official.

33. The Midland Volunteer Force was launched in Athlone before the Irish Volunteers were formed. See Oliver Snoddy, 'The Midland Volunteer Force 1913,' in *Journal of the Old Athlone Society* vol. 1 no. 1 (1969), pp. 39–44.

the further distinction of being the first organised body to join the Irish National Volunteers (applause). Dr. Arthur Dobbs said they were all Irishmen and should join the National Volunteers. When the crisis was over, having fought shoulder to shoulder, it would be easy to be better friends in the future and to get rid of their grievances. He proposed that they all as the Protestants of Athlone join the N.V.s in a body. Mr T. Parsons seconded. They finished with a cheer for John Redmond, the King of England and the Volunteers." Pity about the second, but I hope that this was only "staged" . . .

Sinn Féin is brave, courageous, determined, nationalistic, as always. "We've no Government to defend, we have no Constitution to defend." "All know that Mr. R has made his offer without receiving a quid pro quo . . . The spectacle of the Nat. V's with English officers at their head and the Union Jack floating proudly above them, "defending" Ireland for the Brit. Gov:, may appeal to the gushing eyes of Mr. Redmond, but his eyes are not likely to be blessed with the sight of that apotheosis of slavery. If England wins this war she will be more powerful than she has been at any time since 1864, she will treat an Ireland which kissed the hand that smote her as such an Ireland ought to be treated. If she loses the war, and Ireland is foolish enough to identify herself with her, Ireland will deservedly share in her punishment. . . Let the British Government pass in the same space of time (six hours) a full measure of Home Rule, and Irishmen will have some reason to mobilise for the defence of their institutions. At present they have none. In the alternative, let a provisional government be set up in Dublin by Mr. Redmond and Sir Edward Carson, and we shall give it allegiance. But the confidence trick has been too often played upon us to deceive us again." There's more, but this is the gist of it . . .

Diarmuid told me in a letter this morning that he is Assistant Secretary to the Inspection Staff of the Irish National Volunteers from yesterday. He will be working there, 44 Dawson Street, from 10.30 this morning. He had resolved to go into the Volunteer camp, but Colonel Moore said he would be helping much more if he did this. (Fallon of Mary Street much prefers it. Weeks ago the English seized the bandoliers he was bringing in. Then he started making them himself. Diarmuid will help with this.)

Today when I was in Blackrock, I saw a man driving sheep to Dún Laoghaire. I went up to him. "Where are you taking them?" I said. He said, "I think to the Corporation in Dun Laoghaire." "Not to be embarked for England?" I asked. "No, miss", he said. "That's right, they

53 *Sketches of Diarmid Coffey, 1914*

mustn't be, any of them," I said. "No indeed, miss, we'll keep them", he said. The same thing happened with another man, and I talked about it also to a man in Findlater's grocery. They can't do anything naturally, but it's a good thing to get the thinking right . . .

7 August 1914. These days I'm a little anxious about Mother because she was to stay in England for the bazaar. She doesn't want me to go there, but yesterday I got a letter from her saying that she wouldn't be able to reach Seaford or Ireland until the end of next week because there are soldiers on line in each place. Then she will be coming here, thank goodness.

I left the Coffeys the day before yesterday in the morning. I was troubled and sad, and anxious for news of my Mother, and they were all "bricks" to me. Especially Diarmuid. But! I wish he wasn't so humble. We understand each other so well now, and know so much more about each other's thoughts. Margot is at Rostrevor now for her lung. They'll give her renewed health, please God . . . It's said in the papers today that the English had a victory in the North Sea, but it isn't confirmed. I thought, days ago, that an English victory would be a cause of joy for me, but it isn't true. It's a cause for regret. Partly thro' contradictoryness, partly since I read *Sinn Féin* yesterday. If she wins, she will be stronger than ever. I wonder how it would be if she were to be beaten on sea and France to win on land.

Mrs. Coffey was telling us one night how she met Mr. Coffey. (Diarmuid and I were sitting on the floor on each side of her in front of the fire.)

She started a Workman's Club. She began planning it when staying with the Lawrences in London, and when she came back she began. It was difficult for her because the priest thought that she wanted to proselytise, but when they saw that wasn't the case, the club went well. They had musical entertainment or a lecture as a rule every Sunday, so that the men wouldn't be drinking. These things were arranged by the people who founded the club, and they didn't bother to ask the opinion of the men. Some one suggested that Mr. Coffey should come and give a lecture, and asked him to call on her so that they could discuss it. Mr. Coffey thought at first he wouldn't go because he hated "philanthropic ladies", but then he saw a picture of her in some exhibition,[34] the picture that's in the main room in Harcourt Terrace. She is wearing a red dress. After that he thought he would go. He went. Then he helped her a lot with the club, and persuaded her to allow the men to arrange things themselves, so that they would be more independent. He must have been a glorious lover to have.

To return. Diarmuid is definitely a cooperative young man. We went walking on the cliff the night before I left Howth, "au claire de la lune". Mrs Coffey went back after a little while but we were left together. For the whole time he said not a word over the hardly definable limit we both agree to recognise. Oh it was so hard not to be sentimental!!! He must really be very strong, if I felt that! How funny it is not to know whether I'll be married to him five years hence, or to some other person who I don't know – or maybe not at all! . . .

10 August 1914. I didn't write anything yesterday. *Must* keep up *every* night however tired I am . . . A depression. The Germans are in Liège, they say, but nobody at all knows did they win or not. They themselves say there was a great victory, and the other people speak of the thousands of soldiers captured by them. I don't know what's going on but only that it's a bitter battle, and that the French are in Alsace. I wonder was Frère Georges there with them. I'd like to see that, them going across the Frontière. We little thought in the month of May when we were there that it would come so soon, and oh! how are Simon Marchal and the other friends. This "Great European War" that has been coming for a long time, and I didn't really believe that it would come in my lifetime. Every kind of ambulance work has been taken up by the Irish Volunteer

34. The Royal Hibernian Academy annual exhibition in 1881. See John O'Grady, *The Life and Work of Sarah Purser* (Dublin, Four Courts Press, 1996), p. 174, no. 44.

Ambulance Association, and I'll go and see them tomorrow. I wish to goodness that I had more money.

Mr. Best[35] and Mrs Best came to T with the Coffeys. They have just come back from Germany, but they wish victory to the English. He says that the German would be worse for us than the Saxon, but for all this he is a true Gael. She too. He can't publish *Eriú* yet this month because he hasn't had anything from Kuno Meyer,[36] and he thinks it won't come out until the War is over . . .

Saturday. Seosamh Laoide[37] came with *An Chéad Cloch*,[38] the first copy I have seen, with Salome on the outside. When I showed that to the cousins, two of them said that it was profane, and the third took no notice!

. . . Yesterday in Capel Street, I met that man I had spoken with at Howth. We talked for a long time on the footpath. He told me that there was a Volunteer Meeting the other night, and that half of them were extremists and half of them loyal to Home Rule. They were having a talk, and discussed whether they would be ready to fight for the Empire or only for Ireland. "Every man who is ready to fight and die for Ireland come to this side," he said. And, "Everyone who is ready to do the same for the sake of the Empire come to this side," and they were half and half.

Then he felt he should go to where the Provisional Committee was sitting at the time, and say to the Committee that they had absolutely no desire to be loyalists, but that they would fight for Ireland alone; and nobody would support him. Instead the Volunteers went themselves to send their officers in, and they presented the delegate – they were in uniform and equipped with guns – . . .

I was silly to tell the cousins I'd seen the Howth Coup. I ought to have held my tongue again, that was brought up this evening as occasioning "*such* pain". I suppose when one is 86 one can't be expected to take anything in proportion . . .

35. Celtic Scholar and connoisseur, at the time Assistant Director of the National Library.
36. German scholar of Celtic languages, and translator of Old Irish poetry.
37. J. H. Lloyd (1865–1939), Protestant member of the Gaelic League, who wrote for *An Claidheamh Soluis* and published books in Irish until 1915, but then turned against the language.
38. See Ill. 49.

There was a meeting the other day, where Mac Giolla Bhríghde and Úna Ní Fhairceallaigh[39] were speaking and saying that "England's difficulty was Ireland's difficulty, and any man who said other was a fool." She is too certain, I think, I have my doubts about her. She is a Catholic, and under the thumb of the Church, I'll never confide in her.

39. Agnes O'Farrelly (1874–1951) worked for the equality of women and became a member of the first Board of National University in 1909. She was Vice-President of the Gaelic League and supported Hyde when he was challenged by the Volunteers. She chaired the foundation meeting of Cumann na mBan in Wynne's Hotel in 1914, when one of the objectives agreed on was to launch and administer a fund to assist the arming of Irishmen for the defence of Ireland. At the same time, according to *An Claidheamh Soluis* (5 Oct. 1914), like Redmond and Mac Giolla Bhríghde, she still saw Ireland as part of the Empire and could not envisage an independent nation.

54 *Uillinn Piper*

7
The Volunteers and Cumann na mBan

Cesca's three brothers joined up when War was declared – Herbert according to Margot, who was still in Rostrevor Sanatorium, 'for the excitement of it'. Herbert had gone to Belgium, she told her sister, 'I daresay he does care a little about fighting for England . . . but not much.'[1] Cesca had heard earlier that it was France he was going to, and wrote in her diary:

> 12 August 1914 . . . He will be a despatch-rider for the French army, he hopes, speeding from place to place on his motorbike. His experience of accidents will come in useful, he says. "This is what I've been waiting for for four years." Mother gave him £15 for the journey and he has debts as well. I wish I had some more money. Eddie B. is also going. May they come safely out of it!

Reggie's fiancée, Clare, was doing her bit.

> A letter from Clare some days ago, very unhappy and detailing all the preparations they are making, poor little thing, fifty beds at the Village Hall, the things necessary to be got on loan of which they have the promises.

1. Margot to 'Darling Nut', 17 Aug. 1914.

She and the other Red Cross people are to have a day probationing at the Cottage Hospital. It doesn't seem long. A great battle is expected, two million men engaged, the evening papers say it has begun and French and German cavalry. It was for this that their mothers suffered for them and brought them up; for this their fathers worked to feed them, I suppose, that they might be torn to pieces by shells and shot at and sabred and killed in every way for one country's aggrandisement and another country's greed and another's interest . . .

Diarmid was in Dawson Street, Personnel Officer for outlying units on the staff of the Volunteers, and assistant to the Chief of Staff Colonel Edmond Cotter. Both Cotter and Colonel Maurice Moore – retired professional soldiers and among the six members of the Volunteer Military Council – gave their services voluntarily, Cotter directing the training and military organisation of the men. 'Mrs. Coffey says that they are in two rooms now, he and Cotter in one, and Col: Moore and Erskine Childers in the other. Cotter is giving him more responsibility now.' Cesca herself was studying the School of Civics programme, and got the information she needed about First-aid classes at St Vincent's Hospital. She continued to write her diary:

13 August 1914 . . . It's a good thing the Friday night episode, i.e. the Volunteers' visit to the Provisional Committee, didn't get into the papers, but I'm glad they did it, it probably influenced the Provisional Committee against handing them over to the British War Office, which would have been a calamity and which would have caused serious disunion. Col. Moore wanted it done. In the *Independent* today I see it "is understood" that the Volunteers will only accept arms unconditionally[2] . . .

14 August 1914. A stifling sultry day, thundery skies, two warm showers this morning. I think men are fighting today, it's in the air. There's a mist between us and Howth, blue, faint, and still. So far the English have left the fighting to the French and Belgians. I suppose when the Germans are thoroughly weakened the English will come in and win a "great victory". "Routed Germans". "British troops in pursuit"

2. The position of the Volunteers as a citizen army was still unclear. According to *The Independent* (13 Aug. 1914), no arrangement had been made between the Government and the Provisional Committee of the Irish National Volunteers as to their status, or conditions under which men would serve. Most Volunteers objected to fighting with regular or reservist army forces, but would be willing to cooperate with the Ulster Volunteers in repelling hostile invaders and defending Ireland against foreign aggression.

etc. Mother isn't coming till Wednesday. She is staying in London for the same reasons Máighréad and I came here, wishing to be with the country one loves in its bad time. I wish she wouldn't tho', she feels the sorrows and anxieties of the English as her own.

Mr. Gill showed me a French paper, *L'Echo de Paris,* of Saturday, about the English troops landing, so they must have on Friday. Four regiments left Dublin yesterday. I saw one, an English one, going down Grafton Street. A few girls were at a window and they were waving a Union Jack and cheering, but this was out of enthusiasm, some of the soldiers were cheering themselves. I said to a man near me, "once they've gone, we won't let them back again". He seemed doubtful whether I could have said such a heretical thing . . .

In the evening my tram going back into Dublin was held up with lots of others for soldiers to pass, there were crowds over O'Connell Bridge. It looked so beautiful up O'Connell street, dim and blue and the pale flames of the trams moving, and Nelson's Pillar blue and towering against a pale delicate sky, a green so fine that you couldn't paint it, with soft clouds flushed with faint light, frayed at the edge. You could make a good picture of that and call it, *The Conquered City.* I remember it every time I see Nelson . . .

In the morning I went to the Sinn Féin office. The man there told me the Dublin Volunteers were in a highly excited state and asked me if I knew what had happened on Friday night. It appears that they had had to shut the doors on the Volunteers that same night to let them cool down a bit before they went off to the Provisional Committee. It's an anxious business. He also said a couple of months from now developments might be expected if they got more excited about anything. A good many are prepared to take arms if the British Government gives them under conditions and then break the conditions. One can't approve that attitude but one can be glad it exists. Many more are not prepared to accept any conditions. It's a good thing there should be strong feeling here as a counterblast to the country Volunteers, who go playing *God save the King* all over the place. Diarmuid is fearfully cautious as usual, I daresay it's a good thing, someone should be, tho' I can imagine having a serious disagreement with him on the subject . . .

First-Aid class last night, Room packed, far too many to see properly . . . We're going to have a practice at 7 next Tuesday for an hour before the class, everyone bringing one triangular and one roll bandage, and wearing blouses the sleeves of which will push up and the collars of

55 *Studies from a Sketchbook*

which will undo. On my way back there was a crowd on the other side of the road in O'Connell Street. I went over to see what it was, 10.15 PM or so. Imagine! – five little gamins with sticks, in a row, and a sixth drilling them. They had bandoliers made of corks strung together.

15 August 1914. Today Sinn Féin sent *Ireland and the War* pamphlets to me, and after dinner I went to distribute them in Blackrock. I left some in the telephone office, and some in each shop that I know and in some that I don't, and they were all friendly. I had a little argument with the man in the town hall, but he took copies and said he would give them to people all the same . . .

In the afternoon I went to Dublin on my bicycle to get a book on veins, arteries, etc. so that I could draw pictures of them, but nearly every shop closed. Then I went to the Museum, and I looked at the spears and the swords and the razors and garments of the Bronze Age . . . Coming back my brown bag was on my shoulder. The O'Rahilly went past on his bicycle and looked back. I greeted him, and he slowed down and said, "When I saw the bag, I knew that it was some one dedicated to the Ireland's cause." He was dressed like a Volunteer, it suits him, but I think that he is becoming too full of himself. He didn't say a word worth remembering, except that they had planned to bring in six thousand rifles at Howth, and with fifty Volunteers from every company in Ireland there, but they hadn't enough money. In his opinion, we won't get rifles from the British Government until the Germans defeat them, and it's not likely that that will happen now. I'm in total agreement with him about that.

16 August 1914. The day before yesterday there was a storm . . . in the afternoon. Thunder like big guns, and lightning like their flashes as they kill people, and then rain. Sweethearts and wives first, and then sisters and mothers. The way I knew which was the tears of which was because it was more passionate and intense at first, but the other went on longest. I drew myself, rather a ghastly affair, and later painted myself by candlelight so that it all looks bright yellow in the daylight but not so bad at night.[3] Cousin Fanny and I played patience and Cousin Maria insisted upon reading us all the highly coloured narratives in the London *Times* and indulging in a perfect orgy of emotion, incidentally getting the paper between us and the light the while.

I went out to the Coffeys today to lunch and missed a train as usual! Col. Cotter was there to lunch too. He and D. and I came up on the tram together. He started talking at once and didn't stop at all. D. says he's like that all day in the office. "Fancy, that chap at the head of an army of 200,000 men." It gets on his nerves, it must be fearful. That office is a queer place, according to him. Col. C. has no more idea of method or a businesslike way of working than D. has, who is forced to invent methods of correlating letters etc., buy proper paper, files, even chairs and tables. It's just the same with Erskine Childers and Col. Moore, the latter hasn't much more idea. He got some paper, thin bluish grey like a kitchenmaid uses, and without any sort of official stamp until they got him some decent paper and hid the other. The main difference in the offices is that Erskine Childers knows something of the work and D. knows almost nothing, according to his own account anyway. Probably true, he's had no experience but he'll soon know a lot. He has to! Col. Cotter is a nice old boy tho' and is sound about the Volunteers not being handed over to the British Government . . .

Such a perfect afternoon, we walked over the hill to the drill, and Mrs. Coffey and I watched while D drilled and Col. C. talked to the instructors and looked on. That same priest was there who made the long drivel the last time I went to a drill, but thank Heaven he didn't this time.

---

3. See Cat. no. 5, and col. plate 4.

They were of better physique than the average Tommy, said Col. C., one company 'specially good, drilled by a little fellow with a strong voice. Mrs. Coffey went back by tram, and Col. C. and I walked back over the hill, he still talking. I didn't have time to get tired of it, but I think one would quite easily. He's a simple-minded man but sincere and patriotic, and not appreciative of D. I suppose the latter will have him under his thumb quite soon, he's begun already! I must write some of this to the Goat under *geasa*[4] not to tell, it wouldn't do for it to get about and every member of the office trying to let on that it's run on highly businesslike lines.

In Derry the other day, Cotter and Moore were sent to arrange privately about the celebrations of the 12th July so there shouldn't be rows . . . It took them a long time to get the people on our side to consent to approach the others on the subject. This is the order of peace-lovers: soldiers, civilians and priests . . . An hour before they went, who turned up but the Ulster Volunteers to arrange the same thing. They respect each other there.

Howth is a delicious heavenly place. Mrs. Coffey and I went to see Mrs. Pike, who was a beautiful Miss Howard with marble features when she was young, up at Sherewater, but there was no one in but a pompous butler. We came back across those wide sunlit fields with the sea below us, a blue mist: and life was lovely, in spite of the war. We went up to see Beatrice Elvery (Campbell)[5] too. She has rather a picturesque husband, with hair standing up over his head, and features like her drawings of heroes in rough. Her red hair is the prettiest thing about her, at least she would be much more if she wore decent clothes but anything so dull and characterless I never saw. An artist too, it's a crime. Mr. Sinclair[6] was there in flannels, with shirt open upon a hairy chest, of whom many tales are told, including that he is like Æ only more so (Beatrice E.) and that he has orgies and makes people drunk on purpose (Mrs. Bellingham) . . .

19 August 1914 . . . Yesterday I was in Dublin. To Pym's where I found a nice girl, who said their four Irish-speaking assistants were away on their holidays, and promised to learn . . . After that to the Vege.

4. Under a taboo (Old Irish).
5. (1883–1968). Married to Gordon Campbell, later Lord Glenavy. A distinguished artist, painter and illustrator for the Cuala Press, which espoused the national movement.
6. William Sinclair married Cissie Beckett (aunt of Sam Beckett), who was at art school with Beatrice Elvery. They kept open house in Howth for the poets, writers and artists of Dublin.

restaurant. After a while Diarmuid came in. I don't know whether it was that the last time he came in he had been so cross with me, but it seemed nicer than ever to see him this time. We had lunch together and we walked to my train through the College.

We were just beginning a discussion . . . in reference to the Volunteers and Redmond. He goes on about the Empire fit to make you sick. I think he's an Imperialist at heart. D. thinks he's not . . . "At this moment," says D., "there's a conference going on at the Gresham Hotel between Mr. Redmond, Col. Moore and a man called Mahon,[7] I think representing England, with full powers from Kitchener." I wish I knew what they had decided. I did D. an injustice, he's almost for extreme measures now in regard to the Volunteers . . .

The idea is that one third of the Volunteers should be under the Government's orders for six weeks defending the coast, then another set come on, in turn, so we'll always have two thirds more of them at our disposal anyway; but we agreed that to surrender them at all for however short a time was a surrender of the whole principle and not to be thought of. We hardly talk of anything else, there seems nothing else to talk of . . .

A sort of despair came over me tonight . . . but I suddenly heard a horn while I was sitting at the window, and I ran down and saw some Volunteers going past, four men on their own. I called out, "Good men" and "Good luck to you"; and one of them came back to talk to me. He was steady enough, it seemed to me, and I would say that more than half of them are Sinn Féiners, according to what he told me. They have decided to buy the guns for themselves whatever happens, and I encouraged this and rang the changes on "England doesn't change."

Friday. Another chaotic meeting last night, but perhaps cosmos will come out of it . . . There are a lot of big ships in the port today, fourteen of them, and nobody knew why they were there. Bingham said to transport horses from Ireland, some woman told the Coffeys that there was a German cruiser around and they had been told not to go out (they were staying there without moving), but in the afternoon two of them went off, and I think that most of them are gone now. Another person said that it was to take food away from Ireland. Mrs. Coffey and I deplored that. "Whatever happens, the troops must be fed," said Mother.

She was beautiful at Howth this afternoon, but Mrs. C calls her "Mrs. Trench", and she calls Mrs. C "Janey", and that's not right. I am

7. General Bryan T. Mahon, Commander-in-Chief of British Forces in Ireland 1916–18.

ashamed when I think about it. We went to a meal there. Diarmuid wasn't back before we left though we passed each other going down on the tram. He looked tired, and his slim shoulders stooping more than ever, I looked back after he'd passed, but he didn't. So like him! This reminds me that the reason the cousins were hurrying Mother to come over was because they wanted to know what my relations were with the Coffeys. Cousin M. wrote an anxious note! Mother replied calmly that there was no need for perturbation as she was perfectly satisfied about it. I knew they must be tho' they pretended not . . .

I got a letter from Diarmuid yesterday, in the afternoon (when I was on my knees in the hall cutting a shirt pattern for the soldiers!) saying to me not to be afraid that the Volunteers are getting too English, because there is no danger of this, "as the tendency at the Civil Headquarters is all the other way."

24 August 1914. This is his letter, or part of it . . ."The Military Headquarters see certain difficulties in the attitude of the Civil Headquarters, as it is impossible to run an army without all the services comprised in the Army Service Corps, Paymaster's department etc., and it would be impossible for us to organise these for the next six months. I don't know which side to take as I see both quite clearly. If only one could invent some means of reconciling the two it would be grand, for neither party wants to have more to do with the War Office than can be helped, but the military side can't see any way out of it. . . . Of course you won't tell anyone what I say. We are supposed to be a most harmonious crowd" . . .

I saw him today. Tho' I still think it's dangerous in the extreme to go under the War Office in any way, it seems the only thing. The situation is impossible at present. Here we have an army, undisciplined, above all unarmed, without officers, without commissariat, clothing, or transport. It has practically said it will defend Ireland. To do this efficiently it must be able to mobilise 40,000 men in a couple of days. It couldn't mobilise 1,000 in a fortnight. If the Germans do come here, well we've no quarrel with them but we're going to try and prevent them landing. Unless we get organisation and control we can do nothing of the sort. At present none of the Volunteers have any idea of discipline.

Col. Cotter's way out is a scheme by which we bargain with the Government to provide clothing, that is all except actual uniforms, equipment, bandoliers etc. and arms, also officers from the British Army who know their work, none lower than Colonel so that they should be in a distinct minority, all the rest being Volunteer Officers.

56 *Diarmid Coffey*

No questions are to be asked about these latter officers, and no oaths to be extracted. In return for this, 40,000 Volunteers are to be under their control for three months, with court-martial and the other powers to their hand. This would leave us two thirds free to object and bring pressure to bear if they did anything we did not like. Then 40,000 more, and so forth, till at the end of 9 months we would have an organised though rudimentary army. – We could then bring much more pressure to bear than we can now when no one controls anything or is controlled by anyone, in the way of securing a Government that decent men could respect . . .

I went into their office today with a note for D to ask him to lunch . . . We sat in Stephen's Green and talked about them as we always do, on one of those benches round the bandstand in the shade. I ate an apple, and he smoked a pipe, there was no one around hardly, so no fear of spies. Last year I used to think to myself I would instantly fall in love with him if he wasn't so ridiculously slim for his height. I don't care if he is now, I just think it nice and uncommon and attractive, so it shows how much nearer I am to being in love. It's a better kind too, than the sort that has physical perfection to feed on, I think. If I fall in love with him it'll be because he is my anam-chara.[8] M'elle Genoud said once if I fell in love I should do it in a way to "correspondre à votre type physique", by which she meant passionately. Well now, I wonder.

I've no experience, of course, but, from what I've heard of it, passion sounds the sort of thing one wouldn't like. I suppose there must be some of it all the same in love between husband and wife or they could never bear the physical contact with each other, and in that way it must be right and pure and natural, but if there's nothing but that it'll be all wrong when the senses change, for it stands to reason they are not always in the same condition. It's then that the anam-cháirdeachas gets the upper hand, tho' of course it ought to have been there all the time and to have first attracted the people to each other . . .

26 August 1914 . . . Some of the girls coming in [to First-Aid] started a rumour that there was a "conscription proclamation" out. They probably meant "the militia ballot", whatever it is. Kitchener said tonight, "if the war should be protracted and if the fortunes should be varied or adverse, exertions and sacrifices beyond any which have been demanded will be required from the whole nation". That means conscription and they'll try to take our people, for their own won't fight and ours are only too ready. Here or in the other towns they'll resist, but in the country it'll be hard for them. Meantime people subscribe no more for arms as they say Redmond said the Government'd give them. They say Namur has fallen, but it may only mean the town, like Liège, and not the forts. If it has, the Germans have begun a march on Paris.

Mrs. K[incaid] took Mother house-hunting this morning and she saw one she thought'd do, at Killiney, it seems nice and peaceful to be taking a house.

30 August 1914 . . . Asquith is coming here. To help recruiting assuredly. The Allies are being beaten. Mother believes all the "German-atrocity" stories. They report today a British victory in the North Sea, we must try to make Asquith's meeting a failure. What I'd like to do'd be, give him a guard of Volunteers to wherever he means to speak, several hundreds. Directly he starts let the loyalists cheer and spare your breath. Then when they stop let the Volunteers begin. Let him try to speak and mistake it for enthusiasm, and raise his hand, and they go on, detachment

8. Literally 'soul-friend'.

by detachment, so that it is absolutely impossible for him to make any speech . . .

The *Irish Times* is in a panic and calls on us all to enlist, and the rest to submit to the War Office. I was awfully afraid about that latter at the beginning of this week, but now one can say "no fear". Mary Spring-Rice was in in the afternoon, saying that the doctors of Co Limerick have refused to work at first-aid classes under the Department's Scheme, thro' hostility to Lloyd George[9] it's likely, and if so, they ought to come round. When she'd gone out, in with Mrs. Clarke.[10] She said Mary Spring-Rice had come hot-foot from a soldiers and sailors cutting-out-clothes-for-them meeting and was inclined to doubt her sincerity for that. It struck me very much her suspecting us, as she's the first I ever met who did, when so many times they might have. It's *so* reasonable, and *so* rare. But her man was 15 years in prison, a Fenian, so it's natural . . .

I never realised before how the official nationalist despises the physical-force man. This presupposes my presence at Howth on Sunday. I found the air full of thunder, discovered afterwards that Mr. Gill had been giving Diarmuid advice as to what to say in a letter to Mr. Redmond, which the latter didn't want. He was in the diningroom writing it when I went in, and stayed there to finish it. He meant to say something to this effect, "If the Home Rule Bill isn't passed there'll be a great anti-enlisting movement thro' the country". Afterwards he came in and sat in a low chair looking absurdly young and long.

We had a heated argument coming back from bringing Miss Culverwell over the hill. He thinks anti-English outcry at this time worse than useless. I think it's better than anti-German. He thinks we have no strength with which to execute pressure from what he knows of the unorganised state of the Volunteers. I think our strength is unrealised by us when we consider the difficulties England is in. She wants men and not to be bothered more than anything. If we keep the men and bother her she'll give us anything, even repeal of the Union, I believe. His idea is to pass the Bill, "get tips from the War Office" (that's all right but very different from going under them, or getting arms and equipment from

9. Chancellor of the Exchequer at the time.
10. Kathleen Clarke (1878–1972), daughter of Limerick Fenian leader John Daly, and wife of nationalist Tom Clarke who organised the IRB from his tobacconist's shop in Parnell Street. She was a confirmed feminist, and eventually became the first woman Lord Mayor of Dublin.

them) and use the efficient army thus gained for pressure. Meantime the English may have won and they'd be stronger than ever and able to bring their army back to suppress us. D. says the police could do it now. But at any rate they couldn't so easily and the English wouldn't dare excite hostility anyway. Meantime the Volunteers are getting impatient. If the Germans come here and they try to defend the country they'll be massacred by the thousand.

30 August 1914. Dear Phroinnséas,[11]

Sorry I was cross today, I was beastly irritable but should not have let it out on you.

I think we were rather at cross purposes about things in our talk. What I meant was that as long as things are in their present state (i.e. the HR. Bill on the verge of passing and the Volunteers unarmed and hardly disciplined at all) we must avoid any political move which would bring them up against the English for two reasons.

(a) Because in making any *definite* statement of policy towards England there is bound to be a strong difference of opinion in Volunteer ranks, though the majority would do what Redmond told them as long as they get or are convinced they are going to get the HR Bill. (This is a fact as anyone who knows the Volunteers in the country will tell you.)

(b) Because for a body, which has by its great majority and by lucid acquiescence in Redmond's speech said it is prepared to defend the coasts of Ireland, to fly in the face of the only practical means by which it can become fit to do so is absurd.

To get a government, as things are, one must either get the Home Rule Bill passed now or be in a position to insist on HR as soon as this war is over, or when a suitable opportunity may arise. By keeping quiet, and avoiding open expression of hatred of England, we are practically sure of getting the HRB now. There will probably be a new amending bill later and then we must be organised. To be organised we must have some men with practical experience and a certain amount of authority behind them to help us. For the moment it does not matter whence that authority is derived because if the interests of the Volunteers and their superior officers come into serious conflict it would be the superiors who would go to the wall. At present we have no one with enough authority or experience to run a pig sty.

11. Diarmid still used this Irish equivalent for 'Frances' (Cesca's baptismal name), even though Cesca had established her name as 'Sadhbh'.

I firmly believe that if we go on organising and don't talk politics more than we can help, we shall be able to get what we want when the time comes without the least trouble or fuss. Meanwhile pick holes in this letter and tell me what a wrongheaded cuss you think me when next we meet.

I am your devoted friend always, Diarmuid.

57 *Self-Sketches, c. 1914*

8
Following Leaders

As the signing of the Home Rule Bill continued to be delayed, and there was no guarantee of its implementation, Cesca grew more and more concerned about the political situation, and particularly about the influence Carson seemed to wield. Something had been decided between Carson and the Government, she felt – 'he has his way and that is the reason he is going to talk to his people in Belfast now.'

The Coffeys had moved from Howth into town, where they now lived in Harcourt Terrace; and Mrs. Coffey invited her to stay.

> 5 September 1914 . . . Mrs. Martyn was there in the afternoon, very melancholy and saying the Volunteers had done all the harm in the world, that only for them we'd have had Home Rule in May, only the English were afraid of civil war . . .
>
> Miss Mitchell[1] was there too, very cheerful. She had heard from a very high up source that the Bill was to be passed next week, that Carson had been told he'd got to put up with it and that he'd gone there and then [to Belfast] to tell them. It certainly looked like either that – when we saw this morning that the Ulster Volunteers were taking all steps to go under the War Office – or that he had won his point and was able to tell

1. Susan L. Mitchell (1866–1926), poet and satirist, assistant editor of the *Irish Homestead* and a passionate nationalist, who was friendly with Diarmid Coffey.

them that the Home Rule Bill was to be held up indefinitely, even if, for reasons of recruiting, it was formally passed and signed . . .

Diarmuid hauled out my letter and set of questions at dinner, and read them all out and disputed them. At least he did the first which was, are we, or not, able to give England the things she most needs? He says that the answer is "no", while I think still it's "yes". Men! Otherwise we agree, which is rather a comfort.

My questions were an answer to his letter, which was a *suite* to our heated argument of Sunday when we both misunderstood each other. At the same time, I believe he has changed his position slightly . . . It was rather joyful, and pleasant a thing, to dwell together in unity with the F.O.G.L.[2] again on a serious matter. I told him so, he said same here, or words to that effect. I was sitting on a sofa at one end, and he at the other, and I began to say pensively that it was impossible there should be anything in the whole world so absorbing as this country . . .

This is a curious life I lead, a real double one. I do sympathise a lot about the war and suggest hopeful ways in which the Germans may be beaten, and I've given up trying to persuade Mother not to believe all the atrocity stories. Maybe this is wrong but it's easier just to keep one's mouth shut, tho' rather depressing. I have a sort of surface gaiety and cheerfulness, and am as near being an anti-nationalist as I could be – and when I go out I make up! The Allies are still being beaten, they say the Germans are at Senlis, that sweet village with its 18th century houses and gates and its Cathedral, and the woods where we pulled the cowslips and walked in the sun and shade – Rodica Manín and Yvonne, and the two young Bernands and I. I wonder where they are now – fighting, or killed maybe. We hear nothing of French losses. And I suppose the Germans are in the wood and on that great sandy plain where they exercised and drilled – and what are the Melles Genoud doing? Is it – Paris – beseiged yet? Mother had a letter which cheered her greatly from Raghnal, speaking of a camp, and casualty lists of half the English army had been published so that the other half must be somewhere . . .

8 September 1914. The joyful and pleasant thing is no longer, I thoro'-ly disagree with the F.O.G-L. – he won't bring his influence on the side of enforcing the Act. He always beats me in argument which I hate, 'specially when I'm so sure I'm right. He's got too intricate a mind or else he'd see what the national issue was. It is shameful for us to range ourselves openly on the

2. A nickname for Diarmid, taken from 'Fear Óglaigh', 'Man of the Volunteers'.

side of England while she holds us in prison. The Home Rule Bill is not worth the paper it's written on while it remains unenforced. We could make them enforce it by an anti-enlisting campaign. The one hope for us is that the Bill shouldn't be signed. Then we could unite, but they're too clever for that. It'll be signed, and then the recruiting will begin.[3]

Mother had a letter from Clare today describing how they had gone to Richmond Park and met and had lunch with Reggie drilling there, and how they had brought the rifles back to the gate for them in the G.W.K. It makes me so jealous. They have guns and money and organisation, and grounds and union and everything, and we – nothing . . .

12 September 1914. Summer lasted till the day before yesterday, but it's gone now. Lusk was the last day of it. We went along there at midday, and saw the sea round Malahide lying pale blue and still, like an enchanted loch, and wide stretches of pale blue water on the other side, and flat pale yellow sand-hills, and yellow-green seaweed nearer hand, and overall the pale blue misty sky and the sun dreaming and glowing on the earth. I thought I'd go out and paint it some day, but one couldn't paint the magic . . .

Michael Dwyer is such an angel, he goes to sleep quite suddenly on my knee after tormenting my silk persistently for fifteen minutes, and doesn't mind how many times I throw him away. That's a characteristic of cats I think, and I don't suppose anyone else'd see anything particularly angelic in it, but I do. He's so comforting to stroke and think about, when Mother exults over British victories (alleged) and the wickedness of the Germans (alleged) and believes that all British troops are paladins, and reads out Reggie's and Herbert's letters about their work for the British Empire . . .

14 September 1914 . . . Last Wednesday I was at the office early in the afternoon. I went in thro' *Irish Freedom* and found Séan Mac Diarmuid[4] in charge. I suppose he's the editor, and thro' that little partition door which shuts all the part behind the counter, so to speak, off from the rest. Michael O'Malley, as big and fat and with hands as dirty as ever, and two other men (one moustached, and rather large than small, and a nice

---

3. The Home Rule Bill, which had been postponed by the House of Commons on 30 July because of the growing crisis, was passed on 18 Sep. with a Bill suspending its operation for an indefinite period. Two days later Redmond called on the Irish Volunteers to join the British army and nine-tenths followed him becoming the Irish National Volunteers. Eoin McNeill remained in charge of the remnant.
4. Sean MacDermott from Co. Leitrim, a member of the Military Council of the IRB and Sinn Féin, and later a member of the Provisional Government and signatory of the Proclamation at Easter 1916. Crippled by polio, he was manager of *Irish Freedom* (effectively an organ of the IRB).

ordinary face, and the other I didn't notice) in conclave . . . They went soon after. S. Mac D. gave me the key to keep for the assistant. Beautiful blue eyes he has, S. Mac D. I mean, and a saint-like face, but I didn't remember he was lame. I was talking to him on Tuesday. Of course he'd not touch the War Office with a forty-foot pole, but he wasn't bitter and made me ashamed of myself . . .

There are two things we need in the Volunteers, guns and officers. The latter we ought to be able to get from America. That's so obvious that I'm afraid there must be some impossibility about it that has prevented them doing it yet. I can't believe that it wouldn't have occurred at once to any of them, tho' D. says it didn't to him. The arms-factory – O Rahilly is supposed to have got into communication with a firm who said they'd start one if they'd guarantee to buy 1,000 a month. 52,000 a year, that's £208,000 at £4 each. We ought to be able to do that, tho' it'd be an effort – no doubt. County councils could strike a rate or whatever they call it.[5]

Besides that we'd want money to pay men to teach the officers, and a thousand other things. It'd be hard, but it's the only course. D. says the firm's offer was rejected, but that may be only provisionally. The Government won't want to help us as Volunteers if it thinks it can get our men as real soldiers. It's all very fine to plan about this, but it all depends on what Redmond does. If when the H.R.B. is passed, he tries to bring them under the War Office, he'll succeed to a large extent. But he *would* be influenced by what he thought was their feeling. Then let them show their feeling that they're more prepared to do it themselves than to go under any rotten British War Office . . .

16 September 1914 . . . Redmond made a speech today which filled me with sorrow and shame, and Mother with delight. I went to the office with lead in my heart, and came away with stars in my heels. When I got in, there was a good woman from Dungarvan there who will do a little organising work. I was working pretty hard at a list of Volunteer Secretaries to be asked to co-operate, when in came Mrs. Murray Roberts and Mrs. Curran . . . They returned later after giving me some details in re Achill. The people there aren't enlisting but they're full of the war, and absolutely empty of Ireland. She said Claud was very much depressed. He'd been last seen riding out of Keel on his bike, only it's certain not to

5. O'Rahilly did buy the output of Martini Enfield single shot .303 from W.W. Greener in Birmingham when it was legal to do so.

have been his really, a week ago, hoping to reach Belmullet that night, it then being 4 o'clock. Mrs. Wyse Power[6] says Redmond is out of touch with the country and that he'll get a warm reception if he and Asquith come here recruiting, only that if they hear of it they won't come . . .

This P.M. I came out of the office at 6.20 or so. O'Connell Street was pale misty-blue, the pavement gleamed faintly and the lamps were yellow stars. There was a mist all about. I went on up towards the river instead of turning down to the right, as I usually do, and thro' that narrow street where the unpleasant woman sells *The Volunteer*. When I got to the end of D'Olier St., revelling in the beauty, and turned the other way, the tears nearly came into my eyes, it was so beautiful. Pink flushed clouds in a clean green sky behind the great blue silhouettes of the Parliament House and Trinity College, and the street gleaming. I walked on, my eyes on the sky, and thro' numberless puddles no doubt. It was then I felt the stars in my heels. Partly the fresh air and the movement [of] keen clean air – not that we're stuffy in the office. Unless there's a terrible wind we invariably take out the windows, the cord is broken so that's the only way of opening it . . .

Today's paper has a manifesto issued by Redmond appealing to Irishmen by all their best instincts to do the worst thing for Ireland. Not a word about England or the Empire, as Diarmuid pointed out, on the other side – but that's what makes it so infernally clever, and not just clever as he thought it, but all at Poland and Belgium and France. Mrs. Clarke is one of the most militant of women-nationalists I ever met. I can quite believe she's not afraid of anyone as she states, but I have some ado not to be afraid of her. She condescended to argue with me tonight about Miss Ní Fhaircheallaigh's speech, which was rather a step, but I can see she looks on me with suspicion. What would she say if she knew I had three brothers in the army!

Miss Cunningham was here the day before yesterday saying she thought Madame Gonne a spy, an unconscious if not a conscious one – on account of the Red Cross incident, Geneva not recognising it except thro' a government. Col. Cotter hasn't enough money to go on Volunteering, so D. is in charge of that office. Col. Cotter has gone back to England. I went to say "Slán leat" to him on Wednesday, poor good man.

6. Jennie Wyse-Power (1858–1941), first President of Cumann na mBan, patriot and feminist, who became a Senator of the Free State after Independence. See Marie O'Neill, *From Parnell to De Valera: a biography of Jennie Wyse Power* (Dublin, Blackwater Press, 1991).

58 *Nóra Ní Choinneagáin (Miss Cunningham)*

It's a pity, but it'd be fearfully hard for him to choose if it came to the point, and it seems it will, and he depending on his half pay.

There's so much to write I can't do it all. Mr. Redmond is promised a warm reception if he comes recruiting here. The rifles he sent to Castlebar were sent back to him, by the way. All the money he got for the Volunteers, he didn't fork out any to the Provisional Committee yet. That, by the way also, is gone bankrupt according to Diarmuid, and refuses to pay various expenses the military people had been running up. Mrs. Murray Roberts said she had been contradicting what those who told her that the Howth rifles were useless said, and had been saying they were very good ones. She's a regular "London Irish", come over this year full of Dark Rosaleenishness, and is now desperately depressed after school at Acaill, trying to learn Irish under Claud's auspices.

18 September 1914 . . . Mother doesn't want to take a house permanently yet. The only thing is to wait. I hope rows [will be only] for Ireland's sake, and not for our chances of living here. There's a glorious article in *Sinn Féin* this week that merits copying out. It shall be. *The Volunteer* too, "that scurrilous little rag" as Mother calls it, is excellent.

22 September 1914. Yesterday there was a map in the *Independent* purporting to be the reproduction of one on sale in Berlin, which showed

the remodelled map of Europe. Germany stretches all along the sea from Finisterre to the Baltic, inclusive. Norway and Sweden are intact, England is a German protectorate and Ireland and Scotland are independent kingdoms . . .

The Germans have bombarded Rheims, and partially destroyed the cathedral. It's absolutely heart-breaking. I suppose it must be true, they say there is not much more than four walls left. Jeanne D'Arc and St. Michael might have done better for it, I think . . . The former might take a leaf out of St. Geneviève's book, who fills her rôle of protectress of Paris with such distinction. Melle Genoud says that, [on] the 3rd day of the devotion to her, the Germans turned from Paris, the whole square of the Panthéon being black with *monde* outside St. Étienne Dumont.

Mr. Biggar [sic] has given the Warrior Volunteers in Lusk rifles, whether each one, I'm not sure, but certainly a good many. There may not be a split after all among them. The War Office seems inclined to insist on impossible terms as far as one can gather – Diarmuid says they don't seem in the least likely to help so the less they have to do with them the better. This is a great change.

Col. Moore was over in London, supposed to be talking with Kitchener and Roberts, but he's very reticent since he came back. Redmond will bring it out at the Friday meeting. Whether they really mean to kidnap him or not, by the way, is conjecture, but it's quite on the cards that they may. Some plan they have – so much is certain. Pádhraig Ó Glasáin told me nothing was settled yet yesterday, but something is by now. Seaghán Mac Diarmuid told me so, he had a copy of a Proclamation which his correspondent told him had "plastered" Limerick last week, ending up, "Remember the Empire comes first and the Poorhouse after", and "God save the King" . . .

Séamus Caomhánach[7] gave me a lecture today at the Coffeys on how we ought to support Redmond at this moment. He said when he was my age he thought just the same, but as I'd get older it was likely I'd get sense. Mrs. Coffey thinks the same, that we should support R. for the historical reason that it's always been our destruction not to follow one leader. That would seem to imply that we should do so if the majority are going to, and what if they're not? Séamus Caomhánach says the working men are all for him, but I've found a most extraordinary feeling against him among the few I've talked to. Where there is not hostility,

7. Séamus Kavanagh from Dunquin, brother of the famous Kruger Kavanagh.

there is an uncertainty about what to think, and everywhere a certain resentment of any recruiting campaign.

They are being awfully particular about the tickets for the Mansion House meeting. Sighle Nic Fhionn[8] sent her brother to try and get some: and you are passed in on the night by a Vigilance Committee, they say. Diarmuid is sorry the War Office won't help them, but I'm glad as it may avoid a split. That's being unduly optimistic. But anyway I'm glad. It may be bad policy to refuse help but it's very good nationality.

I wish Sir Roger Casement would bring over twenty American officers to help us to organise. D. says he heard he had been making foolish and extremist speeches (probably what I should call wise and national speeches, that means), and Mrs. Wyse Power says she had seen some in the *Gaelic American,* very good ones, so now I know just the kind. But for the last three weeks "they", whoever "they" are, won't let the *Gaelic American* thro', probably because it's turned against Redmond. I asked D. to write to Sir Roger Casement, who he knows slightly, and ask him for the officers, and he said he wouldn't! Strange young man. Sir R. C. went off quietly just after Redmond took over the Volunteers, and is supposed to have been impressing on the American Irish to send guns, not money. The *Freeman* is plastered with congratulations to Redmond today, as was to be expected.

25 September 1914. Twenty members of the Provisional Committee, i.e. the majority of the original ones, have issued a manifesto repudiating Mr. Redmond and ousting his nominees from the Committee. It's rather sensational and very well expressed – the text is on a sheet separately, as it's long. They have the whole place full of police today. I passed the Mansion House and saw a good many youngish men on the steps watched over by several immense policemen apparently having their tickets examined or given out. There were a crowd of loiterers watching.

Yesterday I said to Pádhraig Ó Glasáin, "You'll have your work cut out for you tomorrow." He gazed at me gravely and said, "Oh, will I?" Mrs. Wyse Power was at the Mansion House yesterday seeing about the room for the Food Conference today at 4, and they wouldn't open the door but that >|| much, and she says there was a soldier's sleeve stretched across inside while she was waiting. *Sinn Féin* says they have machine guns inside too, and both ends of Dawson Street are to be guarded by infantry, while an enormous force of police is to guard the House and

8. Sheila Gwynn.

Square. Only ticket holders are to be allowed *into the street* from an early hour before the meeting starts.

I don't know what the plan is, but they have some plan so much is certain. It's rather an amusing situation that the Leader of the Irish Race at Home and Abroad should speak to his devoted followers on a subject, with which they deeply sympathise with him, from a platform guarded by soldiers, guns and police from the protests of the devoted followers. If only he would come out now at the last moment and drop diplomacy, the whole country would rally to him. There are a very few irreconcilables who wouldn't agree to loyally support an executive Government. We would get our Volunteers trained, we could help the French and Belgians, but he won't. He daren't now do anything but what his paymasters tell him. Now that he gets so much less from America, he has to support the Liberals thro' thick and thin. The *Leader* and *The Volunteer* are in agreement and extraordinarily good, at least the quotation from the *Leader* is. At the first-aid last night, I found most of the girls against enlisting, one who said she didn't see what we had against the English vaguely, and one fiery Sinn Féinidhe.

Diarmuid was here this evening while Mother was out at church. He came in in a desperate sort of a way and said, "I wanted to speak to you about this meeting tonight". We sat down and he went on hurriedly, "If there's a split, it seems likely that you and I will be on different sides". I agreed. "Well I wanted to say that it won't make any difference, before we say extremist things to each other. I wanted to say this before it begins. I'd rather anything in the world, except the disruption of Ireland, rather than a serious quarrel with you". "I'm not going to quarrel with you, Diarmuid, so you needn't think it", I said. "I think we can get on alright, we don't really disagree so very much". "No we don't", he said, "I agree with you in theory, besides, only" – he clasped his head in his hands. "You're a Separatist aren't you", I said. "Well, then, that's alright, it's only a difference of method" – "Anyway", he said, raising his head, "I shall know you're doing it because you think it right – *we* needn't make a split".

He was awfully unhappy. I hate him to be and told him so, but it comforted him rather to realise we hadn't got to quarrel, apparently. "We've had nothing but trouble since the first Englishman landed in this country", he said fiercely. "I sometimes think I'd give anything for unity. Look at those orange people, they've kept together for three years and we can't for one. Of course this may be a storm in a tea-cup that'll blow over, only it happens to be the tea-cup you and I are in" . . .

They are shouting evening editions all down Clyde Road as I write this, but no one has come here since 6.30 when they had an edition of the *Evening Telegraph* with the news that Asquith had had an enthusiastic reception at Dun Laoghaire for all the stop-press. I hope that means nothing particular has happened. Cathal Power[9] told D. that the Sinn Féiners are holding a meeting in Thomas St., which of course is miles away, so that'd be alright; but D. says Cathal Power lies when he thinks there's anything to be gained from it, so he doesn't know whether it's true. He's inclined to believe him. I'm inclined not to in the light of Pádraic Ó Glasáin's remark.

He was going down to Dawson Street to see what happened if anything did. He kissed my hand before he went away in the same hasty desperate manner in which he had come in. Tomorrow I will copy the Volunteers' manifesto and write a resumé of the war. They are still fighting on the Aisne, neither side winning, and both killing each other for all they are worth. Mrs. Hunter is in great anxiety about Noël as his regiment has suffered greatly. D. says the revolters who issued the manifesto are holding the office by force – in Kildare Street! Barbed wire entanglements etc.

Sunday 27 September. It seems that they have to stop fighting soon, there are so many killed on each side. The Allies cannot shift the Germans from their entrenched position. It's nearly a fortnight since they started there. There was no row the night before last, the nearest approach to it was when Mrs. Sheehy Skeffington[10] attempted to speak and was prevented by the police. Enormous crowds were all about and Larkin was announced to address a meeting at the head of Dawson Street, but he didn't. There was no meeting in Thomas St. either. Diarmuid went wandering all about looking for one and found nothing!

I was so thankful when I read it in the paper that I gave 1/- in the offertory. Today hundreds of them are to parade, to process after the body of Sylvester Pidgeon who has died of wounds received in Bachelors

9. Son of Jennie Wyse Power, b. 1892, he was an enthusiastic member of the Gaelic League and joined Sinn Féin at the age of 13. He graduated in 1913, and was afterwards called to the Bar.

10. Hanna Sheehy Skeffington (1877–1946), daughter of David Sheehy, M.P. and member of the Irish Republican Brotherhood. With her husband, Francis Skeffington, later editor of *The Irish Citizen* and *The Nationalist,* and Margaret Cousins, she founded the Irish Women's Franchise League. They worked with Connolly in the labour movement, Hanna going on hunger strike during the 1913 lock-out. Both were actively opposed to recruiting.

Walk. They were drilling out at Fairview, and had sealed orders, dealing with today they were sure. I wonder who gives the orders now, the Revolters, I suppose. There seems to be such a strong party on that side that it'll make the split worse. I believe the Friday night demonstration is only put off till today. I wish I could go, it'll be a fine and impressive sight . . .

Asquith made a beautiful oration on Friday. I'm sure I should have gone out and joined if I'd been a young man. They evidently thought so too for they opened recruiting offices in Grafton Street, but the result of their packing was rather amusing, as no one of enlisting age was at the meeting and no one at all enlisted after it! Six men did before, but as a result not one.

There'll be a good few *intranségeants* who will irritate the others by aggressiveness, I suppose. I wouldn't like to say they are wrong but they may be unwise. Séamus Ó Lorcáin[11] was speaking to what the *Irish Times* described as "a few hundreds" in College Green, which really meant the whole place packed as close as you could stand, according to Mrs. Reddin. He kept a lot from going, she says. Dr. Hyde says he never remembers any time during his life when the spirit was so strong and alive and feelings ran so high in the national line in the people. The *Irish Worker* is rather violent. The Lord Mayor's speech was a gem, he said nothing in a few well tuned phrases. I think the last sentence was "that the only possible solution (of the war) should be a satisfactory termination", tho' I can't swear to it.

I spend my spare time in Nationalist circles collecting volunteers for the collection for the Volunteers that we may have in the near future. Miss French-Mullen,[12] Mrs. Salkeld's sister, a tall pretty girl, who'd get any amount, I should think, and Mrs. Salkeld[13] herself, and another girl whose name I don't know[14] and a Mrs. Brown, wife of a professor at Trinity College. Miss F-M is really wonderfully pretty, reddish brown hair close against her small head, an oval face, beautiful brown brows over brilliant eyes. I sometimes think the latter look a little hard but I may be wrong. She could act too, I should think. Professor Rudmose

11. James Larkin, leader of the labour movement.
12. Madeleine French-Mullen, friend of Dr Kathleen Lynn, who worked with her in St. Ultan's Hospital.
13. Bláthnaid Salkeld (1880–1959), poet, spent much of her early life in India, and joined the Abbey Players when she returned, as Nell Byrne. The Salkelds had a house on St. Stephen's Green where they held regular 'at homes', frequented by writers and artists.
14. Una O'Connor inserted later.

59 *Deóra Frínseach with Seán Beaumont at a Meeting*

Brown keeps up a cynically jocular pose, which is occasionally witty and at times faintly amusing. I thought he was an Englishman at first, he has such an English accent.

Mrs. Dix[15] and Mr. Dix came in about six, they're nice people, a little man with a beard who, you'd believe, as he says is the case, to have French blood in his veins and she a biggish, frank, simple, kind-looking woman with the best of intelligence I should think. I don't know that this is a good description of her, she isn't exactly handsome but you'd like to be looking at her. She looks so human.

Wednesday. We had a committee-meeting last night of the Craobh to consider whether we should "wait for a lead from the Provisional Committee, in the present emergency, or take a line of action, and if so what". I went to the Provisional Committee meeting at 4. There's no chance of avoiding a split, I think. Mrs. Wyse Power would never consent to neutrality in reference to enlisting, which is the only way. She's not the only

15. A member of the Gaelic League, she wrote short stories and drama. Her husband Ernest Reginald McClintock Dix was a lawyer and bibliophile, as well as a writer.

member, to do her justice, in fact Miss Gavan Duffy[16] and I are the only ones who would. I should think we could count on Miss O'Flaherty, but she is only one . . .

When I got to it, Miss McSwiney,[17] Mrs. Clarke and Miss D. were already there. Mrs. Clarke hates me I think, because she thinks I'm a spy, very probably, or else because of my accent and general appearance. Anyway she doesn't approve of landlords or their relations! She always adopts a distinctly hostile tone to anyone who disagrees with her anyway tho', so I don't know that it's more hostile to me than to others. I found what they wanted to do was to send a resolution to the Provisional Committee and to the papers, affirming their entire confidence in the Mens' P.C. etc., which they declared would be merely an expression of opinion on their part, but which would pretty obviously be jockeying the P.C. into the same position.

They didn't want to wait till Saturday, every minute counted, we must stand out for Ireland, show our colours etc. (Mrs. Clarke uses all the phrases with conviction). Luckily we managed to wait till Mrs. R. came, she is a great influence and was listened to (Mrs. C. resents my being a member of both committees, by the way). In the end, Mrs. Reddin, who seems a sensible woman rather, suggested a mild resolution, to be put to the Branch at Tuesday's meeting . . . Thank goodness we have delayed it at any rate . . .

2 October 1914. Things are looking up – Mrs. Creed Meredith told Mrs. Coffey her man said there was some chance of reunion. *The Leader*[18] is acting excellently and it's such a clerical paper it'll have lots of influence. Mr. R. says, "If Moran is taking that line, it shows he sees his way". A man in the *Irish Freedom* office says, "He's got the priests, and that means everything". Wexford Volunteers decided to parade on Sunday for Mr. Redmond on condition he made no recruiting speech!. . Diarmuid still goes on referring to the Provisional Committee as contemptuously as possible, which I find very annoying, but Redmondites are really in such a ridiculous position. "We'll follow our leader but we won't go where he leads". D. ought to enlist if he really believes in Redmond.

16. Louise Gavan Duffy (1884–1969), daughter of Sir Charles Gavan Duffy of the Young Ireland movement. Reared in France, she returned to Ireland at the height of the nationalist movement and taught at Scoil Íde, after Pearse's death founding Scoil Bhríde.
17. Mary McSwiney (1872–1942), a renowned republican, sister of Terence McSwiney.
18. An Irish-Ireland weekly edited by D.P. Moran.

The Leader says the country won't stand the M.Ps being recruiting sergeants, as it gave them no mandate . . .

3 October 1914. I was dining with the Coffeys last night. A.E. came in after, he's not at all like the Municipal Art Gallery picture of him.[19] He'd got rather a fat face, under a glib of hair which he seems to enjoy, and spectacles and a bushy beard and small fat hands which he waves a good bit . . . We most of us sat silent all the time and let him talk, which didn't seem to bore him, and occasionally he'd lean forward in enthusiasm and his eyes would light up in rather an attractive way . . .

He said we were wrong to be such a wretched little imitation of England and that if that was all we were going to do under Home Rule, get an English civilisation only on a smaller and pettier scale, he'd be against it. "But Mr. Russell, how can we get rid of that and reorganise ourselves until we get rid of them?" said Diarmuid. Then A.E. started off saying we must do it, and what he objected to in England was the capitalist system, and how wicked we were about labour. Here he gave instances of low rates of wages, 6/- a week to a labourer, and the reason for that was that we had no place to discuss and settle these matters in, which was rather a support of D's point. He talked about the Upanishads and the Irish legends, and against recruiting, and against what he called race hatred of the English. Yet it isn't the English we hate, but England, that is, all she has stood for in Ireland . . .

I can't understand a man like that who has seen something of the booklessness of a bookloving nation, of the lack of brotherliness of a brotherly nation, saying he doesn't hate England. Not one of the national vices or misfortunes but is traceable more or less to her rule. Diarmuid said, "It seems to me that the fact that we are Irish and they are English, and that they have got Ireland, is enough reason to hate them". A.E. interrupted and said he didn't agree. Diarmuid said had he ever sailed into Cork Harbour? "Well, when you do, you see all those forts, and the Union Jack and white ensign flying over them. You really do feel you haven't got a country."

Today Máighréad and I went to the picture exhibition at Craobh na gCúig Cúigí, quite a good one with some nice things of Estella Solomons and Miss Josephine Webb. Lily Williams introduced me to

19. The portrait of George Russell (Æ) by Count Markievicz hung on the staircase of the Dublin Municipal Gallery of Modern Art, Clonmell House, 17 Harcourt Street, with portraits of his Irish contemporaries.

Miss Ella Young and Maureen Fox.[20] After that on to 19 Dolier St. for Committee Meeting.

Well, we had the meeting, and we decided to publish a manifesto embodying the best in two of Miss Bloxham's and Mrs. Wyse Power's. It was definitely anti-recruiting, but it didn't mention the P.C. Then Mrs. W.P. said – and if branches wrote up to us what side we were on – what to say. This started a fresh discussion of the thing all over again . . . Finally we decided to say that, as far as this was concerned, we approved of the action of the P.C. I forget exactly how it was put, but it was Miss Bloxham's idea, who was in the chair, to phrase it so that it made it clear that we acted as an independent organisation, free to approve one or the other.

So now we're in for it. Everything is in such a ridiculously topsy-turvy state, the nationalist papers reporting the welcome part of a resolution of the Wexford Volunteers saying they'd welcome Redmond *on condition he made no recruiting speech,* and the unionist papers, such as the *Irish Times* and *Belfast Newsletter,* reporting the conditional part, headed "A Snub for Redmond". Meantime, I have heard from two places of Orangemen walking out of church for "God save the King" as a result of the passing of the Home Rule Act. They are also getting angry with Carson and say that his new wife is a Roman Catholic. Our leaders are losing us.

Séamus Ó Lorcáin has some green, bright green, anti-recruiting papers, leaflets, out. Mrs. Wyse Power had a number which had been left with her in Henry Street. She didn't know who had left them but the end, "England wants men, but by God she will not get Irishmen", is characteristic of his violent style. He had a manifesto on the food question out too, ending "God save the People", and on good lines about holding the food. I saw lots of people reading it on that hoarding round the statue opposite the Vegetarian Restaurant, and I suppose it must have been that one the police were tearing down in Henry Street, in view of a large crowd of sympathisers with the poster.

They have a military censorship in Belfast, and the *Irish Times* has got something about extending it to us in regard to the many anti-recruiting manifestoes, proclamations etc., and the tone of newspapers like *Sinn Féin, The Irish Worker, Irish Freedom, The Volunteer,* whose poster last week was "No recruits", now were added to the number. Miss O'Flaherty is going

20. The daughter of a Middlesex lawyer from Scotland, she had got caught up in the Gaelic League, and was known as Móirín Nic Shionnaigh.

to find out exactly where we stand tho' of course we shan't be arrested any of us. Or any prominent person connected with it either, for that'd stop recruiting at once.

5th October 1914. To Killiney yesterday, where we heard Cousin George Lefroy preach and mention how many fine types of soldiers we knew of in "our English history". His sermon was an argument that war isn't altogether bad because so many types of Christian life were taken from it.

Irish Freedom is really a very striking paper sometimes. Wednesday, 7th October 1914. What strikes me most about it is the extreme youth of everyone connected with it. Seán Mac Diarmuid can't be much more than 25, with his cleanshaven, boyish face, and dreamy blue eyes, and the others must be younger, from their looks. Then the way he writes, it's so young and honest and certain of himself and extreme, and yet every now and then there's a suggestion that if England would do the decent thing an arrangement might be arrived at. There's no bitterness.

A most unfortunate meeting took place last night in regard to the manifesto, which is very good, as follows. "As the women's section of the Irish Volunteers, we wish at this crisis to remind our readers that they should abide loyally by the constitution of our Organisation. We came into being to advance the cause of Irish liberty and to organise Irish women in defence of that object. We feel bound to make the pronouncement that to urge or encourage Irish Volunteers to enlist in the British Army cannot under any circumstances be consistent with the work we have set ourselves to do. At this time when powerful influences are at work to confuse and obscure the National issue, and when Ireland needs all her sons, we call on Irish men to remain in their own country and join the army of the Irish Volunteers – the army that was founded to gain Ireland's rights and guard those rights when gained. We would point out to our members that it is their duty in all controversial matters to abide by the principles of nationality, which are the bed rock on which alone any vital national movement can be safely built. Since its inauguration Cumann na mBan has aimed at uniting those who, while differing on minor matters, were resolved that the integrity and honour of the Irish nation were their first consideration, and we rely on our members to lift every difficult question out of the region of personalities and parties on to the high ground of our country's welfare".

Mrs. Wyse Power read it, I moved that we adopt it, or heartily endorse it, and Mrs. Reddin seconded. Then no one spoke and Mrs. W.P.

asked them to. Up with Mrs. Dudley Edwards, who began by saying that she agreed with the manifesto, then she went on that she was however a follower of Redmond's, who had for forty years worked loyally, and that we had no business to judge questions of policy against him, and then that Germany – . Here Mrs. Wyse Power told her not to discuss continental politics. She got angry, they both did, and Mrs. D.E. said she was being stifled, which I think was true.

Mrs. W.P. wasn't a very good chairwoman, a lot of the annoyance among people might have been avoided. Lady O'Connell[21] got up and spoke from behind, and some of those silly young girls in front hissed at the mention of Redmond's name. Everyone went wandering away from the point, and Mrs. W.P.'s rather angry attempts to bring them back failed. I said what I thought was the point, not the merits of this or that leader, but recruiting, and that we could not afford more men. I wish I had quoted Mr. Russell. Anyway it calmed them, but it got just as bad afterwards when a vote was to be taken on the two sides, and they separated to be easier counted: we were a majority of course, 88 to 29, but it split them up. Oh what a frightful thing human nature is to deal with. If only people could be reasonable and not lose their tempers and misunderstand each other . . . Oh how silly this all is, we all want to do the same thing, and Diarmuid says he's hopeful about the Volunteers rejoining, and if only we could have held together, those of us who are against recruiting. There is a very strong case, for the other side, that we are splitting, and Carson is holding together, and getting his men trained at no expense to himself . . .

I was on duty at the [Gaelic League] Exhibition yesterday. Mr. Dix dashed in and asked me how much *The Cloak* was as his wife wanted to buy it. After some consideration I said £2.10. I hope I'll get that for it . . . The *Irish Times* says my picture of the Strand is the only one with any suggestion of mirth.[22] I'm glad I sent it, no one will want to buy it tho'. Miss Webb sent a card to Mrs. Coffey saying she thought my things the most interesting and impressive there! I felt fearfully bucked as she's an

21. Wife of Sir John O'Connell, who was in charge of food and provisions for the Volunteers when drilling in Dublin.
22. *Irish Times,* 5 Oct 1914. The reviewer of the exhibition mounted by members of the Branch of the Five Provinces at 7 St. Stephen's Green commended Cesca's work also because she showed 'a foreign view' among 'nature's messages – nearly all messages of Ireland and the Irish.' (The picture was *Domrémy Church,* painted while she was in France).

artist. She had some pretty things, two jolly good watercolours, and some others in line and wash.

I went out with Diarmuid to Glenduff on Monday to pick blackberries. Mother said she was sure we wouldn't get any, and no more we did because we only got as far as the wood of Glenduff. We started rather late, and anyway the ones we passed were all dusty and unripe. It was absolutely heavenly. We talked joyous nonsense all the way there, and ranged about from the arching sky to the earth coming back. When you turn to go down from the wood, you see the plains of Meath, Kildare and Co Dublin, spread out blue before you.

I supposed the Wicklow clans must have often seen it like that. "How they must have cursed!" said Diarmuid, I've no doubt following their example. "It's awful to me when I think of that sore-always-running of the Pale, and how now it's spread its disease all over Ireland, till we hardly know we're sick, and we talk about loyalty to our pestilence". I absolutely love going out for walks with him, and pretending I'm twelve, and sitting on my purple cloak on the green grass, eating apples and thinking I haven't a care in the world but Ireland, and that that is all coming right . . .

Thursday 8 October 1914. I went out to see Miss Ella Young and Maureen Fox yesterday. They live in an old pink house on the Kimmage road with a garden behind, and a piece in front smelling of autumn leaves, and damp big trees, and dark. Nice to walk about in in the dark, Miss Young says. The house is all grey-white and cream-coloured, with a few choice pictures about on the walls, and uncertain coloured covers to the chairs, and cushions of a misty blue or violet. When I went in they were sitting over the fire, she in a blue national dress and Maureen Fox in a pinkish one.

They are both very Celtic Twilighty. I felt rather inclined to scoff at first, and even now I wonder what they do all day, and think they are a good way removed from realities of life, but this may be wrong. Only when Ella Young says all life is joy and ought to exist for purposes of soul, she ought to believe that enough to have some solution of the problem of how to persuade the working man's wife, whose man is out of work, and she with 11 children, that all life is joy. It's all very well for her living there in mystical independence of the ruder necessities of life! To theorise and even feel like that about it – everything round them is lovely.

It's rather ungrateful to be talking like this, when I got rather Celtic Twilightly myself, and certainly came away feeling rather happy, tho' that may have been because she was talking about me in connection with a period of Irish history and country in which I am particularly interested i.e. Armada and Spain, or because she was transmitting to me waves of joy!

Miss F. doesn't talk much. I think the only thing she said was that Christianity was the only religion that had rejected the symbols (and that was silly because it hasn't), and that she did her writing at the top of a tree – showing me the tree. But E.Y. told me she remembered me as a young Spaniard, maybe on a mission to Ireland, maybe in Smerwick Fort, when she was there in Red Hugh's army that came too late. We went into the garden and I took off my black felt hat and held it under my arm and it was that that reminded her. She took it as a confirmation of her theory when I told her how I had always loved Spain, and had wished to know that period well.

I was and am still divided between the desire to treat that as a most ridiculous conversation, and a high mysteries one! On the whole I take it seriously. I wish I could remember back to then, to write a story about it. I've begun to make one up. It would make a very good story really. We talked a good deal about religion. I wish I wasn't so ignorant.

They have several pictures of A.E.'s there, one of the Sidhe[23] he used to see about on the mountains, tall and beautiful, with an opal light in a crest changing and living on his head. I'd like to see that Sidhe. I wonder does he see them now. When I was on duty at the Exhibition, a girl, Lil Duncan,[24] came in, and as she went out she said "Beannacht leat". – I said "Beannacht Dé leat". It's rather delightful and wonderful when you think of it that there should be a country where people say naturally "Blessings with thee", when they are going away, and reply, "Blessings of God with thee".

9 October 1914. Yesterday I was drinking tea with the La Touches. The two Godfrey girls were there, it's a wonder to me how any people in Ireland today can live so out of touch with realities . . . Miss Brennan came in from above. She said she was at dinner the other night where some people, barristers, were talking of what would be Ireland's position if Germany won. Not sentimentally at all but logically. The majority were of the opinion that it'd be better for Ireland than if England won, as then

23. The fairy people.
24. Lil Nic Dhonnchadha (1891–1984), a member of the Gaelic League and close friend of Neilí Ní Bhriain, was one of the first women graduates from Trinity College. She was a devoted republican, and a founder member of Cumann Gaelach na hEaglaise.

we'd have to pay huge taxes. Whereas it'd be quite in Germany's interest to wipe off our land debt to England. It'd hit England hard, and might be quite good for Germany to have us strong to keep a menace to England.

For us to be enabled to contemplate calmly being a menace to England in our independence shows how far we have travelled in this last six months. The Germans are nearly into Antwerp, at least they've got across the Lethe and that means they're onto the last line of forts. The Government has gone to Ostend. Miss Brennan says she thinks they are in already, as they were saying just the same things about Liège as they are about Antwerp (she's on the *Irish Times*), and that it will be very serious for the English if they really get it as it'll make a raid easier.

She thinks the war will go on two years or more and that America will be drawn in. It appears Roosevelt said a fortnight ago that she must be, and that he would ask Col. Armstrong, who had something to do with organising another army before, to organise another. This may mean they are annoyed with England for her action in regard to the Japanese, or that the anti-German feeling there is very strong, as Miss Stephen says it is, who has papers from there . . .

The *Leader* is preaching peace between two kinds of Volunteers this week, and seems cheerful, very keen to make it clear that it's not absurdities like Sinn Féiners who are responsible for the stand against recruiting. It doesn't really matter who is [so long as] it's made, but I fancy the future historian will see reason to modify that opinion of Moran's. It is a hateful little paper . . . The difference between it and *Irish Freedom! Sinn Féin* is fairly confident, 'specially since the *Daily Mail* wants seditious papers suppressed. We're under martial law of course, so they could.

The *Volunteer* has a paragraph congratulating itself on the same thing. "We are winning, winning, winning", it says, and "Don't wait for something to happen. Drill and drill and drill and something will happen." It certainly has some cause to be cheerful. The Volunteers are not enlisting. How silly and trustless it was of me to write some time ago in my diary that it would be good for us if the Home Rule Bill wasn't signed. I might have known they wouldn't enlist anyway . . .

9 October 1914. It is said on the paper today that Antwerp has fallen to the Germans. The poor Belgians! They are getting all the kicks and none of the ha'pence . . .

14 October 1914 . . . The Irish Neutrality League meeting on Monday was largely attended. Arthur Griffith spoke, and James Connolly,

and other "very neutral men", as Pádraig Ó Glasáin said, and there wasn't a word about it in the *Irish Times.* That's the best way. Miss O'Farrelly says the Northern Volunteers won't go into the army whatever you say to them, and she is certain about that from what she has seen of them this summer. Mrs. Power still saw it as a threat . . .

15 Oct 1914 . . . Yesterday at the 1st Irish class I've been to for a year, they gave us some proverbs, one of them was "Misneach do bhuadhainn cogaidh – ní arm: Courage is what wins the battle – not arms." I wish to God that was true . . . After the class, Sighle Nic Fhionn held out a little paper to me. I took it and read "misneach do buadhainn" etc. She gazed at me with a slight delicious mocking smile under her black velvet hat as I read it. "I thought that would appeal to you", she said softly, her soft innocent blue eyes shining. I must draw that girl, she's delicious, and Dora French, her profile looks so fierce and keen and unhappy, and sometimes she has such a bitter curl in her lip.[25] I was too early for the class so we sat over the fire and talked.

25. She drew Deora Frínseach on 12 August 1918; see Cat. no. 76.

60 *Susan Mitchell, 1916*

9
The Split in the Volunteers and Cumann na mBan

16 October 1914. Last night we went to one of the most delightful parties I ever was at. In the afternoon there came here Mrs. Backhaus, an old friend of Mother's, who also lives in Harcourt Terrace . . . and is rather nice. Then when we were recovering from her, Wilbraham[1] [came in], a perfect dear, just a scrap like Uncle Henry now and then in his way of looking at you, and he told us about a house out at Blessington to take, just opposite him. I asked him were his children being taught Irish, he said he wished they were, etc. Mother said if we went there we'd teach them, then we talked about that for a bit and about what day we'd go out to see the house. He was silent, then said suddenly, "Oh. *Do* come and live at Blessington and teach my children Irish and talk to them about Irish things", in such a nice impulsive way.

It'd be miles away from anything, of course, no one'd ever come and see us if we lived at Blessington, 1 hour in the steam-tram from Terenure, but it sounds rather jolly, 'specially as to rent . . .

1. Wilbraham FitzJohn Trench (1873–1939) of the Woodlawn, Co. Galway branch of the family and a graduate of Christ's College, Cambridge, was Professor of English Literature in Trinity.

> We settled things fairly satisfactorily at the Committee, amongst others to make a collection for rifles on Sunday at the 1st Gaelic Football match of the season. I've got to make the badges. Then on to the Coffeys, where I'm glad I found the Goat – looking awfully pretty, and talking eagerly to Mrs. Fisher Unwin, who seemed to enjoy it. I was planted down with Mr. Fisher Unwin, who knows Uncle Alfred, and says his wife's best memory of Caddenabbia is Uncle Alfred's figs, and who had met Father and Mother eighteen years ago in the Dolomites. Mother remembered when I told her. I wish she had been there. I succeeded in shocking him by saying, "Are they?" when he said, "Of course one's assuming that England and the Allies are going to win."
>
> He was very English and told me he'd like me to *try* German rule for a bit, and what *he* wished was that a Zeppelin would drop a few bombs here and wake us up. One couldn't say anything really rude of course, tho' Diarmuid and I both managed to assure him when he talked about our talking a foreign language before him, i.e. *Gaedhilge,* that the only foreign language here was English . . .

The real joy of the evening for Cesca was Miss Mitchell's singing of her Carson ballad – 'The latter is one of the most delightful ballads it's ever been my good fortune to hear. She sat there and sang . . . how he was arrested and tried and executed and he made a dying speech, and "the first to welcome him in heaven were Mitchel and Wolfe Tone." I'm going to get it, [it's] published in the *New Statesman*[2] . . .'

On 15 October she had a tragic letter from one of her friends of the atelier – 'poor Róisín. Not having heard from Frère Georges since June, and she doesn't know is he gone to the war or not, and "*why* doesn't he write?", poor little thing. I pray he'll get back safe. Is there any way one could find out, except by asking Melles [Genoud] to search the list of casualities in the French papers? tho' it may have already passed. I wish I could get an answer to my letter.'

> 19 October. Yesterday I saw the authentic picture of Jeanne D'Arc. I've never seen such a good likeness before. Most of the portraits of her don't resemble her in the smallest degree. A rather broad fair skinned face, yellow hair parted on the low broad forehead, enthusiastic fearless grey green eyes, a straight strong nose not pointed a bit, just parted lips, shapely and small, over a square chin set on a strong white neck and slim

2. 2 May 1914, pp. 114–5.

boyish shoulders. Peggy Nic Fhionn[3] it is, and she's gone into a convent in England. She's about 19 or 20, I think. I've never seen her, but that's what the picture of her by Miss Harrison[4] is like . . .

20 October 1914 . . . Such a delicious story of the Citizen Army, going up O'Connell St to go to Capel St. Arrived opposite Henry St. "Left wheel" was ordered. Nothing happened. "Right wheel" then. Still nothing. "For the love of Heaven," shouted the agonised commander then, "Will yez go up Henry St.?" The army went.

Mrs. Coffey came to lunch here. After it, I went back with her. We were talking of Miss Mitchell's Carson ballad. I was rubbing Mr. Coffey's hands, which were cold. "Rather irreverent, I think", came from the lengthy form on the hearth-rug. "Irreverent?" I questioned. "Putting Carson in the same breath with Mitchel and Wolfe Tone." I hadn't thought of that before but of course it is. Mrs. Gallogly told the Goat the Ulster Volunteers were getting out of hand, that they no longer trust *Carson,* that they're furious with him for having married and daring to be happy, that he's losing his grip of them. At several meetings where he spoke for recruiting, he didn't get one, etc. Curious and rather thrilling. Redmond in the South, Carson in the North, God send us a leader. A.E. says it's either the last flare up of the dying candle or a new spring of inexhaustible energy, and that it can be the latter if Irishmen don't turn their arms against each other, and that the Isle of Destiny is nearing her hour of fate . . .

The Céilidh on Saturday was great fun. I flirted enthusiastically with the eldest Reddin, and talked to Mr. Creed Meredith about the colour of skies, and enjoyed myself enormously. Liam Beag mac Giolla Bhrighde said to me, "You're like your pictures." "Why, do I look so strange?" said I. "You look so big and vigorous," he said: and indeed he might think I'm big and he so small. The Fisher Unwins were there. I talked to them. They said they supposed they were foreigners there. I said polite things, tho' I meant them more or less, really, and he said, "Oh, it's alright now we've passed Home Rule, isn't it?" I smiled.

---

3. Peggy Gwynn.
4. Sarah Cecilia Harrison (1863–1941), from Co. Down, a great grand niece of Henry Joy McCracken, trained at the Slade and settled in Dublin. Her portraits were admired for their piercing realism. She was close to Hugh Lane, and helped to establish the Municipal Gallery. A promoter of feminine and social concerns, she was the first woman to be elected to Dublin Corporation.

23 October 1914. To Blessington the day before yesterday. It promised rain but became so lovely as we went on, in bursts of sunlight, and streaks of blue on the mountains, and emerald grass. You get very high among the Wicklow and Dublin mountains there, in the most awful little steam tram anyone can imagine. It was a half hour late arriving, and it takes more than an hour anyway.

Mother went to the conductor when we had got past Crooksling and said sweetly, "are you often as late as this?" "Late?" said he with some asperity, "we're not late at all". "Oh, what time are you due?" said she. "We're due at 25 to two", said the conductor firmly. "But the time-table says 1.20," she said. "Ah, never mind the time-table", with deep contempt . . .

The house we went out to see is delightful, and so is the garden, rambling and full of dead leaves, and a yard with grass growing between the cobbles, and stabling where I could have a studio . . . Wilbraham says nationalist Ireland is becoming imperialist, that it hasn't had time to do so yet and that explains what he is pleased to call "the Progerman[5] movement" led by Eoin MacNeill: tho' of course all those on that side are people with *no* influence. It's a funny point of view, and must be rather depressing; but it's very Trenchy and I don't think I should have been disappointed at it if I'd remembered he was a Trench more definitely, and thought less of what I'd heard of his nationalism.

In the evening to the Irish Guild of the Church where Eithne Culverwell read a paper on Irish Ancient Literature, and An Craoibhín spoke, and Mother enjoyed it thoroughly. The Bishop of Tuam was our President, such a darling, and so plain. Someone got up at the end to propose a vote of thanks to him, so up with him "No, not at all Mr. Dix, you're quite out of order". Fisher was there, and the Dixes, and the Miss Warrens, nice people who live in a house with cream coloured walls and Æ's pictures scattered about all over them, Nationalists and middle-aged . . .

Monday 25 October 1914. Last night we had an Irish service in St. Patrick's Cathedral . . . I didn't understand most of the sermon. There were two Volunteers there in uniform, St. John Ervine, and another boy. They looked awfully nice and sat during the prayers for the King of England, which I wished I'd thought of myself!

We supped with the Coffeys before going, and they showed us a letter from Miss Eleanor Hull about an association the Irish Texts Society was going to start in view of the altered circumstances, and the great change

5. Pro-German.

coming over the feeling of Ireland etc., which would be "not merely a recruiting organisation" but a sort of general vehicle for the propagation of Imperialist ideas and hatred of Germany. This latter was speciously veiled under a reference to a series of "lectures dealing with the real causes of the war", and saying that Mr. Rolleston[6] and Mr. Graves[7] both think Diarmuid would be the person to act for them in Ireland.

Well even I never thought as ill of him as that. He wrote back in Johnsonian phrases refusing, and saying that fifty years hence historians might be able to decide the causes of the war, but that at present the stirring up of hatred towards Germany or any other foreign nation could only lead to counter movements which would militate against the success of the cause she had at heart . . .

26 October 1914. 160 of the corps are loyal to the "constitution". They were in the Abbey Theatre on Sunday, and Mrs. [Wyse] Power says they were very enthusiastic. I saw a copy of a new paper yesterday, a daily bulletin they call it, called *Éire,* with a full account of the proceedings in it and names of loyal corps, so we shall get those for the Cumann anyway. She and I were talking, and agreed that perhaps the split didn't matter so much, tho' regrettable of course, if it meant a rivalry for efficiency as we'll hope it does. She says they really hope to capture the country in the end as all "the younger elements are on their side and the effete are on Redmond's". Also, "many of the men who left when the manifesto was read are coming back" . . .

Diarmuid Coffey has a most profound contempt for James Connolly,[8] and doubts the Government will ever bring in conscription chiefly because Connolly expects it. I find his attitude rather annoying chiefly because everyone else listens to him with such respect . . . Dr. Hyde and his daughter, Nuala, came on Saturday to see us. He was awfully diplomatic when Mother made enthusiastic remarks about the British navy standing between us and destruction, and the duty of loyalty. He smiled and said, "Ah but you see, you can't get everyone to agree about that,

---

6. T.W. Rolleston (1857–1920), first secretary of the Irish Literary Society, and author of *The High Deeds of Finn* (1910).
7. Alfred Perceval Graves (1846–1931), poet and assistant editor of *Punch,* he was the author of 'Father O'Flynn' and other renowned Irish songs.
8. (1868–1916), socialist leader, originally from Edinburgh. In 1912 he assisted James Larkin in founding the Labour Party, and he later became involved in the Irish Citizen Army, which joined with the Irish Volunteers in the 1916 Rising.

Mrs. Trench."[9] Nuala is very fat just now after stuffing for a bad lung, and anyway she's not as interesting as Úna. Dr. Hyde was rather annoyed with me for Mór[10] not being there, as he wanted to compare her and Nuala!

In a letter from Dorothy yesterday, she says she's almost sure Art will have to go to the front. There's a bad time before us if he does. Noël is slightly wounded in the head and coming home. They say the Germans are trying to get thro' to Calais, to terrorise the English from there.

27 October 1914. A floating mine sunk a ship off Tory Island the day before yesterday. The battle is getting more and more frightful and violent every day. The Rebellion in S. Africa is spreading. De Wet and Beyers are supposed to be in it now, and Botha has left for the Front. I wonder does that mean down there, or France, where he was preparing to lead a commando.

Mr. Pearse lectured at Cumann na mBan on Tuesday. He concluded by saying not a generation had passed that had not done some desperate thing for Ireland, but that this one seemed to be passing away without, and that maybe that fear would be falsified, and that this generation would yet strike for a bigger thing than the Home Rule Act. His words were received with enthusiasm, to judge by the clapping, and by me with enthusiastic doubt. When you look at the material the things have got to be done with, it makes any idea even of that sort seem desperate in the extreme. People seem so Anglicised, so content with English rule, so easily duped, so Imperial, you wonder what strength extremist feelings have in the country as a whole, and you know that what there is is not organised, or conscious hardly, in the majority of places.

Of course one is wrong to expect exceptional people to be all round to do things with, it's the doing that makes them exceptional, and it was always with the ordinary people the leaders worked . . . Pearse will be in it, so much is certain, it's a pity he's rather fat, and has such a soft hand when you shake it. I do *not* like soft hands in a man. It thundered and poured with rain early this morning before it was light. I wondered vaguely was it guns when I heard the thunder . . .

Diarmuid Coffey came yesterday to help us with those charts. He seemed to think it rather a waste of time, for which I regret his coming. A committee meeting on Tuesday, by the light of two candles, extraordinarily

9. Later in the journal, on 20 December, Cesca quotes An Craoibhín's comment on the shelling of Whitby Abbey – 'They're getting a little of what they did to us now. Our old abbeys, they didn't leave *one* stand up.'

10. Another nickname for her sister Margot, or Máighréad, who also had a bad lung.

picturesque, the room filled with blue dark and the ring of faces at different levels lit by the yellow flame. Very becoming to most people it was too. There aren't enough chairs, so some have to kneel, and some to sit on a box back to back!

2 November 1914. It's a great pity that I have lost so many days. That day which started with thunder was followed with so spacious and splendid a sky for nearly all the day that you'd be filled with a piercing sense of joy to look at it. I was in Dublin, and I went about chuckling to myself with joy because of the street, blue, misty, and wet, and the great delicate clouds, till I thought I was out of my senses. It was the same day or the next that I was there walking along, and I saw everyone as such interesting types. They were so vivid and so vibrant to the sight . . .

Wednesday, 4 November 1914. Mrs. Wyse Power told me yesterday, she'd seen the paper sent to the Press forbidding them to publish the loss of the *Cendacious*, but that it had been sunk off our north coast, and that the *White Star Olympic* had seen it, and had turned into the loch for that [reason]. Also she had heard that it was a Belfast boat laid the mines for Germans for money around there. Lots of people are expecting them to land in the North any time now.

How will that affect the Volunteers, both kinds, there? Turkey has joined in (which gives Germany a port on the Bosphorus, of course), and is preparing to invade Egypt. Dorothy may be coming home on 29th, up the Suez Canal, as Art may be ordered off any time now, or the Indians may rise, and it'll give the child such a much better chance for her to be in England, but it's frightful for her. Three long weeks, and of course she wants him more than ever now, and if the Turks get near the Suez she might be delayed longer. And if Art gets sent to the front she may not get news of him for ages.

The more powers join in, the more chance there is of the war stopping soon, and then the black days will come for us, blacker than now. How far off are we from conscription, I wonder, and famine to a large or small extent. A boy was sent to Spike Island the other day for having *Irish Freedom* in his house, on the information of a soldier called Scully; and two Volunteers have been chucked out of their places in the Post Office in Cork, and the latter filled by two Englishmen. They say the conscription will be preceded by an attempt to get Irishmen to give up their arms . . .

Mary Spring-Rice and Dorothy Hill have split off from Cumann na mBan [and] are sending a circular to all the branches they founded giving an incorrect sketch of the Volunteer movement, and advising all women who wish to aid the cause of unity and peace to join the Irish Volunteer Aid Association.[11] Of course they've absolutely no business to send a circular to begin with. The Cumann wanted me to go down and talk to the branches, but Mother objected so strongly I couldn't go on. I don't know who they will get, there must be thousands of people much better if one could just think who. Anyway the defection of 19 branches is serious. And just on the question of recruiting on which we are all agreed. It does seem silly. Miss O'Farrelly threatens vaguely the disruption of our organisation entirely, but we've had that before, and anyway, if a rival one is to be started, it's started already, in the I.V.A.A.

8th November 1914. I haven't written for ages, one day because I was so angry and wanted to forget it, and since because I was sleepy or lazy. I pass from moods of philosophic calm to fierce rage with Diarmuid. The latter when he says he's writing round to corps about "McNeill's party". If I heard aright it was recommending them to see that the organisation got into the hands of "our men" as he calls the Redmondites. Col Moore seems to think a good deal of him, which annoys me more than that he should be on that side, tho' I always knew he would be really and anyway this beastly state of affairs can't last for ever. It does make a division, there's no blinking it, between us. I'm rather glad, tho' I don't like it. You can't talk frankly to a person who is working against what you think are the interests of the country at the moment . . .[12]

I believe the two bodies will come together some day anyway, and not really both die like "Chaud" in the *Leader* says. At least he says the National will die from inanition, and the Irish will more and more be driven to extremes. He draws a parallel between now and the '82 Volunteers. Rather interesting but very depressing, says they will be disbanded when the Bill passes, danger will call for a partial revival, discountenanced by officials, like United Irishmen – and the sequel.

. . . I'm making out a scheme for tableaux beginning with Macha Mong Ruadh and ending (with) Anne Devlin. They ought [to] be good but I have . . . such lots of pictures in my head. There's one called *The Trumpet* which came one day, suddenly with the phrase "a blast like a scarlet flag", with all it holds of a thrill. A man blowing one, on the top of a hill in front of the snow white walk of a dún, and riders below in the

---

11. Founded to collect money and assist where appropriate in the activities of the Volunteers.
12. The Redmondites faded away, though Colonel Moore attempted to revive the remnants in 1917 and re-unite them.

foreground, stiffened into listening by the sound, and sworded and armed and smiling. And another pastel of *Nodlaig na nGaedheal,* and an illustration from the Bible which I'm doing now. "Thy sons shall be taken from thee and given to another nation, there shall be no strength in thy hands".

Whether we shall get that house at Terenure depends on me very largely. Maighréad is so terribly unselfish, she wants us to take a house in London or near, or somewhere in England in the spring, and put our furniture into it. This was the result of the blow-up we had the other day, when Mother said she thought she'd better live in England, and leave us here, and not take a house at present as we couldn't be happy together. Since then she saw Temple Hill again, and came back full of it, and told me all the things we would do about the apples and the rent and all, and M. said she thought we oughtn't to settle to it as it'd be so hard on Mother being so far away from all she cared about . . . [13]

12 November 1914. Someone told Miss Harrison Ireland was nearer a revolution now than it had been since '98. It'd be fine if one could believe that of the whole country, but I can't of any part but the towns and 'specially Dublin. Because the King's Own Scottish Murderers aren't forgotten here yet. But in other places they haven't that. We started to go to the National Literary Society to hear Dr. Sigerson on "Ancient Irish Friendships" on Monday evening, and met the postman and got letters from him, and read them in the tram; and there was one from Aunt F and Uncle C saying Max had been killed. He and Sybil had been married seven months. There doesn't seem any doubt about it either . . .

The *Emden* has been caught and burnt. She landed a party off Cocos Island to destroy the wireless station there, and the *Sydney* came up with her, and they fought and "the crew lost heavily in personnel". I am awfully sorry as she was such a chivalrous little ship, and never lost a single life of all the lives she had in her power if she could help it. £2,000,000 worth damage she did to British shipping. All the beastly old moneymakers on the Stock Exchange were frightfully pleased.

I go and eat my lunch in Stephen's Green on Mondays and Tuesdays. It's delicious in the sun, and you feel at peace with all the world. In spite of the idiocy of the Depository,[14] where they are supposed to supply you with materials and have only *one* kind of canvas, and no chassis, which all have

13. In the event, the three women took this house in Terenure.
14. A Day Class admission ticket among Cesca's papers records her registration at the Dublin Metropolitan School of Art for the five month session from November to March 1914–15, the fee £26.

61 *Studies from a Sketchbook*

to be got from England! I said were there no capable carpenters in Dublin, and he said there were, but that it was cheaper all the same to get them from England. But I don't think he has tried, from his way of speaking.

We tried to go and call on the Hydes on Tuesday, and couldn't find Earlsfort Place, so we went into the Coffeys to ask them. I had to go in at seven, so we didn't get on to the Hydes, and Diarmuid walked to College Green with me. I tried to pierce his armour of gentleness the whole way and failed. It won't do, brothers aren't so humble . . .

Saturday 14 November 1914. The Thomas Davis centenary celebration, which the Gaelic Society of Trinity College was to have had in Regent House, is forbidden there, Mrs. Salkeld told me last night, because Mr. Pierce [sic] is speaking. Someone else says they'll allow it really after all.[15] The last time I heard Mr. P. speak he ended up with the

15. Because Pearse had been invited, Provost Mahaffy banned the Davis celebration and dissolved the Gaelic Society. However, the meeting, with W.B. Yeats, Pearse and Tom Kettle, was hosted by the National Volunteers on 20 November 1914.

remark that maybe we would strike for a bigger thing than the simulacrum of Home Rule, but surely surely the time is not yet. Eithne O'Kelly came here today, and we discussed the pictures we would have for the Gaelic League. She is a very nice, pretty girl . . .

We were at Loughlinstown last night, and it was bitterly cold. Mr. Good and his sister came straight to where we were going. I spoke to him about the conversation we had about the Dean and the Bishop in Cumann Gaedhealach na hEaglaise. "But surely you don't want parsons in it", he said. "Oh yes we do", I said. "Think of all the harm they can do if they're not, with their influence". "I wish you'd tell me where a parson's influence is", said he. "If you knew anything of a parson's life you'd know he has no influence, for good or ill"!!

All the correspondence in regard to the Gaelic Society is in the *Irish Times* this morning. The Vice President is rather arbitrary I think, but Cathal Power got his own back in one remark about freedom of speech. We wanted Mother to go to it, and it's rather a good thing we tried to persuade her now that that has come out, for it shows at any rate we didn't anticipate any anti-recruiting danger any more than there is. I'm afraid there'll be a row about it tho'. Diarmuid and I had such a pleasant walk back from Irish on Thursday. I like him when he shakes hands carelessly as if he was thinking of something else.

A ridiculous little rhyme that came out in *Sinn Féin* this week:

"Ten little German armies fresh from the Rhine
The *Castle Journal* shattered one and then there were nine.
Nine little German armies out one night too late
Met the *Evening Telegraph* and then there were eight.
Eight little German armies heedless all of heaven
Crossed the *Irish Catholic* and then there were seven.
Seven little German armies feeling in a fix
Up came the *Independent*, then there were six.
Six little German armies glad to be alive
Down swooped the *Evening Herald*, then there were five.
Five little German armies very sick and sore
Faced the haughty *Irish Times* and then there were four.
Four little German armies beaten black and blue
Ran into the *Sunday Freeman*, now there are two.
Two little German armies always on the run
Soon they'll meet the Dublin Press and then there'll be none.
No little German armies - hip, hip, hooray!
Home Rule in College Green at no far distant day!

. . . Yesterday morning I was cycling about Dublin, I went to take 5/- to Miss O'Farrelly and she rose up from her chair by the fire in a grey dress looking so pretty, with a "Tá fáilte romhat" that delighted me; and we sat down and discussed Monteith's dismissal.[16] She thinks it means things are beginning to move, and that it'll go on with the arrest of Griffith and Seán Mac Diarmada and the like gradually, also that conscription is inevitable . . . *Éire* was full of Monteith, and T.C.D. forbiddings. Mother didn't think anything impertinent in Cathal Power's letters to the Provost at first, but yesterday morning Mrs. Coffey came here wanting me to go to lunch to meet Mr. Barton,[17] and said Diarmuid had thought it rather impertinent, and, since then, the impertinence has been discovered . . .

On Sunday evening a large meeting in Stephen's Green about Monteith, at which several very violent speeches were made – "the day nearer than anyone knew", etc., which may be true, but not of *successful* revolution. Diarmuid told me Monteith had taken his men out on manoevres at Swords (true), that he had drawn them up in front of the police barracks and shouted "To hell with the police, to — with the army, and three cheers for the Kaiser". I asked Mrs. Reddin last night, she said her sons were out with him, and that nothing of that sort had happened. It probably was that his job gave him knowledge of and access to maps, and that they didn't want to risk anything. A decent quiet man, she said. The *Irish Times* says it was that he refused a commission, according to Maighréad.

I'm painting Xmas cards with a blue cloak on Muire, and a bright scarlet background and yellow haloes and red-yellow hair . . . I went to brekker with the Coffeys yesterday to meet Mr. Barton, rather a pleasant man about middle height with the manners and accent of an Englishman to a curious degree, and the appearance of one too, considering he is a nationalist. They are a funny type, these English-Irishmen. He says his step-grandmother was a Trench so we're cousins. I can't make out what sort of cousins you are under those circumstances.

Saturday, 21 November 1914. On Wednesday, Miss West came here and told us ridiculous stories about the Ulster gunrunning. On Friday Mother and Maighréad went to a meeting of the National Volunteers to

16. Robert Monteith, former British Army captain and associate of Casement, was dismissed from the Ordnance Survey in the Phoenix Park for his association with the Volunteers.

17. Robert Barton, cousin of Erskine Childers, was secretary to Colonel Moore. He joined the British army at the beginning of the War, but resigned in 1916 to become a Commandant in the Volunteers. In the 1918 elections he was chosen as Sinn Féin MP for West Wicklow.

celebrate Thomas Davis, at which Mr. Yeats delighted Mother, and Mr. Kettle was hissed. He said he had come there because he knew he would be. Mother was very sporting and took all the pro-Germanism in good part. Mr. Yeats said something at the end about Nietzche (cheers). "I mentioned Nietzche on purpose", said he, "because I could not deny myself the pleasure of hearing Nietzche cheered by a Dublin audience, as it never can happen again".[18]

Sunday. I went to see Miss Purser[19] this evening, she greeted me with "Well, Miss Trench, who stole the guns?" I said, "Which guns?" She, "What, were there more stolen?" I, "Well, if it was the Howth ones, lots of people stole them." She, "The ones that were stolen yesterday?" Me, "Oh, were there some stolen yesterday? Whose?" She, "Fancy your not knowing, I thought you and Countess Markievicz[20] would have been doing it, of course there were some stolen. Going from Ringsend to Dolphins Barn, fifty men sprang out and took them. National Volunteers they were for". "It sounds rather like the Citizen Army", I said, "but I may be doing them an injustice". This pleased her immensely as she hates Larkin.

She wasn't nearly so aggressive as usual, and I put this down to company, but I was wrong as usual. She wasn't well, and had only just got up, so I expect that was why. Still she wasn't exactly conciliatory. But she didn't seem to despise me so much as I thought before. . .

Thursday 1914. [26th] November. On Monday came those adorable children of Wilbraham's to T. Diarmuid came too, to help play with them. He sat on the floor and was an earthquake, which Síghle immensely enjoyed. He went in about an hour tho' because, he said Col. Moore might be back at the office, tho' we tried to persuade him he wouldn't be. Yesterday Mrs. Coffey told me he hadn't been. What an inconvenient thing for everyone his conscience is. After the children had gone, we were quite stiff . . .

---

18. See J. Hone, *W.B. Yeats, 1865–1939* (London, Macmillan, 1965) p. 293.
19. (1848–1943), portrait painter and founder of An Túr Gloine, the stained glass co-operative. Her immeasurable services to the arts in Ireland and to young artists have been widely acknowledged.
20. Born Constance Gore-Booth (1868–1927). She met Count Markievicz at art school in Paris and with Ellen Duncan they founded the United Arts Club in Dublin in 1905. In 1908, as a member of Maud Gonne's Inghinidhe na hÉireann, she founded Fianna Éireann, where she trained boys who would subsequently be Volunteers. She supported Connolly and Larkin and received a testimonial from the unions for her campaign during the 1913 lockout. During the 1916 Rising, she was second in command in Stephen's Green.

We have been in anxiety about Herbert, his H.A.C. having been under fire. Mother wired to Mrs. H. to ask her to find out anything for her, tho' it was such a long time ago they were engaged we thought we should have heard if he'd been wounded, and she went to the War Office in London and asked them, and they said of course that we might assume he was unhurt. In Ireland on Tuesday [it] was reported that Sir Roger Casement had been to the Foreign Office in Berlin, and had been received there, and there assured of Germany's kindly intentions towards us. Reported from *Daily News* and *Daily Mail* also, who stated that as it was only from German official sources, it might be treated with reservation. We all thought he was in America . . .

Saturday [28th]. Yesterday we sent off another pound of spare lumps of chocolate from that dreadful sixpenny place in Grafton Street and one and a half lbs gingerbread, soap and matches, 3 boxes. I went to leave a message at Wilbraham's in the morning. As I was going away, he said, "I like that torc brooch you have fastening your dress." He always makes remarks about one's clothes. I said, "Oh yes, it's rather convenient isn't it? – saves a button or hook". "I like it better than – that rifle of Cumann na mBán"[21] (as he always calls C na mB), he said hesitating. "It's rather exotic, isn't it?" said I. "It's not that", said he, "but I don't like your kind of Volunteers". I laughed. "I was afraid it was that", I said as I rode away, but I'm sorry now that I didn't take that opportunity of saying we were neutral. It's not at all clear.

A committee meeting last evening in which Miss G[avan] D[uffy] proposed, and I seconded, a motion to restrict members of committee from writing to papers on matters connected with policy of Cumann na mBan. This was to stop Miss O'Farrelly. She construed it into a personal attack, she knows Miss G.D. doesn't like her . . .

Tuesday [1 December] . . . The céilidhe on Saturday night was great fun. I wore my green silk dress, succumbing to the temptation after a prolonged struggle. Diarmuid was there and looked simply delightful, he has such a shapely head and shoulders and Máighread says it's true that he never looks raw. An Craoibhín told them that neither Parnell nor he liked green, that it was an unlucky colour. But it did look ripping all the same, so picturesque.

He introduced a straw to me, which greatly delighted me, a history professor at TCD[22] who speaks Donegal Irish. Why I call him a straw is

21. He refers to the Cumann na mBan badge consisting of the initials 'CnamB' mounted on a rifle.
22. Edmund Curtis, author of a history of Ireland.

because he shows which way the wind is blowing. "Are you Sadhbh?" said the history professor. "I am," said I, laughing. "But how did you know?" "Oh, I saw your name in the papers." said he. "In the papers?" said I with a movement of horror, so that An Craoibhín and Diarmuid laughed and said, "Don't be alarmed!" He sat down, and D. and he began to tear Professor Mahaffy's history to bits in a manner of respectful contempt if such can be. An Craoibhín proceeded with his compliments to Eithne O'Kelly. After a bit Peadar Ó hAnnracháin came up and started the same game in his usual vigorous style . . .

Later on The O'Rahilly came to sit by me, and said, "Where are you living now?" I told him. "May I have my letters addressed to you there?" said he, "I don't get a letter at all now that hasn't been opened, and the post office knows my sister's address now."[23] "You may," said I, "That's all right. They'll come under my name, is that it?" "That's it," said he, "addressed to 'Sadhbh uasal Trínseach', and there'll be a letter to me inside." "And I'll bring them to you every day. I think I can do that," said I. "I'll try anyway." . . .

On Sunday . . . The Irish service was more heavenly than usual. Going along we passed St. Sepulchre, which is a police barracks now, and used to be the archbishop's palace. In thro' a small gate we looked and saw the house gleaming blue white, with yellow lights in it, under the moon and a great space in front of it. I wish and I wish and I wish there were no Protestants in it, for that would mean no English, and no police-barracks in a palace. Canon Carlton rose to the occasion splendidly and gave the blessing in Irish. It was thrilling and sporting of him to learn it up, as he did so well, and a prayer too. Mr. Duncan and Diarmuid had to take the plate round. Their elbow level is about the height of most of our noses, however I just managed to see over enough to observe that it was all sixpences and shillings, except one twopence . . .

Last night to Miss Ella Young's. When Madame Markievicz came in there was a little desultory conversation first, then she said high spiritedly, "Isn't everything exciting?" This started us. Every omen of the downfall of the Empire, from a falcon in the King's house at Tara to the wrecking of the *Empress of Ireland* and the *Delhi,* and the chipping of the coronation chair on the orb side by the bomb setting of suffragettes in Westminster Abbey, was quoted . . .

23. The O'Rahilly was engaged in the purchase of arms at the time, hence his concern for security.

62 *Sketch of Celtic Heroes*

I told about the prophecy from *Irish Freedom.* They hadn't seen it, and won't be able to get a copy now that the police have it all. Lucky I got a copy Monday. They raided the newspaper shops yesterday and took all the copies, also all in the office, or [all they] were supposed to have. The prophecy foretold the year of this war, and Carson, and the Boer War and the death of Victoria of England on account of it, and also the burning of Dublin and its destruction, and many other sad things to Ireland, ending that a pure king should reign,[24] and peace and happiness and prosperity be on us till 7 periods before the ending of the world. And the time of year of this war he told, and the Volunteers . . . Maureen Fox [and I] . . . were sitting over the fire, I in a low and comfortable chair and she on a stool with a huge fan between her face and the fire. She looked like a squirrel, probably because her hair is so bushy . . .

Friday. They have intimidated Devereux Newth and Co. into not printing *Sinn Féin* this week. I wonder what Arthur Griffith will do. In today's *Éire* there is, "Look out for *Nationality,*" edited by A.G. Maybe a substitute for *Ireland* or for *Sinn Féin,* who knows. The printers of the *Leader, Freedom, Volunteer* and the *Worker* have been warned too. It's clever and mean, instead of attacking the people responsible, to attack the printers who do it in the way of trade.

24. On December 20 Cesca writes, referring again to the prophecy, 'Sir Roger Casement of course'.

Mme. Markievicz has a private printing-press on which she brings out those violent anti-recruiting green and yellow leaflets that were much in evidence lately. She declared triumphantly, "We brought out two thousand of them and got them thro' the length and breadth of Ireland," as she sat at ease on the floor, her long legs stretched out to the blaze. I said, "Oh those were yours were they – I thought I perceived the hand of Mr. Larkin in the tone of them, an oath at the end, which he seems in the habit of using." She laughed and said rather apologetically, "I got one of the scouts to write it, you see to appeal to a certain class of people, the ones we wanted to prevent enlisting, you must get one of their own class to write for them, they *know*". Miss Young and Miss Fox sat and looked dreamily at us all as if they were seeing into our minds but I wonder were they? . . .

Sunday . . . Diarmuid says, "If I was sure the Germans were going to win this war, I'd want Ireland to throw in her lot with them at once, the only reason I can see against our identifying ourselves with them is that we are pretty sure she isn't going to." This was à propos of Sir Roger Casement, I *would* like to see that man, he must be like a hero of romance. Mme M. says he's the only person she'd seen who looks like a hero, even the critical Diarmuid says he's quite sure anything he did he would do from the very highest motives. It's worth considering of course that he on the spot knows more of Germany's chances of winning than we do . . .

Saturday 12 December 1914. M brought in *Scissors & Paste* this evening, a newly dressed *Éire* to come out every Saturday and Wednesday. Did I mention that the latter had been suppressed together with *Sinn Féin* by the simple method of intimidating the printer? The *Volunteer*, purified by suffering, has come out under Eoin MacNeill's editorship, no more verse, only a front page article, a leader, and technical notes all the rest. The Aonach[25] has been going on this week, very small, and when we went on Tuesday afternoon not ready yet! I bought a lovely brooch thing for the Goat, but she'd sooner have had *The Demi Gods*,[26] I think. I got a read of that in Hanna & Neals the other day, such a heavenly description of "Mary" and her beauty, and you can see her.

The Aberdeens are going, someone said yesterday at the committee. It was because they were against proceedings being taken against heads of the Volunteers, and that gradually all those who were a bit friendly would go. They're going in February.

---

25. The Gaelic League Art & Crafts exhibition.
26. James Stephens's new book, published by Macmillan.

63 *An Crois: Cuirm Ceoil –*
At a Musical Evening

10
Love and War

Tuesday, 15 December, 1914. The Convention was held on Sunday so I couldn't go. I wrote a letter stating my views and we went to leave it, after church at St. Anne's. Ahead of us in College Street we saw a woman walking, very badly, no stays, dressed in green! "There's a Cumann na mBan delegate," said M. I said to myself, "There's only one person in Dublin who would wear just that particular shade of aggressive green," but aloud nothing. She crossed the street, and turned the corner and joined Mme O'Rahilly just outside Remingtons. I caught Mme O'R up to give her my letter, and saw, as I suspected, the shall I say famous or notorious countess. I rather liked speaking in Irish to Mme O'R in her presence. Political nationalism isn't the beginning and end of patriotism – "Notorious," Wilbraham would say.

He was here last night, he invariably trails his coat just as he goes to take his bicycle from the tree against which it leans. If I step on it, he throws down a gauntlet with the upmost speed, and pauses with one foot on the step to see will I pick it up. I usually do, and we make a pass or two and then mutually conclude to put it off to a more convenient season. Last night he said, "Yes, interest in Irish things – ought to make you more *broad*minded – not narrowminded." I said heartily, "Yes indeed. Fix well thy centre first, then draw thy circles round, as the archbishop says". He was silent at that, digesting it, or wondering whether I was really as flippant as I seemed, or more obtuse, I don't know which. I felt a moment of remorse and said, "Don't you think – there's a stage when people seem to be narrowminded – but then they get past it". "It isn't 'seems to be'," he said with energy, "You are". "Do you mean me personally," I said, "or Gaelic Leaguers in general?" . . . He began to lead his bike down the path and paused under the first arch of the pergola. "Believe me", he said, "our civilisation is in the melting pot."

Cesca wasn't in the best of form. Diarmid with his 'practical politics' had been accusing her of being pro-German and supporting a party whose actions could not lead to anything, though, as they walked the roads near Lios an Uisce after her rejoining 'tirade', he withdrew his remarks. 'I'd been wanting to get it off my chest for a long time, an excuse for vehemence so seldom occurs with that young man,' wrote Cesca. 'Also I often get mixed up as I go on, but this time I had my batteries marked and my disposition made. Alas it was too easy a victory . . . I went to the Irish service that night, and when Diarmuid came in late, after I'd given up hoping for him, I got such a thrill of joy that I'd have done anything he asked me – if he had!. . . He's in Clare now in an officers' training camp at the Lysaghts' house[1] for the National Volunteers.'

Her mood, heightened to extremes of nationalist passion by the tension of current events, was tempered to restraint when the war crisis thrust in upon the family personally.

3 January 1915. Raghnall and Claire are here, arrived Friday morning in pelts of rain after an awful passage, so we put C. to bed with a fire and hot bottles, and Michael,[2] who discovered the bottles, and lay steadily on them the whole morning. She slept for 3 hours and arose a different woman. They'll be married at the end of this month. 28th. It's not quite settled whether Margot or I should go over.

The day they arrived they went to Loughlinstown with Mother, and I went to read to Mr. Coffey. On Wednesday here came Father Brown, Mother's pal, Miss Bloxham and Claud. The latter had a soft little beard on his cheeks which gave him an even more Italian Renaissance appearance, and he coughed most of the time and was lame from two abcesses

1. Diarmid's friend Edward MacLysaght (1887–1986) lived at Raheen, in Co. Clare. An Oxford scholar, genealogist and nationalist, he used the Gaelic version of his name rather than 'Lysaght'. He worked ceaselessly for Irish culture and the Irish language, organising a Gaelic Féis and Volunteer training camps at his house, where he would also host the 1917 Convention. He kept a diary of the period, *Leathanaigh ó mo Dhialann* (Dublin, Clódhanna Teóranta, 1978). His life by Seán Ó Ceallaigh was published by Coiscéim in 2003.
2. Michael Dwyer, the cat.

on his leg. He had not been to see a doctor, and was not proposing to. He also refused to speak English even on Mother's account. We thought[3] he looked as ill as could be. If R. hadn't been coming, we'd have arranged to take him to see a doctor, or to take one to see him ourselves. As it was we wrote to Mr. Martyn, who undertook to look after him.

Thursday. Tuesday was a day of great emotions. Claud turned up in the morning when the others were all out, and talked to me for an hour or so on end – this wasn't one of the emotions but it began it. He looks better slightly, and has his neck very carelessly tied up with a handkerchief, and a huge piece of cotton-wool sticking over the top by way of a collar I suppose. He was on his way to see Mr. Martyn, but didn't go there. At luncheon time, for which Miss Johnston (Anna) came, a telegram arrived for Clare, a long one from Raghnall. She read it and handed it to Margot, my mother asked about it. She said it was only a long rigmarole from R. We thought no more of it. After lunch I went into the diningroom and found Margot and Clare standing together. Margot said, "Herbert's back in England". "Why?" I said. "In hospital at Leicester," said Clare. We waited till Miss J. had gone and told Mother.

Thereinafter all was confusion. Mother's packing, who was making ready to go over when the wire should come saying how seriously he was hurt that the hospital was to send, tying up meccano for him to play with when he'd be better, looking out trains to get there on, and she and Clare were to go together so Clare could help find rooms, as she wasn't expected till the next day, cutting the lace off M's nightgown in case he wanted a soft extra one to wear.

I dashed out to get a Bradshaw, and no wire had come when I returned. Soon it did tho', and a great relief with it. "Nervous breakdown only trouble, home Sunday". We all went about grinning foolishly at each other for the rest of the hour, and when Cousin Isa Tisdall came to T, she and M made us all shriek with laughter. On top of that we went to church. I wrote to Ballyfin saying I couldn't come, and I should be going probably to bring him over. Yesterday we got a v. cheerful card from himself and a wire from R. saying he looked quite well. In the

3. There is an insert here, at the top of the page: *The Free* [by] Æ
'They bathed in the fire-flooded fountains
Life girdled them round and about
They slept in the clefts of the mountains
The stars called them forth as a shout.'

64 *Claud Chevasse*

evening a letter from him saying, "It will be GLORIOUS to be home again, probably Monday morning and 28 days leave . . ."

On Tuesday evening, as Herbert wasn't wounded, we went to a committee meeting and settled a few things in spite of any amount of talk. Those meetings are frightful. Miss Doyle says Dr. McCulloch may not be our medical inspector of V.A.D. now as he's so pro-British, and she was talking to him about it. It isn't exactly rot that she talks but it sounds like it, when we've got everything to do to make ourselves in the least degree efficient . . .

A letter, it was on Monday, from Palmer, and we arranged on the spot that he would paint a picture for Clare for her marriage on the 28th courant. His letter of yesterday showed he was very happy about it. Yesterday afternoon she and I went to Dun Emer to see some things. Needless to say she was delighted. After that I went to Upper Rathmines to tea with Claud, and I found Maighréad and Druncet na mare (namely: Diarmuid Russell) there already. He is a strange little boy, he can't stay still for a moment – though that is not unusual in a little boy – and he is fond of Claud, though that's not strange in a little boy either – [but] he was there like a "chaperone".

He has eyes with a sort of glow in them, tho' they are grey, I think. It may have been just the fire, but when I said something about a former life, he looked at me suddenly and I saw this glow, which gave him a most weird look, as if someone else's eyes were looking thro' him and his. Anyway with that sort of father and mother[4] you'd think it's natural . . .

Ballyfin, 10 January 1915. Now I know all that this name connotes of religious belief, prejudice, hospitality, comfort and anti-Irish sublimity. If you weren't very temperate here you'd wash yourself away there's so much hot water and jolly soap and soft towels. If you aren't very stupid it's easy to go out by yourself and no one be any the wiser. If you aren't very admiralty, you're no sort of a good guest. These are three simple rules . . .

15 January 1915 . . . I found a lot of books I wanted to read, and my only real chance was at night, so I did it, and then was too sleepy to write and too lazy during the day . . . On Saturday Max arrived, a nice lad, very young and merry, and in the afternoon I went out by myself and [with] the *Oxford Book of English Verse.* I went by the lake and thro' the woods, and found a dead jackdaw, frozen I think, for it had no wounds, and covered it with leaves; and the sky was clear and clean, and I got to the demesne edge and saw the view and a straight dark cloud above and a pink one over it, "as still as a brooding dove" . . .

When I got back [home] Eireamháin had arrived and had gone to meet me . . . That evening he went early to bed and since then, till this morning, he was rather bad, he's still bad with bronchitis, but less tired. He dropped into a ditch on their way back to billets, after 3 days and nights in the trenches, and lay there unconscious till he was picked out by ambulance some hours later. A rather nice Dr. Boxwell is attending him . . . Since then I have made a lovely white linen gown with painted patterns for Gráinne Ní Mháille,[5] likewise a cherry coloured coat laced with silver braid.

24 January 1915. Eiremháin is gone to Loughlinstown, and Maighréad and Mother to England to Raghnall's wedding. I've got a cushion broidered with tulips for Clare and R. from Miss Yeats, lovely it was but rather hard, and sewed it up in Irish manufactured canvas and brown paper.

I am by my lone which gives me a fine lot of time. Eiremháin was nearly well when he went, we gave him his brekker in bed each

---

4. Æ's wife, Violet Russell, was a member of the Dublin Hermetic Society, and had published *Heroes of the Dawn* (illustrated by Beatrice Elvery) with the Maunsel Press.
5. Grace O'Malley, in one of her tableaux.

morning, and one night he went to dine with the Coffeys which he greatly enjoyed. D. came here one day, and folded himself up in a low chair, and talked to E. to such good effect that the latter said after he'd gone that he was an "awfully nice man," and that if he began arguing pro-Germanism itself he'd probably agree with him. And Mother said he always seemed so temperate, didn't he, and to take such a large view, which set me wondering what I could say to D. that'd annoy him most next time I saw him.

My opportunity came when I saw Mrs Coffey a day or so later, for it was part of the annoying process to try and avoid D. himself, which I did successfully. She mentioned various friends of his who had or were going to enlist. I said, smiling, "Diarmuid ought to enlist himself". She looked rather shocked, and said, "Oh no, he wouldn't do that". I said, "Oh wouldn't he?" with a laugh. She said, as if anxious to justify him, "They called him a Fenian down in Clare, didn't you know?" "They knew very little of him to do that", smiled I. "Oh no", said she, "I think he's a Fenian, aren't you?" "No indeed", said I, "A Fenian's a very antiquated thing to be". By this time I'd reached the gate, smiling still. "We're all antiquated," said she, "only we don't want to fight the other island". We parted then. I hoped she would tell him, which I expect she did.

On Friday night I went there to ask Mrs. Coffey to come to a lecture at Cumann na mBan with me. Crawford Neil on ballads. She couldn't. I was saying something about our drill when she said, "Did you read his account of their work in Clare, the drill they did there?" "No, I didn't", said I, "has he written one?" "He" meantime was standing by – "In the *National Volunteer* this week, with his portrait," said she. I experienced a sense of loathing towards my young friend. "In the *National Volunteer*," I repeated with some of my feeling in my voice. "Oh really?" I smiled in what I imagine must have been an unpleasant manner at Diarmuid towering over me. If it expressed any small part of my emotions, Diarmuid said nothing and looked at the back of his father's armchair. "You didn't see it?" said Mrs. C. "No", I said, "I don't read the *National Volunteer*". "It's greatly improved," said she . . ."I'm glad it's improved," said I, "it needed improvement"; and with that we parted and I went to Cumann na mBan with anger.

I don't know why I should be so angry with D., for I don't feel much or any resentment towards the National Volunteers as a body, in fact I feel quite friendly to them and I always defend them when attacked by Irish V.'s. C na mB was really rather cheering, we had drill and all our names were taken, and the course of 12 lessons were mentioned and explained, and the exam at the end, and altogether we were much more businesslike than usual. As I left and right turned, my indignation died away, so I think it's partly built upon a fear that we are inferior to the N.V.'s . . .

3 February 1915. Last Sunday, Mother being still away, I had a rehearsal of the tableaux, at the Craobh. In the morning I wrote a letter to Diarmuid in which I said that there was a stream between us which was growing, and would grow steadily bigger. Several other things too which I thought would hurt him. I gave this to him at the Craobh, with some money I owed Mrs. Coffey. That evening Siobhán and Úna Hyde, a charming person of 18, came to sup with me and Miss West. We went to the Gaelic Service. Halfway thro' it I saw Diarmuid; when we sat down he glanced about once or twice and finally looked round full at me. I felt a thrill of anger, it was during the sermon. The next day Mrs. Coffey left a message asking me to go to T. there as the Lysaghts were coming. I debated, and, while I was doing it and having luncheon, there came a note from Diarmuid Coffey saying there was only one possible reply to my letter and I knew the reason, he couldn't make it. I thought, "If I go now, it'll be the beginning of the new terms for us to meet on, this note shows he had accepted them."

So I went, after working hard at a poster of Naomh Brighid[6] and was rather late. Mrs. Lysaght had gone. Mrs. Coffey and I talked a little, and then when D. came in I got up to go. She came some of the way with me, and we talked about my intolerance of their opinions, and how I always seemed to think those who differed from me traitors. A long time we walked up and down, and I defended myself as best I could, but at last it came out that I felt a good deal of hostility to Diarmuid and that was why I always seemed to show it to her when she quoted him. She and I debated what to do for a while. At last we decided that, without saying anything to him, we'd arrange between us for me not to see him for a couple of months. My committee I thought to be at 7. I said I was going straight on. She had to invite me to some brown bread and honey, I accepted.

I knew D. was up reading to Mr. Coffey: but I'm not sure whether I wanted him to come down or not. Anyway not much sooner was I devouring food than he came in. Then Mr. Coffey called out and she had to go. Diarmuid stood over at the fire-place. We talked a little

6. St. Brigid.

about his shooting that night. Then there was a pause. Then another self in me began to speak. "I've just been telling your mother that I feel hostile to you," it said. The "subject" of the experiments said, "That seems a great pity", with a slight smile. "Only just what I said in that letter, only I thought it might interest you to know what we were talking about," said it smilingly. "Very much," said Diarmuid. "Nice thing to say when I'm eating your bread and honey, isn't it?" with another smile. "Not nice particularly," he smiled back. "Do take off your glasses", I said, "I can't see your eyes". "Well now I can't see you," said he, removing them. "Small loss," said I. "What time is it? It must be late". He told me.

"May I just warm my hands?" said I, suiting the action to the word. Diarmuid moved with apologies and leant his arm on the mantelpiece. "I still don't know why you wrote that letter", he remarked composedly. "I wrote it because I wanted to hurt you," I remarked with equal composure. His face became rather white – "You know there's only one reply to it and I can't give that reply," he said below his breath. I glanced at him with cold curiosity and said, thinking aloud, "Did you ever want to hurt anyone you were in love with?" as I gazed into the fire. He never made love to me before but he did then, and I don't know whether I love him or not.

Tuesday 9 February 1915. In bed with flue [sic] induced partly by overwork in connection with tableaux, partly by thinking about D., and partly by it's being about. It's a rotten disease. On my birthday I got a little note from D asking could he come see me between 5 and 6 and a flint arrowhead made into a brooch, also a letter from Claud and three sheets of poetry, which really was poetry, I think, but much more passionate than ever before.

I went and telephoned to D not to come as I thought Mother would be in, and he said it was me he wanted to see. She went out to a Quiet Day, and the last thing of it was a[t] 5.30, so I thought I'd risk it later and went again to say come.

And so he did, and we sat by the fire in the drawing room, and I wondered again whether I loved him, and he said that he hadn't told his mother but that he had come in so late and so excited that he was sure she suspected most, and that he knew he had done everything wrong, but that he'd never felt such a glow of satisfaction for 48 hours on end before and that he knew it was lunacy but that he was tired of being wise (with that he took my hand and kissed it, I offering only a faint resistance) and I tried not to acquiesce in his assumption that I loved him and found it rather hard.

I said, "The question is what are we to do now?" He agreed, and he sat silent, and I looked at his thin brown hand and wondered whether I wanted to hold it all my life so to speak, and want years and years for it, and be poor with it and perhaps very poor – so I said, "I don't know what to tell my mother, because she'll say if I tell her I kissed you "you don't kiss a person without being in love with them", and then I shall say, "yes, because I only did it to stop him calling himself a cad" – "Oh Diarmuid, I really don't know whether I love you or not –" (the thin brown hand took hold of mine at this) "you're quite convinced I do". – "I don't think you're quite as uncertain as you say", said he.

Thursday 18 February. Whether I do or not it was an extraordinarily sweet and pleasant interview while it lasted, and when he went away I stood at the door and rejoiced in the wind which was high, and some of my uncertainty went. That was a long time ago, and I didn't see him since, except on the day we kept my birthday when he and Claud came and played childish games with our boisterous little cousins. We had forfeits and Pádraig insisted on the "Bow to the tallest, kneel to the prettiest and kiss the one you love the best" one, which came to me. I had a mad impulse to go and kiss D., which I successfully restrained.

That evening I told Mother I thought I was going to fall in love with D. She wasn't pleased as you can imagine, and began to rub in all the disadvantages of being poor. The next day I got a temperature and had to go to bed, so that I saw neither the rehearsal of the tableaux nor the things themselves. Dr. Boxwell came here and told me I should faint if I went, so I remained where I was. It annoyed me very much when Margot came back and said Gráinne had such lovely hair, and that D. looked splendid in his Spanish clothes, but apparently they went off alright in spite of my absence, which was surprising indeed to me and not altogether pleasing. But not really displeasing either.

On Tuesday I was still in bed, and in the afternoon Claud came to bring back some things and talk to Margot on his way to Dun Laoghaire. I heard him waiting in the hall, so I called out to him to come up and talk to me. He did. "When are you going?" I asked. "Now", said he from outside the door. "But – to England?" I said in dismay. "This

65 *St. Patrick's Day 1915: Cuirm Ceoil*

evening", said he. "Oh, Claud, I wanted to see you before you went", said I, disappointedly. "Hmm – ," he said. "I wanted to see you." "Oh dear," said I, "you can't come in, or you'll get the *fliú,*" said I. "Oh, no I won't," said he, "And I wanted to show you the new kilt." "Have you a new kilt? I asked, "Oh, I'd like to see it." "Me too", he said, "I'd like you to see it." "Well, you can't come in", said I. "If I come blindfold?" he said. "What good is that?" said I. "You'll get the flue whatever, for sure." "I'm not afraid", he said, "and I'm going away this evening." "That's true", said I, with a sigh. Pause. Then. "Come for one minute so, but you mustn't stay." In he came and stood near the table looking awfully handsome in a new kilt of dark greeny-brown, the colour that suits him best, and looked at me and we talked a little about the tableaux, and then Mother came in and was rather shocked at finding him there, and we hunted him away between us, and he made [a] most beautiful bow when he went.

66 *National Volunteer Review, April 1915*

With this account of the sorting out of her emotional entanglements, Cesca's diary comes to an abrupt end for the next fourteen months. It is tempting to think that another scribbled exercise book may be found some time, which will fill in the gap in this important period of Irish history. It could be that her demanding life – busy with art, the Gaelic League and Cumann na mBan – as well as her contentment at recognising her love for Diarmid, left her no time for writing. Another explanation is that, during the tensions of 1915, for a member of the Cumann na mBan executive to record events as she had been doing was inappropriate, even risky.[7] There was a feeling abroad that there would be a Rising within the year.

7. Margot was in Dublin now, an active member of Cumann na mBan, and maintaining a link with 'our unionist sisters in the north'. In her brief journal of 1914, she noted, 'A policeman is always outside *Freedom* office, watching those that come in and out. Cesca is having a dress dyed on this account!'

A month after the break in the diary, Cesca's student days at the Dublin Metropolitan School of Art came to an end. She had registered the previous autumn to attend the session ending in March 1915. Never once does she refer to her time there in her journal. Two brilliant students, protégés of William Orpen and intent on developing an Irish subject matter, had recently left the College and must have been talked about. The precocious Patrick Tuohy, three years her junior, had already had his first exhibition. Seán Keating went to London as assistant to their master, William Orpen. Sadhbh had no contact with Tuohy, but would note in an engagement diary of 1918 that Keating visited her studio in the company of another Limerick nationalist (and collector of paintings), Stephen O'Mara. The Protestant establishment attitude at the Metropolitan surely grated on her,[8] but what she learned about mural painting from the Belfast-born master, James Ward, who with the help of students was decorating the interior of the City Hall with historic Dublin scenes, was useful when she accepted the commission from Neilí Ní Bhriain to paint murals for the Irish college at Carrigaholt in County Clare.[9]

Cesca's artist friends were members of the Movement like herself; and, though Jack B. Yeats was a generation older than her, and unlike him she was academically trained, Cesca would have been in sympathy with the most prominent nationalist painter of his time, who exhibited regularly in Dublin and, was from a Protestant background like herself. Yeats, despite his political idealism, was apolitical in his painting, and she too, while she sketched Volunteers and their leaders, seems too to have had no desire to use contemporary politics as narrative matter for her oils.[10] Despite her original ecstatic linking of art with nationalism, she seems by now to have accepted that this was possible in theory only. She was slow to detach herself from the romanticism of heroic and historic subjects, retrogressive themes that haunted her and the first writers of the Celtic Revival. Her *Celtic King and Queen* pastel is based on one of the tableaux she was constantly producing. A large scale biblical subject in pastels, *Jesus at the Gates of Jerusalem,* has the same idealism as her mythical subjects but most probably was made while at the Paris atelier, where she learned to handle space so expertly, and worked for a time with Désvallieres.

8. See J. Turpin, *A School of Art in Dublin since the eighteenth century: a history of the National College of Art and Design* (Dublin, Gill and Macmillan, 1995) p. 193.
9. See Chap. 14.
10. Cyril Barrett (*Studies* vol. 64 no. 256 pp. 393–409; vol. 91 no. 363 pp. 223–238) and others have questioned the nature, and even the existence, of a nationalist art in Ireland.

67 *Sketches of Reggie's Daughter, Delle, born November 1915*

Cesca continued to get Parisian art supplies regularly from her French friend Marie (Máire) Palmer, who forwarded them from Broadstairs where she and Alfred were living. They had named their baby daughter Francesca after the Irish artist, who visited the family in August, writing to Máighréad on the sands, as she was 'hearing guns firing all the time from over the sea or on the sea'.[11] She begged her to send papers, 'or tell me how things are going in Ireland. You hear *nothing* here, not a *word.* Ireland might not exist.'

11. To Máighréad from Broadstairs, 12 Aug. 1915.

PART FOUR

'Everything Normal is Abnormal'

68 *Claud Chevasse with a Group of Nationalists*

1. *Gaelic League Poster* (1913; Cat. 85) (National Museum of Ireland)

2. *Achill (or Connemara) Landscape* (c. 1914; Cat. 22) (Private Collection)

3. Æ (George Russell), *Portrait of Cesca* (1917; Cat. 95) (National Gallery of Ireland)

4. *Self-Portrait (1)* (1914; Cat. 5) (Private Collection)

5. *Self-Portrait (2)* (1914–15; Cat. 6) (Private Collection)

6. *Jesus at the Gates of Jerusalem* (c. 1914; Cat. 23) (Private Collection)

7. *Reggie Smoking a Pipe* (c. 1915; Cat. 24) (Private Collection)

8. *Head of Amy* (c. 1915; Cat. 25) (Private Collection)

9. *Girl in Orange Blouse* (n.d.; Cat. 27) (Private Collection)

10. *An Rón (Margot)* (n.d.; Cat. 27v.) (Private Collection)

11. *Celtic King and Queen* (n.d.; Cat. 26) (Private Collection)

12. *Portrait of Móirín Nic Shionnaigh (Maureen Fox)* (1916; Cat. 10) (National University of Ireland, Galway)

13. *Carrigaholt Mural: Claud Chevasse and Maureen Fox* (1917; Cat. 88) (Coláiste Eoin Uí Chomhraí, Carrigaholt)

14. *Carrigaholt Mural: Darina and Herif* (1917; Cat. 88) (Coláiste Eoin Uí Chomhraí, Carrigaholt)

15. *Self-Portrait with Diarmid Coffey* (c. 1918; Cat. 20) (Private Collection)

16. *Self-Portrait (3)* (c. 1917; Cat. 14) (Private Collection)

17. Æ (George Russell), *Portrait of Cesca* (1917; Cat. 94) (Private Collection)

18. *Tree at Temple Hill* (1917; Cat. 13) (Private Collection)

19. *Caseta at Glengarriff* (1918; Cat. 16) (Private Collection)

20. *Portrait of Diarmid Coffey* (1918; Cat. 17) (Private Collection)

21. *Portrait of Margot at Temple Hill* (1918; Cat. 19) (Private Collection)

11
THE EASTER RISING[1]

Cesca's diary resumes in April 1916 when the Volunteers had been marching and demonstrating openly for more than a year, and rumours were widespread about the Rising she knew would happen. Yet even she who was at the centre of things in Cumann na mBan was taken by surprise when it happened.

There had been a false alarm. Cesca scribbled a note to the Goat on Holy Thursday, 'Such excitement the day before yesterday, tho' I'm glad to recollect I didn't get excited & threw cold water on anyone who did. I went into the office & found them all poring over papers & looking grave. Mrs. W.P. looked up & said, "Bad news, Miss Trench." Sorcha looked up & said "Such a thrilling paper," with a ring of genuine enthusiasm in her voice & rather a nice smile . . . Then they all began to talk at once, & described the paper that no doubt you saw reproduced in last night's or this one's paper, that Ald. O Ceallaigh read out. Someone had sent it from the Castle to E MacN[eill]. So they were making preparations. We did our small part . . . took away & burnt papers with names, & all the pamphlets disposed of. As it'd be tiresome to be without literature, I took the Constitution in a packet to the Hyde's & left it there to be called for by me some day. Now of course they say it's a fake, and no one can know whether or not . . . Anyway it won't happen now for some time . . .' However she was mistaken.

1. Cesca's account of the Rising is written in English.

[Easter Monday] 24 April 1916: Cousin Wilbraham came this morning [to] mend the bookshelf in the bookroom, he was at it all the morning and came back after lunch. He said, "Did ye hear that the Sinn Féiners have risen, they're all over Dublin?" I said I supposed it was manoeuvres. He said he hoped so, but the trams had stopped running and he heard they'd got all the principal buildings, Custom House, G.P.O. etc. and the Castle itself. I said to him to say nothing to Mother as I thought it couldn't be serious and knew it'd be diminished in the paper tomorrow.

Marthe and I were going out to Miss Yeats on [the] Dartry tram.[2] I took all the ammunition for a rifle in my bag, also some bandages and compressed food. On the way to do the former there came a ring at the door. I opened it, the maids being at Blessington for the day. A nice faced young man stood there and said, "I'm sure you don't remember me, do you Miss Trench (I'm Conn O'Grady)".[3] I said I did and he came in and explained that his mother had told him we lived along here[4] and he'd come in to see us. We chatted a bit in the drawing room *à trois*, then he said he must go and I accompanied him to the gate. It turned out that his Mother had wanted to know what I was doing. I said we intended to go out to Miss Yeats that afternoon and he agreed to come there and bring us word as Mother must know nothing of it, she knew nothing so far. We started, I took some bandages and a few other necessaries.

On our way down we decided that since the trams were not running we'd go in to see the riot.[5] We came to the tram place, not one to be seen, but all the conductors in groups. We asked them, one said, "Sure we can't run, there's war in the city, the Sinn Féiners are out and carrying all before them". "But is that true?" I said, "did you see them?" "Sure it is", said they; and one said he'd seen them as he was bringing back his tram. Further on we met another group, an agitated maiden lady of uncertain age was asking them was [this what] they wanted after all. One of them looked at me and winked. "Just the freedom of Ireland, ma'am," said he, "that's all". He saluted and we passed on.

We came down to Rathmines, and I saw my peeler-friend who has the little boy and asked for news. He said a peeler had been shot and that it

2. Lily Yeats ran the fabric department of the Cuala Industries in Churchtown and presumably the unidentified Marthe was interested in embroidered cushions and dresses.
3. Son of Standish O'Grady. Conn O'Grady, an engineer, was Diarmid Coffey's closest friend.
4. Temple Hill on Terenure Road West.
5. She uses the word 'émeute'.

69 *Cesca*

was bad work and that I couldn't get over the bridge of Portobello. This proved to be the case, as we observed from a distance the soldiers holding it. We went by the Kenilworth Rd turn off Rathmines Rd, and got to Charlemont Bridge and crossed it. There I saw a tweed-clad figure in the distance on a bike. I waited as it seemed somehow familiar and it resolved itself into Conn O'Grady. He had just started back to go to Miss Yeats. He could find out very little, but confirmed the rumours we had heard.

My chief object then became to get to some Cumann na mBan people to see what was doing. The message to attend a committee on Friday night was now explained as I thought. We went along Harcourt Terrace. Conn said, "Dermot C. and his mother have just gone out, their nurse brought them news that a man had been killed in Cuffe St. this morning, she saw it." As we went along we saw them returning. They'd been to the Green and found it barricaded and full of the Citizen Army.

All this time I found it hard to believe that Eoin Mac Neill[6] sanctioned this apparent madness, and it became imperative for me to see someone capable of telling me. At the corner of Earlsfort Terrace Marthe said she'd go back as she was too tired. I'd made her run, and in her narrow skirt. It was all the better. Conn O'Grady and I went on, we came to the Green and saw the Citizen Army men inside with a sort of low barricade across the gate inside and two big watering engines – they appeared to be – outside, also trenches being dug. We went and talked to them. I asked had they food and 1st-aiders in there. They said they had "Cumann na mBan and all", a nice brown-faced man it was that

6. MacNeill, Chief-of-Staff of the Irish Volunteers, had been opposed to the policy of armed insurrection, but failed in his attempt to cancel the Military Council's plans.

answered us, without uniform but with a bandolier and belt and rifle. He was in great spirits and said they had all the buildings. "Dublin is ours," were the words he used, "and the Castle after 700 years".

We went on down that side – on which is the Arts Club – but near the Green itself. Suddenly there came a rush of women and men at the Merrion Row corner, from what we could not see, round the corner. C.O'G. caught my arm and we ran into the Ely Place turn. Then we found it was a false alarm and we went on. He said that coming up Baggot St. he'd seen a man he knew at the head of some gorgeous wrecks[7] who were supposed to be making for the Green. Thus his object was to get me out of it as soon as possible.

They had a barricade erected in a loose sort of a way across the street opposite the Shelbourne Hotel. We went thro' it and down Dawson Street, not a soul except two men to be seen and the Headquarters door locked. We decided to go on to Henry Street. College Green was perfectly quiet. "I wonder whether they've got the Bank of Ireland," said he. "Doesn't look like it", said I. "No, they'd hardly have up all those notices," said he, referring to the recruiting pleadings with which it is plastered and disfigured.

At length we got to the G.P.O. by Henry St. I went to Mrs. Wyse Power's[8] and we found the blinds all down. We knocked on the door and windows. At length the blind was cautiously withdrawn and she looked to see who it was. Seeing me she came out, while C.O'G. withdrew to a distance. "What is all this?" I said, "is it true?" She nodded gloomily. "But can it be?" said I, "is Eoin MacNeill in it? After all he said –." She said, "Eoin MacNeill has his headquarters at Seumus O Kelly's[9] house in Rathgar Rd". "Then he approves", said I: it seemed almost incredible. I was staggered. "What are the rest of Cumann na mBan doing?" She didn't know.

"I must stay here" said she. "Anyone'd want to be prayed for that stayed in this house – my advice to you is to get back home." "I've got some first aid things here," said I, "I want to get in to give them to them: if the thing is serious, I ought – to help perhaps". She gave a gloomy look, and another person approached and I retired to tell my news to C.O'G.

7. Old soldier veterans popularly called 'Gorgeous Wrecks' from Georgius Rex.
8. The Irish Farm and Produce Company, Jennie Wyse Power's shop and restaurant at 21 Henry Street, was a meeting place for those planning the Rising, and it was here that the Proclamation of the Republic was signed.
9. Seumas O'Kelly (1881–1918), or Seumas Ó Ceallaigh, journalist and editor of *Nationality,* he was also a dramatist and short story writer, and friend of Arthur Griffith. He is best known for his classic short novel, *The Weaver's Grave.*

Part of it was that the police were confined to barracks. Then followed three quarters of an hour of mental distraction. At its height I met Sorcha, just having heard and going in to help somehow.

At length I decided with Conn O'Grady's help to go to Eoin MacNeill's headquarters and ask him whether I'd be more use inside or out. I went in first and left the first aid appliances, guided a strayed girl from Fairview to the other women who were making beds for the hospital . . .

They had Volunteers with arms at every window, of which the glass was all broken and thrown about in the street and a little inside. They were protected behind boards and bags, letter bags, a good many I expect. C.O'G. and I went off by Camden St. There we passed Jacob's Factory, in the hands of the Volunteers, who were sitting quietly at each window while some women were yelling at them below. There were bullet holes in the windows and in some of the shops opposite, hence a lot of broken glass. On the way I went to see [the] Misses MacGrath in Grantham St. They didn't seem nervous but weren't very well either of them. The niece looked so dignified and worthy to be respected, in her chair, with her fine face. Then to S.O'C's and then home. At S.O'C's, who [sic] came out and said, "He isn't here", to my enquiries. "He was before, he was here this morning, he's not now". I came home and made as light of the whole thing as possible: tho' I was far from thinking lightly of it.

[Tuesday] 25 April 1916. The next morning was very warm. I tore various underclothes in strips on Monday night, and again on Tuesday morning, and rolled them up and fastened them with red cotton. Saunders came just as we finished brekker and said that there had been slaughter in Dublin all night. The soldiers and the Volunteers shooting each other and more to the same effect. I collected my bandages into an elephant bag, and made a little list of the other things that might be useful such as needles, cotton and pins. Then I went out at about 10 ostentatiously to S.O'C's for news, but with the intention of going further.

When I got to Terenure, I bought the needles etc., then to Nugent for iodine, lint, cotton-wool and oilsilk. (How expensive all these things are). Then to S. O'C., having left word with Richard, combing the ground round the gate, to tell C.O'G. where I was when he came. I walked down and meant to leave my bike opposite to get the puncture mended, but he said he'd do it for me as the man opposite said he'd take 2 hours, having other work, according to the report of Una the sister, sent out immediately with it. He thought I ought to go out to Eoin MacNeill with news if I was really going into the town. "You're a brave girl," he said. I didn't at the time and

70 *Charcoal Study of Mrs Coffey*

don't now see anything brave in it. It was chiefly curiosity that impelled me. We took the bicycle out in the garden and turned it on its side and mended the puncture. Then another was discovered and proceeded with . . .

Mrs. Coffey had been down town and had just come back. She said it was quiet except for an argument in front of Jacob's, where she passed. C.O'G. and I went off at last and as it was getting late he asked me would I mind going by Harcourt Terrace as he wanted to get Diarmuid to take a message to his people, since he expected to be late intending to go with me.

– We went to overlook – walking rapidly down. The soldiers had Portobello Bridge and weren't allowing passage so we swerved down and crossed Charlemont [Bridge]. I asked Diarmuid would he take a message or send one for me to my people as I thought Mother'd be anxious. He hesitated and C.O'G. asked him to for him too. He said, "Well as a matter of fact I've got something to do that will prevent my doing either of those things". I said, "Oh really, what is that or is it a secret?" "Well it depends what you're going to do whether I'll tell you or not".

So I told him I was taking the first aid things in [to] the G.P.O. He thereupon explained that the National Volunteers were by way of being besieged in their office, and that he wanted to see what about getting food etc. to them. They'd got stuff there that they weren't going to give up. I was aghast, as I couldn't make out whether he meant they'd sided with the soldiers. Conn O'Grady and I went on, and into the house, and Mrs. Coffey tried to dissuade us from going on as she said it was proclaimed, and fearfully dangerous from 12-on. However we went while Diarmuid was telephoning as we didn't believe it was so dangerous.

I tried no 6 H[arcourt] S[treet] first as I heard they had a depot there, but it was shut. Here I lost C.O'G. I went on via Grafton St, which is always nice to ride down, College Green and round by Henry Street to G.P.O., left my bike at 91 for fear of punctures in the glass and boldly to the door of G.P.O. and in – I found Sorcha above, working in the cooking department. I asked her had she slept there then. "Sleep," said she with a smile, "there was no such thing as sleep, there were meals going on all the time." I looked in to the kitchen and saw 4 or 5 men in khaki working away drying plates. "Those are prisoners," she said, "and one of them is a cook and has been working like fury the whole night."

Of course she realises it's madness but felt she must go in. Same way with Mac Gearailt,[10] and with poor O'Rahilly who I met downstairs. Sorcha charged me with a message for her landlady in Harrington St. but I have forgotten the number. It was not pressing, still it was stupid [of me]. I asked Mr. Pearse had he any message he wanted sent to Eoin MacNeill. He said, "Have you seen him?" I told him what S.O'C. had said to me. "What does he think?" said he. I intimated what I believed he thought. "You don't seriously think you'll succeed, do you?" said I. "We would have," said he, "if it'd been on Sunday. Eoin MacNeill spoiled it." "It seems to me mad," said I as I took the little note he gave me for his mother or sister as I was going out that way, "and I thought your idea was to be on the defensive". "Our idea was to win Irish freedom," said he with a glow in his voice.

I am aware that I ought to have spoken with more vigour, but while I'd been walking up and down waiting for his note to be written I saw things I shall never forget, a row of young fellows kneeling saying their prayers, and 2 priests came in while I was there, and began to hear confessions kneeling by the side of them; at a little distance, a proclamation to the people of Ireland – of *Pobluiðheacht na hEireann* ("Irish Republic") signed by Tomás O Cléirigh, Seán Mac Diarmada, P.H.Pearse, Éamonn Ceannt, Seosamh Plunkett, Tomás Mac Donnchadha and Séamus Connolly. I read it, it included the phrase "our countrymen in America" as far as I remember, and "our gallant allies", either "in Europe" or "on the

10. Desmond Fitzgerald (1888–1947), born in London, learned Irish at Gaelic League classes, and for a time lived in Brittany with his wife Mabel, a Belfast Presbyterian Nationalist. In 1913 he joined the IRB in Kerry, and organised the Irish Volunteers. He and his wife served in the GPO during the Rising.

Continent". Of course that will damn them. If they don't win, and it's impossible that they should, they'll all be shot. One part of it was filled up like a hospital and I met Miss McCoy there. "It is mad of course, they oughtn't to have done it, but by Heaven it's gloriously brave". Then I went out with the note in my purse, and to Rutland Square.

I came to the National Volunteers office of which I found the door shut. I went and knocked, a man's voice shouted, "Who's there?" I didn't reply at first, as I thought they'd open, and knocked again. They shouted again, and I said "It's only a woman, please let me in". "How many are there of you?" said they. "Only one and that's a woman, it's alright, really". They opened and I found Mr. — there with two or three other men armed with rifles, and a couple of others without who looked like pals. I said did they want any message taken anywhere or anything of that sort. "Surely you're not going to fight your own countrymen and join the soldiers?" "Oh no," said they, "only they've got a lot of stuff here, we're waiting for orders from the officer commanding now what to do about it". I told Mr. E. of the man's name at Blessington if ever any of it went on again, and went since they didn't want anything, and said Mr. — was coming over just now.

I returned by Henry St. and Liffey St. at which corner there was a Volunteer holding it. I didn't see Clery's, which they say was looted, stupid not to look when I was in O'Connell St. I went back by Mrs. — and told her I was quite safe as she hadn't expected we should be. She said — had just gone out and to tell him to hurry up if I saw him as Colonel Esmond[11] wanted to speak to him on the telephone. I met him on the way and he made me come back and wait a few minutes and then came with me some way. We settled that I should come round the next day for and with news. He said he had advised the National Volunteers to give the rifles up, this was private, as they weren't enough to defend them, and anyway Irishmen shooting Irishmen, "there's enough of that".

It's a long way to — [12] and a lovely place when you get there, with daffs and hyacinths growing in the grass. Mrs. MacNeill opened the door

11. Lieut-Colonel Edmond, a Volunteer, joined the board of military inspectors when war was declared. Other members of the board were Lord Fingall, Majors Crean and Deasy, and Captain White.

12. Woodtown Park, Ballyboden, where Eoin MacNeill had been staying with his brother, James.

to me and brought me into the study where were gathered the following people: Miss MacNeill, Miss Creegan, Mr. Hobson[13] and Mr. Lester.[14]

I joined their circle and acquired the following information. From Friday night to Monday evening Bulmer Hobson had been a prisoner in a private house on the north side, because he and Eoin Mac Neill had tried to stop what he called "an act of criminal lunacy". They were furious. All Thursday night, when Bulmer Hobson discovered it first and came out to the National Volunteers, they were working at a plan for countermanding the Sunday parade which was to be real instead of only a parade. All Friday he was distributing them [copies of the plan]. On Friday night they decoyed him to a house on pretence of a committee meeting and kept him there. They used Eoin MacNeill's authority to imply that he was behind it, in an unscrupulous fashion. "If by a miracle they succeeded, of course, I suppose they'd be justified; but if we'd shot a few of them, I'd have saved the country," said B.H.

They all took the most gloomy views. Miss MacNeill thought there would be orange riots in the north, which made me feel unpleasant. All this time Mr. Lester was sitting there looking in front of him with his head in his hands. We had T., and I returned, forgetting my newspaper, unfortunately, which was a three sheet with the proclamation, and an article on spring fashions, and the rest theatres, a most curious document which will be historical. However I'll get it. I got directions how to go to the Hermitage, but wasn't quite sure of the way and missed it, and asked a little girl. She thought I was a spy because I was silly enough to ask her not to say that anyone had asked her, and said she'd tell everyone. *Tant pis!* I left the note with the man of the lodge who seemed a good fellow. The thing that made the MacNeills so furious was that this should be done just when everything was coming our way, the Orangemen playing into our hands with their snub to Wimbourne[15] showing how necessary it was for Irish Volunteers to retain their arms, and sympathy

13. Bulmer Hobson (1883–1969), from Holywood, Co. Down, founded the Ulster Literary Theatre. In 1907 he became Vice-President of Sinn Féin, but fell out with Griffith. In 1909 he published *Defensive Warfare* in Belfast. He was on the Supreme Council of the IRB, but believed justification for physical force lay in the will of the Irish people and not with a republican minority. He joined the Irish Volunteers and was one of those opposed to the Rising.
14. Seán Lester, journalist and publisher, and later international diplomat in the League of Nations, was born in Co. Antrim. He was friendly with Ernest Blythe and Seán O'Casey.
15. Lord Wimbourne had become Lord Lieutenant in February 1915. He resigned after the Rising, and was reinstated on 14 August 1916.

71 *Portrait of Eoin MacNeill (1917 or 1918)*

coming over to our side. I read St. Malachy's prophecy,[16] which he had on the mantelpiece there.

On my way to Mr MacNeill's house I wrote a note to Mother and sent it by a boy in Terenure to reassure her, tho' it was rather late then. It rained when I was coming back, softly at first, then heavily – I thought there might be a chance to go down in the car of a friend of Marthe's that evening to let S.O'C. know what I'd been doing, but the friend didn't come naturally enough. They said soldiers had been marching up from the Curragh since Monday afternoon and Saunders said in the morning that a friend of his, a detective, knew for certain that three transports had been sent to England that night to contain 3,000 men each, and that they were expected at 2 p.m. I gardened when I came back, the only tolerable occupation.

16. The prophecies of St. Malachy (1094–1148), Archbishop of Armagh, about the popes are famous. He predicted that Ireland would undergo oppression, persecution and calamities of every kind at the hands of England for a week of centuries at the end of which her oppressors would be chastised roundly.

[Wednesday] 26 April. Marthe and I went to the Piggotts . . . They have a lovely burburis in flower and two pale yellow blooms, an exquisite sight. Then I began to start off to Dún Laoghaire to see – I. whether boats were going to England for Marthe to go by, and – II. whether one could send letters from there. On the way there I intended to go to Harrington St. and the Coffeys. I got to Charlemont Bridge and saw no one crossing it but no soldiers, so was turning down by the canal when men in the house windows opposite began to shout at me "Go back". I stared, then saw a soldier standing up who had been in ambuscade in the bridge parapet, pointing a gun at me, shouting "go back" in a loud voice. I went without more ado, and heard they'd got all the bridges. However I thought I'd try Baggot St., and was overtaken by Dr. Maxwell also trying to get in, on account of her profession. She had been out at Enniskerry for holidays.

There was no stop, and I got to — [17] . . . I said I was going to try and post some letters at Dún Laoghaire and especially to Máighréad in Belfast, and heard from them that Mr. Knox[18] was with the Hannays and was expected there and might not have been able to go back. I wanted to go alone, they wouldn't let me as they said soldiers were supposed to be coming along the road and it might be unpleasant for me. So we went together. Mrs. Coffey was as miserable as I. It's a comfort to have something to do.

We went by the O'Grady's and found them giving T. to soldiers who Mrs. O'G. said looked so hot, poor things, and thirsty. "What regiment are they?" I said. "I don't know, I only know they're Irishmen," said she. We got — ['s] bike, and he muttered something about giving T. to people who were going to shoot down Irishmen, as we mounted. Dora[19] passed on a bicycle with L. Mac G[iolla] B[hríghde]. All the way there we met soldiers but couldn't see what they were. (Wilbraham had arrived just before I started, with Pádraic from Blessington, in a great state of mind, and I had a letter of his to post). I suppose they were told to scrutinise every passerby, for they certainly did. We laid bare our hearts in a curiously impersonal way and it was rather a consolation.

---

17. Cesca was writing rapidly, and leaves gaps here and there for names in her hurry. She must mean Harcourt Terrace here, where the Coffeys and the O'Gradys lived. The dash that follows refers to Conn O'Grady, they needed a bicycle for Diarmid.
18. This may be the 'soldier' referred to by Cesca in her letter of 29 April.
19. Dora French.

We came into Dún Laoghaire, and at the turn of the P.O. there were soldiers. I asked one nice little officer could we not send letters, he said not a word that wasn't military. He had had to send a message to his people by the war office, tho' they were in Ireland. So we went on to Killiney, stopped in Dalkey and bought some oranges, and then to a stretch of grass near the Hannays, where we had each half a packet of "Cream & Nuts", a bar of chocolate and an orange. "It seems almost incredible", said D, "that there should be [a] revolution going on in Dublin, [and] that you and I should be having a picnic on Killiney Hill". I felt inclined to say that it needed a revolution to accomplish as much, but refrained.

"There's nothing so calming to the mind as a beautiful view," which he had remarked, was true. The bay stretched round there blue and misty, and the water curled round on the sand. It seemed like summer. We discussed what he should say if I called him as a witness on arrest, tho' he thought it was probable I wouldn't be, and Laurence Sterne's writings, and C. O'Grady's wife, and how incredible it was that she should be – and how he and another National Volunteer last night had seriously thought they ought to join them, and how they had got the N.V. guns, "I'm glad to say," said —. He looked awfully white and tired, not having slept much. We went on to the Hannays. We discussed committees in general, and related what we had either of us seen or heard up till the time we met, and I told him all the MacNeills told me, and he told me about the life of Dr. Hyde[20] he was writing, and what our mutual plans were or had been for the summer.

When we got to the Hannays we found them all there on the sunny smooth lawn, with flowers in all the beds, a great border of purple violets, and the blue bay in the distance. A most exquisite spot. Mrs. Hannay gave us some water which we asked for, and bread and butter, tho' she would have given us more. My heart smote me afterwards. Mr. Knox had been in on Monday. We were telling them of the Proclamation of the Republic and Mr. Hannay took down the names! "No harm I suppose as they'd be known anyway," "and they have the tricolor up on the College of Surgeons," I said, "orange and white and green". "Oh is that it?" said he. "I saw it on Monday, it's very pretty. I admired it immensely and wondered what it was." Madame Markievicz is said to be there, looking after the food.

20. *Douglas Hyde, An Craoibhín Aoibhinn* (Dublin, Maunsel, 1917). A new edition, *Douglas Hyde: President of Ireland*, was issued by the Talbot Press in 1938, when Hyde became first President of Ireland.

They were putting in big loads of flour according to Mrs. Coffey's account when she was down there. Mr. K[nox] was held up trying to get back as his leave was up, but hoped to today, and promised to take our letter for Máighréad and look after her if there were any riots of Orangemen.

Mrs. Hannay is nice, and asked me to go out and see them, "in happier times", said she. "Do you know, of course, I'm very much blamed for saying it, but I'm almost glad they've done this, it proves they're not cowards, shirking their duty; and from what you and D. tell me, they're not on the make, but idealists". "If only they could have borne the taint of cowardice a little longer," I said, "Heaven knows they're not that". We went back by another route, shorter, avoiding Dalkey, in the queerest sort of fraternity.

[Thursday] 27 April 1916. Of course no posts are coming and there's no flour at the Ravensdale Shop in Rathmines, so I have just come back from buying some wheatmeal from the Nutts themselves to make bread for some of the poor. Sacks have been used for barricades which wastes a good deal.

Yesterday Mr. Nesbit said a woman in Camden St told him she'd seen the soldiers bring a Volunteer out of a house and shoot him after making him kneel. – M. Debremie is here, he's going to Limerick by bicycle looking for his wife, and says there is indiscriminate shooting in the city. Probably exaggerated. Mother has started referring to the English soldiers as "we". M. Debremie says they have all the stations now, not the G.P.O. tho', but the Volunteers have the houses. W[ilbraham] was here, had been to Clyde Rd and they and soldiers were firing at each other from that house opposite Lady Aimes at the end of Clyde Rd. He saw a soldier lying dead in the telephone box. He talked to me about my responsibility.

Mr. N[esbit] said a man had told him "we" had won everything in Limerick and Cork, there are persistent rumours of Germans of course, chiefly that they've come up the Shannon, probably originating in the interned having escaped. When I think of all those well-equipped, well-led, well-disciplined soldiers coming along the road from Dun Laoghaire. If the people in the country get to hear of the shooting of Volunteers, they'll get at the police etc. I should think, as Mr. N. suggests, and more Irishmen will be killed. It'll be easier so for the English to rule us – I wonder is this A.E's prophecy? Yesterday I said to D., "I don't care what happens to the other prophecies so long as St. Malachy's comes true, I was reading it yesterday". "So was I," said he.

27 April 1916. W[ilbraham] came this morning, and it was rather nice, keen to know whether I'd got rid of all "incriminating papers" which are really non-existent. Since then there has been intermittent firing from Dolphin's Barn direction, and there is a great fire to be seen that way now, all glowing in the sky. This morning destroyed papers with such vigour that my writing table hasn't been so tidy for years, and disposed of all the newspapers except a few to be dealt with tomorrow. W. is a good man.

Mr. Phipps came by and said that 8,000 English troops were thro' Dun Laoghaire yesterday and today, "Notts & Derbys" Yeomanry they were. Some of those we saw yesterday, I suppose. Since then there was a continual stream of visitors beginning with Diarmuid and ending with W.P.,[21] and including Elmina, full of tales as she had been in Ely Place. It is unnecessary to repeat them as they were chiefly libels on the character of the men whose souls she professed later on to be willing to pray for.

Diarmuid said on the authority of Sir John Lynch that Sir Roger Casement had been shot in London. Henry C.B. came too, having come from England this morning, and managed to get from Dún Laoghaire in some soldier's motor car. They wouldn't give them any food at the hotel, not being in residence there. He read what he says he believes is a fairly correct account of the thing in several English papers, "crazy rebellion", they call it. They're right for once, the brutes. They don't mention any names apparently, and they say that Cork, Tipperary and a lot of other places are quiet, which is something to be thankful for.

Warren's brother said they were fighting at the corner of Grantham St., and three of them were killed in a house and two others surrendered, and they took them and shot them – Conn O'Grady says they're treating their prisoners in Trinity well. There's volley after volley coming from Larkfield direction. "Grey is the evening when Irishmen die".

28 April 1916 Friday. I listened to the shooting last night for a long time but one can do no good by sitting at a window breaking one's heart. Another grey day today. It's a little clearer each day, and consequently a little worse, what the results of this "criminal lunacy" must be. It's like hacking at the chains of a prisoner with an axe and missing the chains or denting them merely, but gashing the prisoner.

W.P. said the soldiers had taken the G.P.O. by pumping gas into it, so that the people had come out and given themselves up. W. said that

21. This must be Warren, whom she quotes later.

they had not been able to take it without knocking down a house or two on the O'Connell Bridge side as the Volunteers were in all the O'Connell St. houses and commanded D'Olier St. and the Rotunda – they'll be awfully anxious in England for us at not hearing – we're going to try and get a letter thro' by a soldier today if we could.

Miss — was here and said a friend of hers had been in and said you wouldn't know Dublin, the law library was destroyed, and Hopkins & Hopkins and other houses down O'Connell St. burned. No one knows whether the G.P.O. has been taken yet. They say that Madame Markievicz has been shot, is wounded in a hospital, and is neither. All today they've been firing in the Larkfield directions, volley after volley, with occasionally a great boom of a cannon. I went to see Mrs. Nolan in the morning, she was almost distracted about her son, having heard he was in Jameson's Distillery which was supposed to have been burning last night, but later on her daughter came up and said they'd seen someone who spoke to him and he was alright so far. Some other young fellows in Thomas St. got a message thro' to their people saying they had plenty of food and plenty of ammunition. The firing goes on steadily.

If you think about it, you are inclined to envy Madame M. if she is shot. In the afternoon I went to Miss Perrin to ask her the name of a Belgian House that Marthe wants to go to. I think from her manner that she thought I had something to do with this madness, so I suppose there will be a lot of that to bear. I tried to get potatoes at Mrs. Fitzgerald's in the morning, but she had none to sell, nor had The Yellow House, that beastly lounge public house at the corner where you turn from Rathfarnham. I asked the peelers, who didn't know either. They have the martial law placards up on each barracks for all Dublin city and country.

In the evening when I was out painting the gate's name in English – the action of the weather had effaced it, tho' not the name in Irish – two motorbikes with side-cars passed me in a cloud of golden dust, straight out of the sunset. Mother thinks I'm going to be arrested any minute which is horrid for her so I hope I shan't be on that account, but I wish I might suffer some inconvenience of that sort at least, on other counts.

[Saturday] 29 April. It began again at 7 A.M., and went on till about 1 or 2 o'clock. In the morning I went out to Mrs. Hollwey to ask her for some potatoes. There I found her, her daughter and Mrs. Phelps. In the course of conversation she, the latter, said, "As long as we hear the guns we know we're alright, it's a great thing to hear the guns". I looked at Mrs. Hollwey restraining myself from saying, "Well it's not your country".

Mrs. H. said, "We don't like to hear the guns and know the poor fellows are dying," in a way that will endear her to me forever. Then to Ravensdale and got more flour, but it didn't come yet!

Warren came in and said that he had been yesterday at Mass and was told there, a) that in Blessington the Sinn Féiners and National Volunteers were killing each other, and that it was on fire, and b) that in Terenure people were lying dead on the streets, and the man who had fled from there was pointed out to him. He found a train had gone yesterday from Sallins to Limerick. He went on into Dublin – Marthe also. She found the bridges, tho' guarded, passable, and was able to get to Mount St. That was the place where Major Clerk saw the fight and 50 casualties on the English side.

The Mercers came in this morning, having tried to get bread in Rathfarnham and finding a tumult there of people on the same errand. Marthe has decided to go to Dún Laoghaire tomorrow and try to communicate with her sister from there. Mother and I put up paper on her wall early this afternoon, and — came and told us rather comforting things. One was that they had Richmond Hospital with two doctors in it. Another that they might possibly offer them terms if they'd take them. A girl from out of the G.P.O. had been taken, and said they were alright in there. So it's not true that they were gassed out. This morning S. said that a young chap he'd met had had a message sent him saying there was nothing to worry about, that they could hold out for another month at least, and that 500 of them had come in from the country along Kimmage Rd at 2 AM, having shot 3 sentries in the North Circular Rd. They say the Germans attacked England with 4 cruisers but that the attack was beaten off. — cheered us both rather and we went about feeling it might not be so bad as we had thought.

Then Miss L. came and said a man had told her he was in Merrion Square, saw 20 of them come out of a house, kneel down and fire at the soldiers who had not even time to take up their rifles, up on their bikes and make off as cool as mustard. "So they're in a house in Leeson St. now," said she in triumph. She hadn't actually seen them, I don't think, but am not sure. She came to say she had a cousin going to England who could take letters tomorrow or Monday.

Warren came back, not having been able to get nearer than Merrion Square, and saying the whole place is crammed with soldiers. While he was here, Maud opened the door and said, "Miss Mercer is here, with news for you", and introduced her. She came in all red from her haste, and said in a tone of triumph, "Have you heard the news? Unconditional surrender!" "No," said Mother in a too-good-to-be-true tone. "Well, I heard that", said W., speaking with a matter of fact voice, "but didn't think it was worth repeating, it seemed so unlikely". "How" – "Unlikely, oh do you think so", from them. "How could they get together to surrender? There's not enough cohesion between them, is there do you know?" to me. "I don't see how there can be, they're all in different houses," I said. It's possible that some small body surrendered, hence the rumour, tho' the silence all the afternoon lends colour to it, so that it was almost a relief to hear it starting again this evening.

While Mrs. Pigott and I were walking up and down talking about her favourite subjects, her little Caris came along on a bike and said, "They say 1,000 of the Sinn Féiners have surrendered" – the same rumour of course. Mrs. Clarke has hitherto been unappreciated by me, but she is really rather nice in her feelings. "Poor brave fellows" is the worst she says of them. It's not at all likely that Birrell is come over to make peace, and thank God it's not true what the *News of the World* says that the National Volunteers are fighting side by side with the military. Miss Langrishe came here yesterday too, but she was only full of faith, not of news, which is preferable really.

There is a sort of stillness in the air, and seems less oppression of misery, is it that we are getting inured to it, I wonder.

[22]29 April 1916

Dearest Aunt F.

You may be anxious about us as the posts are so disorganised we have not been able to communicate. We are alright & shall probably continue to be so, if the food difficulty can be solved, as there is a certain scarcity at present & I fear it will increase. However there are some mills near here. We heard firing going on from 12 noon yesterday & the nights before & since then till after midnight. It was quiet at 7 this morning but has begun again in a desultory fashion now, two or 3 miles away near Dolphin's Barn which is to the north of us, mostly rifle-fire with the boom of a cannon every 10 minutes. It is impossible to know what to believe of the affairs in Dublin, to believe some you wd think it was half destroyed, but most reports *we* have heard have been contradicted 10 minutes later. Wilbraham Trench comes in to see us from Blessington every 2nd day or so, & is rather a comfort in calming Mother.

I got a letter thro' to Margot on Wednesday by bicycling to Killiney & giving it to a soldier I know who was staying with the Hannays & expecting

22. This letter from Cesca to her favourite aunt, Frances Trench, seems relevant to her diary account.

to get back to Belfast the next day. "We are under martial law, of course, but haven't suffered much from it yet except as regards the railways being stopped for ordinary traffic. It is that which makes the scarcity of food, as so far the soldiers do not seem to have organised supply-ships.

This mad affair has done irreparable damage to the cause of Irish freedom which it is meant to serve, as it can only succeed by a miracle which isn't likely to occur. God help us, I think it will break all our hearts.

Yr loving niece C. Ch. T.

In case you are anxious abt my share, I had none, it was done against the leaders of the Irish Volunteers & all the sensible men among them, but there are many who will suffer innocently. Seumas Connolly is a man whose chief merit is his desire to see his country free, but he has no other qualifications for an affair of this kind. Most of the others are high-minded but utterly lacking in judgement, poets, or they wouldn't have run us into such idiocy. This is all in confidence to you. Please don't mention this opinion of mine to anyone who had no sympathy with the cause, as it is an opinion only.

Mother's best love. There's no fuel to be had, we have a lot of wood tho' to give away, thank goodness, & trees.

[Sunday] 30 April 1916. Last night was almost still, and the words "unconditional surrender" haunted me because I had felt somewhat less downcast since — was here, seeming to think it might not be so bad as we thought it must be at first, and if we were going to get anything out of it, it'd be a thousand times worth it. But if they surrendered it was not likely we could. This a.m. to church at Harolds X, on the way back we passed Mrs. Nolan's and called in to see her and tell her to send up for some meal.

She looked a different person from what she had the other day, when her face was colourless except for the red round her eyes, and said that she had a good heart now, and that she'd got a note from him in good spirits – that a little boy had come with notes to all the mothers, and he was in Maryboro St. This cheered us immensely. All the groups we passed were talking of food, it appeared, at about 11.30 a.m.

M and I went to R[athfarnham] to tell Mrs. Fitzgerald that there was a chance for letters and saw up on the police barracks two notices – one purporting to be the copy of a document signed P.H.Pearse, saying that to save the lives of their fellows, surrounded and outnumbered, the Republican Forces were surrendering in the G.P.O., at least I think that was in it, but at any rate they were surrendering. In another document side by side with it, it said that P.H.P. was in the neighbourhood of the Four Courts with a fractured leg, and "the woman Countess Markivich" also, and that they were being surrounded etc.

Part of news yesterday was that the — were trying to get them offered terms. Well this notice was depressing. We returned, and came on the Fitzgeralds coming out of church, and walked down with them as they were bringing goat's milk to Nugents for a sick baby. At luncheon time Mr. Thompson came, and I went out and talked to him on the steps. He had been down in Kerry and had only just managed to get back by train to Sallins, but thought as the fighting had been going on in Crumlin a couple of nights ago that it might be they were trying to drive them out into the country and we were just in the line of fire. He said in Rathmines people were walking about in hundreds with smiling faces saying it was all over, and talking with the soldiers, who were making complimentary remarks on the Volunteers' tactics, and they were generally supposed to be discussing terms in the Castle now. A truce of two hours last night enabled them to remove their wounded on both sides, and terms were discussed then. He had just seen — who had tried to join them in Jacob's, but they wouldn't have him, which was sensible, as they didn't know him. The unmentioned had an appointment with 3 of them who had been out just then, they hadn't had much food for 2 days and had no more ammunition. So they had put away their rifles and bandoliers, and walked out in their ordinary clothes and joined the crowd.

Mr. Thompson himself said he met one, who he knows to be a prominent Sinn Féiner, out foraging in the environs of Dublin. He says the soldiers are letting all women over the bridges, but all men have to have passes. Mrs. — has been taking food in regularly to her husband in Jacob's. It's the oddest situation, but I have been feeling hopeful all day. There was a lot of firing about 7 p.m., which was largely blank shot, if one is to believe Warren, who was told that in Rathmines to keep the crowds away. Also there's been – 11.30 P.M. – a good deal out to the south towards the mountains for the last three quarters of an hour, quite desultory but I don't think it's blank, so that may be the Wexford men trying to get in.

Kut-el-Mara[23] is fallen in the paper, which is rather bad for the Allies but may help towards a rapid and satisfactory solution here. By satisfactory I mean one which will not leave bad feeling behind it. What a lot of moods one goes thro'.

23. Kut is south of Baghdad in the Mesopotamian valley, in what is now Iraq.

72 *Eoin MacNeill*
Commission, 27 May 1916

12
A Frightening Vision

[Monday] 1 May 1916: It seems to me today that there is an end to all hope. We are like *le condamné* waiting for the execution and he doesn't know what kind of death is in store for him. I can't bear to think of it.

[Tuesday] 2 May 1916. W. says the soldiers will be coming to search every house indiscriminately. I would like them to come here soon, so that I will be ready whatever happens so that they will find nothing. Diarmuid came here yesterday and said that he could hardly get his bicycle up O'Connell Street, there were bricks everywhere. Nothing is left of the G.P.O but four walls. they didn't do too much damage to the Four Courts, but half of O'Connell Street is on the ground . . .

W. had many stories from Mr. Turton. He himself saw barefooted women wearing fur coats, and Volunteers trying to put an end to the looting.

[Wednesday] 3 May 1916. Miss Breslin came from Dublin yesterday. She was there last night while there were skirmishes on Mount Street Bridge and Harcourt Terrace. She wasn't allowed through and she had to remain in the middle of the shooting. But she says she wasn't as afraid as the two men who were there, one of them leaping at every sound. She said all the soldiers were saying that they had never seen such "pluck". It's the one ray of light, the respect the Sasanachs have for them [the insurgents]. — came in the morning and said he had a friend who was a prisoner in the College of Surgeons for a week until it surrendered, and the kind of boys who were there were the poor from the most depressed districts of Dublin, but they were so careful not to let cigarette ash fall on any floor that had a carpet. When they surrendered, they had an hour, and he told them to abandon their rifles and get away, and that no one would know they had been there. But they said they wouldn't leave, they would be true to their pledge. And they were. The papers are awful. Nobody knows what has happened to Eoin MacNeill, or Bulmer Hobson.

Miss — came. There is no one that she can talk to at home. After this Mrs. O' — came and we were asking what would happen to us now. She said, "Well, we've had four insurrections and three famines, that ought to content them for 116 years of the Union, they ought to give us Home Rule now." I'd like to be able to believe that they would. I see nothing but an unrelieved darkness before us, a frightening vision.

W. was in Dublin the whole day looking for Miss Breslin. About six the chauffeur came back and said that he had to go in and tell W. that she was safe at the Russell Hotel. I went in with him and up O'Connell Street. The houses up to the Pillar are almost all in ruins on each side, four walls in the place where the parapets and façade of the Imperial Hotel were; and the same in the street all around. The Hibernian Academy is one casualty, but it's little loss except that I hadn't seen it [the annual exhibition] this year. Crowds of people were gazing at the destruction, and there were armed soldiers on every corner. We went up Henry Street as far as Middle Abbey Street and it was nearly all destroyed too, some of the houses still smoking. It seemed to me like a dream. We went along the river as well, and saw the Four Courts with white marks on its dark grey walls where the bullets hit them. Where The Irish Farm Produce Co. was is nothing but a ruin, you wouldn't recognise it.

Last night I heard a shot in the direction of Terenure it seemed. It seemed to me there were about three or four people shooting, and then retreating and shooting again, but perhaps it was only a motor car. Yesterday I went and told the police that I have a pistol and a rifle, and they were to say they would send me a warning if the soldiers were coming. They said that there may have been Sinn Féiners in the fields to the back of the house but nobody knows if they are there still.

The O'Rahilly is dead, and this morning they put Pearse, Thomas MacDonagh and Tom Clarke to death after a "Trial under the Defence of the Realm Act".[1] Colonel Clark told Warren that when they went into O'Kelly's house at the corner of O'Connell Street they found twenty Volunteers dead. — came up this morning. A cousin of his who is a minister in Thomas Street was hit by a stray bullet. When it happened he sent word to the soldiers that he had a good "observation point" here and he gave the keys to the officer who came with some of his men. They went inside and the soldiers were so fearful of there being a "trap" that they forced him to go ahead of them up the stairs with his wounded foot.

There were five Lancers in the Missions near the Four Courts. The caretaker there gave them milk and tea and sugar, and any other provisions she had, and locked up all her money and valuables. When she came back the next day, the cupboard had been broken into, and the valuables taken. She told the tale to W. yesterday, the poor woman. There is another poor woman near here who runs a boarding house, and she told Saunders that the Volunteers came in and said, "Put everything under lock and key, and take your money, and everything will be safe until you come back." She did so, and came back the following day to find everything as they had promised.

6 May 1916. Saturday. On Wednesday W. returned very late from Dublin (Miss Breslin having waited to drive him in her car), and he said he had had to go back because the soldiers said there was a Sinn Féiner hidden in his house, and they asked him what he knew about the housekeeper's husband and he had had to admit he knew nothing. They suspected then that he had let one of them in. W. went back and slept the night in the house of a friend nearby. Yesterday he said that six soldiers and officers went in and they opened everything that was closed, and they were very suspicious about some boxes of "homeopathic medicines", because they thought they were explosives, and about a bullet Pádraic had, and other things of the same sort. But they didn't find anyone; says W., "If there were a few poor fellows wanting to hide, it'd be the most natural thing if he did say they might come into the empty house."

I didn't write this down on the 3rd because that was the day they put William Pearse, Joseph Plunkett, Éamonn Ó Dálaigh and Mícheál

1. The trials and executions were conducted in secrecy and the sentences made public afterwards. Ironically, though no names are specified in the official records, it is almost certain that selected men from the Sherwood Foresters (of one of whose regiments Reggie was commanding officer) carried out the executions.

O'Hanrahan to death. I knew the first three, particularly William Pearse[2] – Joseph Plunkett[3] married Grace Gifford the day before he was shot. Éamonn Ó Dálaigh is Mrs Clarke's brother, or Widow Clarke as she is now, because her husband was executed on Wednesday.

Another reason I didn't write yesterday was because Margot came on Thursday. She arrived safely, after a journey of five hours. The police made difficulties about her pass at first, but she got one in the end saying that she is a "loyal subject". There is a change in this house of mourning since she came.

Miss B said on Thursday, when she was here, that there was talk about searching two houses in Harcourt Terrace. "Which of them," I said. "Oh I don't remember exactly", she said, "the couple next to Miss Maguire, I think; they said that the wife was a "Miss Lestrange" before her marriage,[4] but I'm confused, you know." "Oh, yes," said I. "The son was here today." "Was he?" she said, "Is he a nationalist?"

Yesterday we had a splendid fire in the studio. It would make a nice picture. But now I don't suppose we needed it. Máighréad didn't get the letter sent by me with Mac an Cuine. I hope there was some reason for his not going up there, because if he forgot it –. The post came again at 11.30 the day before yesterday, and yesterday there were two letter posts and one parcel post.

[Tuesday] 9 May 1916. Reggie came on Sunday when we were eating breakfast. He was amiable and good tempered and good-spirited, and stayed the night and went off last evening. It was a terrible day, the weather appalling, heavy rain like the previous day and every day. Miss — came and said that she was at Dún Laoghaire with her third cousin, a Sasanach, and some one else said to the cousin, "This is Éire weeping for her sins." "Perhaps — the other country — has more reason to do so," said the cousin. "May be", said Miss —, "but not such a tender conscience."

The Archbishop is making worse statements than the British. He would like to have vengeance on the "forces of anarchy", the "wretched

2. William Pearse (1881–1916) trained as a sculptor in Paris and taught in the Dublin Metropolitan School of Art. He acted with the Theatre of Ireland in Hardwicke Street, and founded St. Enda's with his brother Pádraic Pearse, where he also taught.

3. Joseph Plunkett (1887–1916), poet, edited the *Irish Review* from 1911 with Tomás MacDonagh. A Volunteer and committed republican, he had gone to Germany with Roger Casement in 1914 to get arms.

4. Diarmid's mother, Mrs Coffey.

73 *Sketch of Reggie*

men". He can't add a favourable word to the debate although the courage of those involved has impressed everybody to date, and they are beaten and a victor shd be generous tho' they were singleminded, and a priest shd appreciate its rarity tho' they were Irishmen, and he aspires to call himself one! Shame on him!

An Craoibhín came in yesterday evening. Soldiers and detectives were in his house looking for arms and they took away his guns and his bayonet, and he offered them some bows and arrows off the wall. "So they said, "Ah, we're not sunk so low as that yet, sir." He said that they went to Mrs. Coffey's house and took Diarmuid's Howth gun, which was a pity because Colonel Esmond was going to collect it in a little while but the soldiers got there before him. Miss Griffin and myself were going to the gate when I saw Claud Chevasse coming up the path.

10 May 1916. He reached Dublin on Wednesday. He was arrested immediately at the station, and put in Richmond Jail in a large room like the — [5] with 39 other men. They weren't allowed to go out at all on any pretext: there was no sanitation, no beds, and they were in with looters and other "criminals", some of them merely on suspicion. Seán Sweetman was there, who is all of seventy-two years, and a scoundrel also who had neither manners nor schooling. They were let go on Monday without a trial – "Aren't I going to be tried?" he said. "No, we haven't the time",

5. This word is unreadable.

74 *Portrait of Douglas Hyde, 1916*

they said. "And aren't we going to get any satisfaction from the Government on account of this?" Oh, you can write to the authorities, but you needn't expect any satisfaction," they jeered.

11 May 1916. On Tuesday I was alone all evening because Mother and Máighréad went to Blackrock. I worked a little, but was so deeply depressed that it affected my thinking. In the end I decided to cycle out to Leinster Road to pay a visit. I was at the gate going out when the "Good Man" met me coming in. He's such a nice person. I could have told him much much more than I did – on Monday after Claud and Reggie left we were worried he was running the risk of being out after 8.30, since he didn't leave this house until 8.15, and he is not unostentatious. But there was no problem at all. (An Craoibhín said he was surprised that Thomas MacDonagh took part in the Rising because he was a person who wanted to accomplish something in his own life. I heard the same opinion from other people, and he was doing well.)

Yesterday he [Claud Chevasse] came here, as lively as ever. He had been to the office of the *Independent* with a report of the conditions in Richmond Prison, but they were afraid to publish anything. He said Mrs. Reddin's three sons were there, and Seán mac Diarmada and Éamonn Ceannt, but [the latter] was shot on Tuesday, and now they are putting poisonous rumours around, as if they were terrorists, Arthur Griffith along with the rest. But I'm not surprised, though I know he wasn't pleased that the Rising went ahead because he's a shrewd man.

Mrs. Clarke came in when CC was telling me his news, and he told her too. She said that her husband went to Portobello Barracks and he found the soldiers shooting anyone who went past, they were so afraid, and they didn't know who was their captain, or anything. It was one of them who ordered the shooting of Sheehy Skeffington and two others – a gentle editor and "The Devil" –.[6] There will be questions in the house about this.

The *Freeman* is becoming comparatively decent, except in its sordidly continuous squabbles with the *Independent,* but Seán R. is calling on Redmond to condone the shooting, and the *Freeman* supports him. Doesn't this show that MacNeill was right when he said Redmond had

6. Francis Sheehy Skeffington (1878–1916), author of a life of Michael Davitt, edited the suffrage newspaper, *The Irish Citizen,* and, with Tom Kettle, *The Nationalist.* He was active in the labour movement, and became Vice-Chairman of the Citizen Army in 1913. A convinced pacifist, he had been arrested on 27 April and shot summarily the next morning at Portobello Barracks by Major Bowen Colthurst, an officer in the British Army, who was afterwards declared insane and allowed to emigrate to Canada where his sanity returned.

no authority in the R[ainbow] Coalition. He admitted as much yesterday, "in so many words", which is rather extraordinary.

M. went to Leinster Road and heard a rumour there that I went as a messenger to Dun Laoghaire "under the pretence of delivering a letter to Killiney." I would like to have asked her when I went there yesterday from whom she heard this, but I forgot.

. . . When I went back to my work at the Museum after the Rising, Mr. Armstrong[7] talked to me for my soul's good. In the midst of the flood of gossip, warning and appeals to my social sense, which passed harmlessly off my back, he mentioned his assistant G.[8] That he had lost his job on the head of some suspicion "they" had of him – I heard no more of this at that time.[9]

14 May 1916. Yesterday Mrs. Cole called and said she would prefer me not to go back to the College of Science at the moment. She asked me as a favour to herself not to go, because there is a woman there who is so bitter that she said she would resign if I was there, and she'd very much like there to be no need for the committee to be in dispute, especially about Mrs. Henry. She was all "tears and tragedy" about it, "but she wasn't vehement enough", "and, if I could say that you are not coming back, it could put an end to any argument." "But what did she hear about me?" I said. She didn't know.

Then I remembered something she herself had said about me. According to Mrs. Lefroy she believes that I am a Progerman. And it's likely that when she remembered it again she was scandalised. She was upset and convinced that there was more damage done now than ever. There was a [rifle] range in the College and a great crowd of people came to learn how to shoot and, as Mrs. Cole's son thought they didn't seem like people who would take to arms, most of them, he put up a notice implying that he hoped the people who were using the range, etc. They tore down the notice and many of them left. But one who was called O'Donovan didn't leave and now he has penal servitude.

---

7. E.C.R. Armstrong, Keeper of Antiquities at the National Museum, was the author of the *Guide to the Irish Gold Ornaments.* The Museum was closed from 24 April–8 May because of the 'Rebellion'.
8. Liam Gogan, who later returned to the Museum and became head of the Art and Industry Division. He was one of the founders of and secretary to the Volunteers.
9. This undated paragraph written on a piece of loose writing paper fits into the narrative best at this point. Many art students practiced drawing at the Museum. Cesca may have been making studies of Celtic artefacts for pageants; there is nothing in the official records to suggest that she was employed there.

What has struck me most about this thing is the immovable incorrectness of the unionist attitude as regards Ireland . . . They talk of "traitors" and "our men", meaning respectively the men who were fighting for the independence of their country and the men who were fighting to keep her a slave. Their own country, mark you . . . This is the most astonishing country, everything normal is abnormal. The College of Science as it is a government institution must needs be anti-national, we'd better not try and be so absurd as to bluff it – we have no Government. We have no State.

There is a letter from Bernard Shaw in an English paper saying that the Irish have as much right to fight for the independence of their country as Serbia *par example,* and it is traitorous nonsense to bark at them. They have as much right to demand help from Germany or any other nation as England has to demand it from Russia. Rather decent to have someone saying that.

Another curious thing is being in agreement with M.P.s! Mr. Dillon made a great speech that angered the Sasanachs so much that one of them shouted out, "You evidently wish they had succeeded". It's a pity he didn't say, "I do", that was the truth of it, surely.

19 May 1916. Another thing he said, that his youngest son was going to join the army on his next birthday when he was going to be 18, but that some officer insulted him, and "Now, please God, he won't".

I was at the Hones yesterday. A letter came the day before from Cousin Henry saying that he had heard "today, that Máighréad and Cesca had been arrested", and if it is true, "I have been told nothing but lies for the last 3 weeks." That's probably because he was told we were in no danger. Máighréad saw Sorcha on Tuesday, she was free, and she wasn't expecting to be taken.

Coming home in the afternoon I went to the D.C.C.S. (it's a deplorable name!)[10] and they were full of hope about the Cumann. They have a shop in Merrion Row and they won't have any counters because that's the new thing; things will be all around, and you do your shopping directly, so to speak, without the intermediary of the counter. Going there, I met An Craoibhín; he was coming from the Castle after leaving his guns and things there. He had to go through the whole Castle to find the man who was in charge. In the end he found a man who said to him, "Come with me, Dr. Hyde, I'll show you the way. This is Colonel — who thinks he's the man, but Inspector — is really." Coming from the D.C.C.S., I collided

10. Dublin City Co-Operative Society.

suddenly with a motor car. I thought I was dead or something broken at least, but I was only bruised, thanks be to God!

I saw Mrs. Coffey then. Soldiers have come twice, searching the house the first time. Diarmuid was out, and they went into every room, except the room where his uniform is, and they took his gun away with them. The second time when she saw the soldiers coming she was certain that they were coming for him, and went to the door. "No 5?" they said. "Yes", said she. "Coffey?" "Yes, that's right". "I have got to search the house". "Oh, but we've been searched already, yesterday," she said. They didn't believe this, but in the end apologised to her and went away. The first time there were soldiers with bayonets positioned on the stairs, and Máighréad and Séamus Kavanagh under guard, their backs to the wall.

21 May. When I was about to go out, Eva Gore Booth[11] came in. She had just been to see her sister. She is "in very good spirits", she says. She [Constance] told her sister that, when she went into court, she said, "Well, it was a grand fight. Ireland's been free for a week anyway and now you can do what you like". They brought a little boy to witness against her who said that he had, standing on the steps of some Club, I forget which, from whence it is apparently impossible to see the front of the College of Science with any clearness, seen her shoot some doctor deliberately. Then this broke down, as it was too bad a tale, and they tried again and brought back the same boy with another tale and for that she was sentenced.

Tall, slender in build, with a voice just like her sister's, is the poetess. We had some talk of the conditions of imprisonment of suspected persons and she said that Madame M. had been very keen to have it known that Dr. Kathleen Lynn[12] had nothing to do with it at all, had simply doctored people, as the students at the College of Surgeons who wanted to were told, "well you needn't come back if you do." I said, "When you see her again, will you remember me to her and tell her we

---

11. (1878–1928). Countess Markievicz's sister, prominent poet of the Celtic Twilight and feminist socialist, involved in the suffragist movement. She worked in Manchester on behalf of marginalised working-class women. With Esther Roper she organised Constance's unsuccessful election campaign against Winston Churchill in north-west Manchester in 1908. See *Eva Gore-Booth and Esther Roper: a biography* by Gifford Lewis (London, Pandora, 1988).
12. She acted as Medical Director of the Citizen Army during Easter Week with the St. Stephen's Green garrison, and in the City Hall area, attending Seán Connolly when he was wounded.

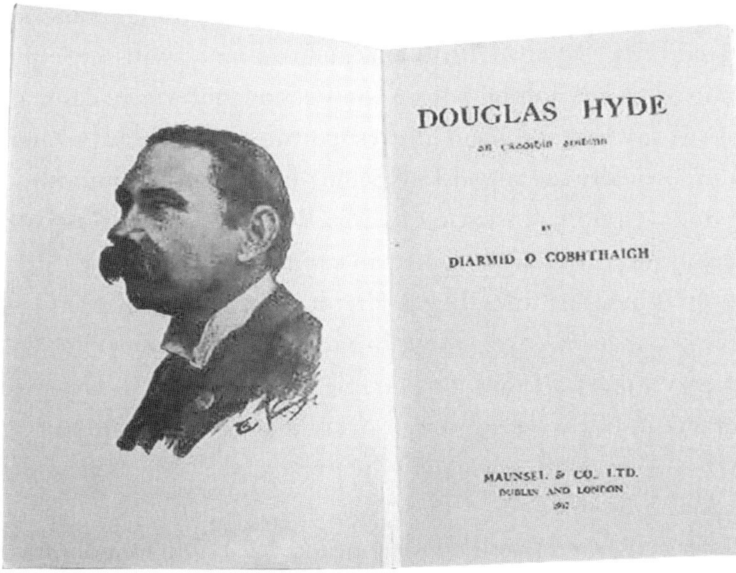

75 *Portrait of Douglas Hyde: Frontispiece to Diarmid's book, 1917*

don't believe all the stories people tell". "No indeed, we were just saying when you came in that we didn't, weren't we," said Mrs. Coffey. "Oh, thank you so much, I shan't see her again for 3 months you know, but she will be pleased," said Miss G.B.

It was after that that I went to the Co-Op, and bruised myself and went back to the Hydes[13] and was petted by Miss O'Brien and had oil put on my ankle out of a tiny bottle by Dr. Hyde, which he said had taken 8 herbs and 3 months to make. It's wonderful stuff certainly. I read parts of Diarmuid's *Living Irishmen* of Dr. Hyde while at No. 5. Acquaintance with the author and his subject gave it a peculiar interest, but I wish I could help him with it, there are things here and there I could improve, not faults of judgement but infelicities of style.

Apparently there is some chance of our getting a sort of Home Government. Today there was an account of an interview with Sir Horace Plunkett, cautious beyond words! and The *Freeman* has been devoting a good deal of attention to articles in the London *Times* and *Daily Express* which talk about the necessity for a settlement. This puzzled and cheered me, I could not imagine why they were doing it, there must be some motive beyond pure boredom with the Irish question (it would be to do them an injustice to suppose them disinterested well wishers of Ireland).

13. The Hydes lived at 1 Earlsfort Place, just off St. Stephen's Green.

On Friday I went to Killiney. We were talking over things there and Mr. H[annay] said the reason Griffith was so keen on a swift settlement was that he wanted to get it done before the Peace Conference came on, so as to be able to say that we needed no separate representation there, having been domestically arranged for. Seems likely, and rather cursed if that is his game. It's no use trusting to Mr. Redmond for his insisting on Irish representation there, still you can't tell what might turn up in politics. I thought when this thing began that it'd absolutely discredit the Irish Volunteers, not as regards their bravery, but volunteering as a policy. It hasn't so much as I thought, people are naturally shouting for general disarmament, but if we get some sort of a government others will say and feel what Mrs. Coffey means when she says, "Mr. Pearse will feel he hadn't died in vain".

The *Freeman* was warned that it'd be suppressed if it didn't moderate its tone last week. Rather an unusually respectable situation for it, it must feel bucked up. A letter from H[erbert] full of such deep sympathy. Sir R[oger] C[asement]'s trial began on Monday. I wish I had known that man. I should have loved him if I had, however, there's a drawing of him in a paper I got today. Eoin MacNeill's trial tomorrow, not open to press, that means not to public either of course, I wish we could have gone. There's still not a word in the paper about Bulmer Hobson – I remarked that to Mr. Hone. He said he had heard it suggested that he was betraying. What is one to believe. At A.E's the other night we heard who it was who had S[heehy] S[keffington] shot. The husband of Sighle's and Deora's friend, who Mother knows and took flowers to. Rough luck on her.

I wrote to the Governor of Mountjoy to ask about penal servitude generally, and Dr. Hayes[14] in particular, but he's not with him. Cousin Henry here to lunch today says there's only one convict prison in Ireland, and that's at Maryboro'. I wrote there. I would like to write to him, but he's probably got lots of people who he'd rather hear from – and if you can only get a letter a month – and at 1st it's once in 4 months. I suppose all those sentences will be revised.

Daylight saving bill came into force today. Rather funny and hard to keep out of an apologetic attitude towards the sun . . .

26 May. Friday. Claud was here yesterday and said that in the fighting at Lusk, or near, when two peelers were wounded, Dr. Hayes ran out

14. Cesca had got to know Dr Richard Hayes when she was helping to organise the Lusk branch of Cumann na mBan. He was sentenced to twenty years for his part in the Rising.

in the middle of the bullets and bound them up and attended to them who were wounded. Just what I'd expect him to do but it's nice to hear of one's expectations coming true.

I saw Sorcha on Monday, she spoke to me about the Reddins, that two girls went to their house looking for them, and that the father and mother took hold of them and talked to them. And that "the poet"[15] nearly went with them, but he didn't go out, and neither did either of them. "And I can understand and forgive their not going out . . .", she said. She said the people who went out were very bitter against the people who didn't go out.

She looked very tired. She is working on her M.A. Before I went to visit her, I went to Mrs. Shorter[16] at Dr. Sugar's house and she spoke to me about the I.N.A.A.[17] that was to be started by a large number of people among the counsellors and others. There was to be a meeting on Tuesday. The people who are involved in it are very lazy, and wonder will they have anything to do with Cumann na mBan: they would like it to do most of the work. Mrs. Clarke has a fund of money that the Volunteers left with her for the Dependents, and Diarmuid is looking after it . . . They made plans for a general rising without telling Eoin MacNeill anything about it. About 6 weeks before they told him, but not the date. He agreed to it – then, a week before, they told him the date. (I haven't the next bit clearly enough to write it and I must ask M. Ní Riain.) It ought to be true, told under those circumstances, and, if so, Eoin MacNeill comes less well out of it than Bulmer Hobson's story leads one to think . . .

27 May. On Tuesday I went to Dolphins Hotel at five and I found the meeting in full flow. Mrs. Hutton and Sorcha and Mrs. Power and Deora F[rínseach] and M. Ní Riain and C. Cealthara and Seumas O'Kelly and Father Aloysius, and Piaras Ussher and Miss O'Rahilly, and Lorcán Sherlock as chairman,[18] and Alderman Corrigan who has a five year old son, George Nesbit, and many others. At the beginning it seemed there would be a fight because of the utter unscrupulousness of L. S[herlock], who said in

15. Kenneth Reddin, b 1895, who was taught by Pearse at St. Enda's. He was appointed a Justice of the District Court in 1922, and had two plays performed at the Abbey.
16. Dora Sigerson Shorter (1866–1918), poet. Her friend Katharine Tynan said she died of a broken heart because of the failure of the Rising.
17. Irish National Aid Association. It was amalgamated with the Volunteer fund to become the Irish National Aid and Volunteer Dependents' Fund.
18. Lorcan Sherlock had been Lord Mayor of Dublin 1912–15.

76 *Æ (George Russell), Two sketches*

practically so many words that we would ask for money for several objects and use it for only one. However the 1st clause of the Constitution was rather well drafted, and came out quite honestly in the end . . .

28 May 1916. It's hard to believe it's the truth, but I can't. In the p.m. M. and I went out to Túr na Gréine, Foxrock, the residence of Mrs. H., who gave us the benefit of her consideration which had led her to the conclusion that the man captured and called Sir R[oger]C[asement] was not him at all. There are certain things against it's being him, his leaving a dagger in the boat, revolvers in the sand and dropping a paper of code from his coat. But the most likely thing is that these three things are invented evidence. M.Nic S. said – "Yes it's possible that they could have got a man to represent him tho' it'd be hard to find his match in England, but a man who'd do that is not the man who'd say of Bailey, "This man is innocent, at any rate", and ask whether he could make arrangements for his defence as well as his own. This was the view of the people at the Mitchells' too, where we went after dinner and found herself and her sister and Mrs. Coffey, Mrs. M[urray] R[oberts], Mr. C[onor] O'B[rien] and later Mrs. D[arrell] F[iggis], also they added that his emotion on hearing of the boys drowning was thoro'ly characteristic. Miss M[itchell] thought they'd try and prove him of unsound mind and shut him up, but I hope to God they'll not do that.

Massingham calls this "The Revolt of the Children of Light". They all expressed with I know not how much of sincerity surprise at my being free. "Why what would they run me in for?" said I with the most innocent of expressions and voices. "You know best, Miss Trench", said Mr. O'B. "I certainly feel that John George Maxwell[19] hasn't done his duty by you". "It really is very trying," said I, with a change of position, "We've not even been searched". This astonished them all still more. What is it that protects us I wonder, Raghnal, or Grandfather, or what, or is it that they despise my puny attempts? Anyway it's no use, as C.O'B says, "advertising oneself to the Raj".

The Darrell Figgis[20] affair was most scandalous. Twenty police armed to the teeth came to his house at 4 a.m. and broke a large hole in the back door and the fastenings off the front, tho' he shouted to them to wait as he was coming to open, and searched their room and bedroom, and took him off in a motor between two of the biggest of them. Mrs. D.F. is a nice little lady of the kind who can wear a high narrow hat and short full skirt and can take her veil down under her chin instead of pushing it up over her nose, with impunity. After a bit Miss M[itchell] came and sat close to me on the ground, and said she'd heard all about me and had been longing to talk to me, so I discovered what she had heard. Martial law is continued. They were angry with L[ieut.] C[ol.] J. Cherry for signing it and compared him with the man of Wolfe Tone's time, who refused, but I can't quite recall the details of that, so it is confused in my mind. Then nearly at the end C.O'B. produced a poem by A.E. called "Salutation", and Miss M. read it aloud and no one said a word when she'd finished.

30th May. With Mrs. Hamilton on Saturday evening, full of rumours of treachery. It's on Connolly that she puts her finger. I inadvertently mentioned A.E. "A.E", said she in a tone. Pause. "I could never speak to A.E again". Another pause. "What is it you feel so strongly about his attitude?" said I. "His attitude," said she. "His blood guiltiness". We gradually drew her on, and she explained that she thought he has behaved terribly in linking nationalism with labour movements the way he did, never before had they been confused, she thought, and this was the result. I suggested that he wasn't quite the first if it was so disastrous. The Land League for instance. She admitted that it was an instance. Then Wolfe Tone did the same. In fact there was a good deal in Irish history to justify the idea that their interests should be linked. I admit there's a good deal that militates

19. General Maxwell, sent over to suppress the insurgents.
20. (1882–1925) Poet and dramatist, who wrote under the name 'Michael Ireland'. He was a member of the Irish Volunteers, involved in the Howth gunrunning and in drawing up the Constitution of the Free State, after which he was elected to Dáil Éireann.

against it too. For instance it was aristocracy won the Irish Parliament and democracy that fought in '98. About equally divided the honours are.

Wednesday 31 May 1916. Sunday passed as Sundays do, only that I refrained from church matters, which was rather nice, and wrote a long letter to Aunt F[rances] – I sent her Æ's poems. I hope she'll feel rather flattered at being the only one. Service in Irish in the evening. Austin [Fisher] and Mr. Quigley. Austin looked sweet, and such a fine face and voice. They will not let him into Trinity College for some innocent remark he made that was reported to the soldier in charge. About 25 people present. I hadn't felt so desperate for a long time and Miss Edith White was there, and came some of the way home with us, which made it worse, I don't know why. It may be [I] was thinking of George Irvine in Maryboro' Jail.[21] Doctor Lynn used to come sometimes too. George Roe came up to me afterwards and said, "Can you come to a committee meeting on Wednesday at Mrs. Dix's house, it's very important. I got a letter from the Bishop of Tuam." "What is it about?" I said. "An official resolution?"[22] "It's Elmina West who's responsible," he said, "and I think we have to procrastinate."

There was some concern about what statement the Cumann Gaedhealach should issue about the Rising, since according to its constitution the Cumann was non-political. The Bishop, however, who was chairman – though he cautioned the committee against showing any political bias – was anxious that they should affirm loyalty to the Crown.

"That's it", I said, marvelling as I began to see light. "That's the resolution there was all the talk about – she was" – "conspiring with the bishop, it seems," he said. "What day is the meeting?" said I, "I'm coming for sure." He told me again and I promised to be there . . .

When I told M[áighréad] about E[lmina] W[est], the thing that struck her was the great damage this move would do to the committee. Certainly that's the worst thing about it. "No wonder she can't ever work with others", she said. Mother agreed when we told her . . .

---

21. Irvine was a member of Cumann Gaedhealach na hEaglaise, as was Dr Kathleen Lynn, who like Countess Markievicz had been incarcerated in Kilmainham Jail.
22. See also *Red-Headed Rebel: Susan L. Mitchell, Poet and Mystic of the Irish Cultural Renaissance* by Hilary Pyle (Dublin, Woodfield Press, 1998) pp. 175–7.

14 June. Yesterday I worked hard in the morning, and in the afternoon, except that I was surprised by Claud making a "prop" of the bicycle. Then I had to go to a committee meeting of Cumann Gaedhealach na hEaglaise. They proposed a resolution to the Bishop, in these words –

". . . That we deplore the recent rising resulting in the death of Irishmen at the hands of Irishmen and the reviving of party strife beginning to disappear in the common desire to work for the country (or words to that effect), and we call on all members of Cumann Gaedhealach na hEaglaise to follow the scriptural text, 'Honour all men, love the brotherhood, fear God, honour the king'". There were seven of us present and three against the motion. Mr. Dix had another resolution, much better in my opinion, and I wanted them to put it in alongside the first, but they didn't. I myself think if it is correct for the Bishop to take this initiative, then it's right to put this resolution on every notice he sends out so that we may know what it is.

77 *Sketches at Carrigaholt*

13
THE AFTERMATH

Monday [5 June]. It was a bad day because I didn't have enough sleep on Sunday night nor on the previous night. On the Friday before I went out for a ride on my bicycle and found an old ruined castle on a quiet road, and loads of cowslips in the field beside it, and I saw wonderful things in the sky and on the ground looking down towards Dublin. On Monday afternoon Ella Young and Maureen Fox came here and I began a picture of the two of them that I think will be a success. In the course of conversation E. said "I should like to have seen the scene would not you, when Mr Lysaght proclaimed the independence of Ireland from the chapel steps?!" M. said "Do you know whether it is true that there was a notice stuck up on the [Redmonds'][1] gate saying 'Traitors to the cause to be shot at sight?'" . . .

1. 'R', and 'Redmond' have both been struck out in manuscript.

Tonight I went to Mrs Curran's[2] house. Alice Milligan[3] was there, and Stephen MacKenna[4] and his wife, and Mrs M. Robertson and Mr Roberts,[5] who is letting his light hair grow too long to be becoming, and Eithne O'Kelly, prettier than ever. Colonel Moore's evidence published in the *Freeman* yesterday was the best thing I have read for a long time. The Commission wouldn't have it read out, and none of the other papers published it . . . Mrs MacKenna said she had been playing with Tomás MacDonagh's little boy[6] and he seemed quite cheerful and gay, she was carrying him on her back at Howth, and suddenly he said to her, "Do you know the soldiers shot my father and he's gone to heaven and he'll pray for me always". She tried to turn his mind off and he let himself be turned and then later said "Are you brave?" She gave the obvious response, "Would you come out with me, when I go out and kill *all* the English soldiers?"

6 June 1916. Mother came in this evening with the news that the ship Kitchener was in had been sunk off the coast of Scotland with all hands and crew. I wonder where he was going off the coast of Scotland, such an odd way for a soldier to go anywhere. It's a good thing Cousin Henry is coming tomorrow as she is naturally in the depths on the head of it . . . There's no doubt that the Rising has made more difference to England than anyone could have calculated . . . America seems to be quite estranged by the "simple soldier methods". I'd no idea they counted so much on America's friendship. It has brought Home Rule forward again as a piece of practical politics, isn't that queer? The Belfast Unionists are saying that any concession now will "only encourage them", quite true. But they're all talking about Home Rule with Ulster cut out. The *Independent* has begun its opposition already. The *Freeman* is cautious – it's hard on our own up there if they are to have merely a vicarious joy in a scheme of self-government.

9 June 1916. The soldiers have occupied Terenure with a view to overawing the populace, I expect. When I passed down this pm, about

---

2. Helen Laird, a member of Æ's theosophical lodge, was a fine comic actress, friend of Susan L. Mitchell, the poet, and other writers. She was married to the connoisseur and collector, C.P. Curran.
3. (1866–1953) Enthusiastic Irish-Irelander, biographer of Wolfe Tone, she was born in Co. Tyrone. With Ethna Carbery she edited the *Shan Van Vocht*, where James Connolly's first writings were published.
4. (1872–1934) Scholar, translator of Plotinus, and committed republican. A close friend of the playwright, J.M. Synge, he had the reputation of being one of the finest conversationalists in Dublin.
5. George Roberts of the Maunsell Press.
6. Donagh MacDonagh (1912–1968), a district justice, was also a poet and successful playwright.

4, the junior portion of the populace was seated on the wall of the school, they are in there, passing remarks about the soldiers' personal appearance. The rest of it seemed to be maintaining its pretence of indifference with a good deal of bravado. Saturday, I went to the mountains, visiting Mrs. MacNeill on my way. She looked thin and anxious and said it had been a great shock to her. "But we couldn't have kept him in all his life." When I think that they can do it if they like and that we have no remedy, I ask myself is there anything so hard as bondage and oppression . . .

After that I ate my piece of chocolate on Mount Venus. The girl in the place where I bought it asked me was I a Sinn Féiner because I told her she should get Irish chocolate. I'm sure she'll get on to the police as soon as possible. Then I went to Cloch Righ. In the afternoon I climbed Three Rock. It was cold and high and beautiful, and I loosed my hair into the wind and climbed up to the Rock at the top, and didn't reach the village until ten o'clock when it was nearly dark . . .

The next morning I started about 10.30, after a large nondescript meal, and walked up Killakee direction, by St. Columba's College, and there I found all the people going down to Pearse's mass in Rathfarnham. Two little girls I asked the way of were going, and I thought of doing the same. I decided that my costume would attract too much attention (I had on a blue skirt and reddish shirt, purple cloak, purple sleeveless coat under, with scarlet borders knitted, and a violet coloured poplin handkerchief on my head, very convenient in all that wind and rain, but not to Rathfarnham . . .).

On with me then till I came to Gleann Dubh, thro' the grey satiny beech trees, with crimson backgrounds of the fallen leaves of many autumns, absolutely wonderful. I got past and on to Glencree Road, very bleak and raining hard all the time. I overtook a woman and man and talked a little with them and passed them till I came to the Cyclists Rest. The woman of the place gave me buttermilk, and showed me a short cut, but all the same I was tired enough when I came within 3 miles of Enniskerry. The sun was out then and great clouds fraying out behind me and I carried my cloak instead of wearing it, and kept my hair on as best I could in the wind.

I found the Campbells' house and knocked on the door, and stayed there for a couple of hours resting and listening to the poetry of Seosamh MacCathmhaoil,[7] new poems that he wrote recently. One of them about

7. Joseph Campbell (1879–1944), who exhibited with Cesca in the Gaelic League exhibitions, was born in Belfast, worked with the Ulster Literary Theatre and collected traditional songs, the best known being 'My Lagan Love'. In London he became secretary of the Irish National Literary Society. He settled in Co. Wicklow but had to leave Ireland later on account of his republican sympathies.

the *crepuscule.* I recited a poem by Æ to them and they liked it. The last time I met that pair was at Lily Williams's cottage where I stayed this weekend, and the O'Rathaile's took me home in their motor. They have orange coloured curtains in the windows, a sort of colour that gives a light in itself, wonderful, and they have 2 sons with yellow hair, 3 and one and a half years.

11 June 1916. The day before yesterday I was on bike in Dublin and I took the turn down Henry St and along Moore St – there are girls selling fruit in shawls and full blue skirts there at the corner of the ruins, just like they used to when I'd see them so often in the evenings going in for Cumann na mBan. I asked one of them where was Moore Lane. "Second lane on the far side," she said. I went, but at the second lane I got off and tried to make out the name. It was Sackville Lane. There was none beyond – I went to a fish shop at the corner with two girls in it and asked them was it Moore Lane. "It is," said she. I thanked her and said I wasn't sure because of the name being different. "No it's not Moore Lane," said the other, "It's Sackville Lane but it's always called Moore Lane". While she spoke I saw white chalk writing on the wall next to the first door on the far side of the lane, that is the left hand side, "O Rahilly" and a †.

I didn't like to be looking at it so I made to get on. The first girl asked me who I was looking for, so I denied looking for anyone and went on down the lane and back, and saw what was written – "O Rahilly died, 24 May" and a † in two places, one large on the brick wall, and one small on a pipe, in white chalk. Mrs MacNeill said he was there a long time, badly wounded, calling for water, and that no one dared to take it to him because of the shooting, and in the end a boy went to him with water, and he was shot. After a while when the firing died down, a litle girl brought him water, and then he tried to crawl to the other side of the street, and he died as a result. Ella Young's story was that he was shot even though he was wounded. Which is true?

13 June 1916. Yesterday I went to the Educational Co: a boy there said, "Oh we'll have monuments in O'Connell St to them yet", and coming back I saw a crowd outside the Pro-Cathedral. I asked a policeman what was happening. "Masses for the Sinn Féiners," he said, cheerfully. I went there and saw the tricolour being raised now and again by somebody in the crowd, and everyone cheered when it was raised. It wasn't possible to go into the church, nor further along the street because there were so many people. The man with the flag started to go through the

78 *Three Sketches of Anne Cassidy*

crowd and they were giving him kisses. Some boys with caps were collecting money for food for the prisoners. I spoke for a short time to Pádraic Ó Conaire, he was looking very brown and thin, but if appearances are anything to go by his hardships have done him no harm . . .

23 June 1916. Partition and Home Rule, if you can call it so, seem to be coming. Colonel Moore keeps on insisting that it's not "permanent exclusion" that was promised. I read in the *Freeman* today a letter to that effect from him, replying to some country member, and just before a short paragraph in the *Irish Times* saying that the Ulster Council got a written promise from Lloyd George that it should be. I must go and see him. This is the second night I've slept in the studio, and tho' the first was one of gloom and darkness, even in the midst of it there was a certain peace in the little place, with the "dreamy gloomy friendly trees" outside. Clare was off at the Park Gate last night, doing canteen for munition workers – *The Master* is over the head of the bed, the drawing I did of it at the time it was produced . . .[8]

Yesterday that beautiful dark girl came, Anne Cassidy. She puzzles and fascinates me. I can never get out of her as much as I am sure is there. She has a strong face, deepset clear blue eyes under fine brows, a clear red and white skin, rather large clear pink mouth, high bridged nose and thick curly soft dark brown almost black hair. She is as tall as I and slimmer. Her face is the face of a heroine of deep feeling, but I can't feel her feeling – I can't get at her, and yet I have a sort of worship for her – she is so beautiful and noble-looking, and so large in all her ways

8. Cat. no. 54. *The Master* by Pádraic Pearse had been produced at the Irish Theatre in Hardwicke Street the previous year.

somehow – she can't pose a bit, or keep still, and if she takes a lovely pose unconsciously and I say – "keep like that" – instantly, and as if by instinct, it's like a wet cloth on a slate, all the interest is gone from the pose and the face. Made 3 rotten little sketches of her[9] – that's partly what makes her so hard to draw I think.

30 June 1916. This morning the papers had the news that Sir Ruaidhrí mac Easmuin had been found guilty and sentenced to be hanged, added that he had made a speech of protest, and misquoted a small portion of it – in Clare's evening paper, the London *Times*, his speech is in full. It's most admirable. I don't know when I ever heard of a man whose words, acts and general bearing I so thoro'ly and universally approved of, that is, what I've heard of. From all accounts his person is equally impressive. I wish I'd seen him ever. The *Freeman*'s "London Letter" said that "people said in court, 'That speech saved him from the gallows', said a learned counsel to me", and "they'll never hang him after that". If they don't, which God forbid, and even the *Irish Times* isn't calling for "an example", and he ever comes here again, I have made Mrs Hyde promise to ask me to meet him if only for the opportunity to draw him.

Met Col. Moore in the library yesterday, very cheerful, considering, and expecting a settlement quite soon . . . The difficulties are something frightful . . .

6 July 1916. On Tuesday I took Maighréad to [James] Stephens.[10] Never saw such clouds, immense pearls edged with fire-opals. Edward MacLysaght was there, and came and sat by me and talked about a scheme he has for a conference. He was to know on Wednesday morning whether Dermot O'Brien[11] would help him, if so, well and good, if not, "he hasn't the nerve to attempt it." "I'm going to try and play the Shawe Taylor,"[12] he said with his nice human enthusiastic open look, as if he was sure you'd be interested, "and see if I can get a sort of Recess Committee to try and come to some arrangement in Ireland. This scheme

9. Sketched heads on the verso of the two sketches of *Mrs Judy Withers*, see Cat. no. 74.
10. Like other writers and people of note in Dublin, the poet had an At Home once a week, and visitors came for the memorable conversation.
11. President of the Royal Hibernian Academy, he was Neilí Ní Bhriain's brother.
12. Captain John Shawe Taylor, cousin of Hugh Lane and a man of action – 'the man that braved the peeler, for Art and Liberty!' (according to Susan Mitchell) – initiated the conference that led to a peaceful settlement of the Land Question dispute between landlords and tenants.

is so beastly". I heartily agreed, "Oh why do people like Colonel Moore support it." "He tried to get me to write a letter to the *Freeman* in support". "Glad you didn't," and we talked about the feasibility of a conference. He has T. Bennet, Sir W. Caomhanach,[13] Dunraven and Monteagle,[14] Col. Moore and a couple of others (who I forget) down to ask from the South, and he's going to write to Bigger to ask him to find "10 of the most humane" from the North - "of course we'll have to ask the politicians but they won't come equally of course, because it's going behind their settlements". He might ask Wilbraham perhaps. I think I'll suggest it. I asked him had he seen that report of a sermon made by a man called Patterson at an Orange lodge saying they, Orangemen, had been betrayed, but they were proud and wouldn't go where they weren't wanted, and surely it might be possible for Irishmen to arrange with Irishmen. He had. "He's one of those I'm going to write to." He has another scheme for publishing a book of Pádraic Ó Conaire's with a translation by way of "making Irish European". He's the only modern Irish writer who writes as a European. I said An Seabhach[15] had hints, but it's more or less true about P.Ó C., he certainly does . . .

14 July 1916. The Orangemen didn't celebrate the Twelfth this year, and are feeling very proud of themselves for that, and for their 1st July fight which has been lauded, adulated and described as Suvla Bay was not.

Yesterday Mrs Stephens sent me a copy of the poem her man wrote called "Spring in Ireland 1916". It is great – as good as Æ's, a sort of pastoral. – "Be green upon their graves, oh happy Spring, for they were young and eager who are dead . . ." There are some lovely lines. "The clouds bloom out again, and live in fire", "Blue is the dawn of day, calm is the lake" . . . – oh it's all most uplifting. Came out in *The Nation.* How odd it seems. Because when the Hones were here the other night, he was telling me how J.S. had been afraid to publish the whole of it here,[16] only that bit that's like a prelude came out in *New Ireland,* and he can do it

13. Rt. Hon. Walter MacMurrough Kavanagh (1856–1922), educated Eton and Oxford, was MP for Carlow 1908–10, and Privy Councillor for Ireland.
14. Two philanthropic aristocrats, who started industries and encouraged rural co-operatives on their estates at Adare and Foynes in Co. Limerick.
15. (1883–1964), most famous for *Jimín Máire Thaidhg,* which went into many editions. An Seabhach also published the proverbs of Munster as *Seanfhocail na Muimhneach.*
16. The poem was published in 1916 by Macmillan, New York, in Stephens's collection *Green Branches;* republished in Dublin in 1917 by Maunsel.

79 *James Stephens*

> without fear in a paper of the nation, against whom the people he praises in his poem rose. Is it the catholicity of letters or the licence of poets – I wonder . . .

A week later Cesca set out on her bicycle, Luke,[17] to ride to Carrigaholt, at the mouth of the Shannon in County Clare. She was going to a course in Coláiste Eoghain Uí Chomhraidhe, the Irish college founded in 1912 by Neilí Ní Bhriain in honour of the writer Eoin O'Curry. She had promised to produce a pageant; and she would also make drawings for what would be her most ambitious art project, two murals in the schoolhouse there. The 'frieze' she describes in her diary perhaps excited her to suggest the idea to Neilí Ní Bhriain, or it could be that Neilí Ní Bhriain had already asked her to consider painting a mural. Whichever way, the use of symbolic images of her friends on the old wall of the Carrigaholt coastguard station expressed her personal notion of a neo Celtic civilisation in idyllic fashion, and the second theme of the murals, the tableau of pageant characters, identified this new civilisation's roots in heroic history.

17. Lucania and Pierce cycles were top of the range Irish models made in Dublin and Wexford factories, sold in Camden Street, Dublin, and in Scariff, Co. Clare, by Thomas McMahon, Market Square, where Cesca may have bought it, appreciating the connection with St. Luke, the artist.

> [Tuesday] 24 July. I was taking a lot of interest in politics . . . and lamenting that I wouldn't have certain papers, but now that seems very far away! Now I'm beginning to work. Until yesterday we had a real holiday, we all ran wild, it was jolly. The memory strongest in me for some time to come will be the frieze made by the white wall, Ella Young in a blue dress and Maureen Fox in a corn coloured and mauve one sitting on it, Claud Chevasse in his kilt leaning against it, and the woman of the house and Mrs Dix, all of them against a still opal sea and sky and faint blue line of land opposite us in Co. Kerry. I sketched some of the attitudes,[18] it was really exceedingly beautiful.

She had a strange retrospective sensation which strengthened the instinctual belief in reincarnation that she now shared with Ella Young.

> We were going to have the pageant of Briain McGowan[19] and the Norsemen next Sunday . . . a rehearsal the day before yesterday in the evening. C.C. had gone on a message and was expected back any minute. When he arrived, it was nearly dark and too late to do anything . . . "I suppose he just forgot", I said, and I went in and she [Ella Young] with me. It was a curious sensation I felt at the time, or rather afterwards, that it wasn't myself, Cesca Chenevix Trench, that was questioning him, and assuming a right to know where he went, and why he wasn't back before – even if I was running a pageant and he was acting in it.
>
> Ella told me afterwards, without my referring to it, that she got confused twice that day about me, once at lunch, I had my hair over my shoulders and that blue shirt on, for I had been bathing for the second time, and I was sitting at the head of the table, and she half saw a great hall and a black-haired king with a great tragedy in his look, and again when I was speaking to him and going into the house. – As if it was bad news that had come and she and I, druid and king, had gone in to hear it for ourselves tho' we knew it already. I was much taller to her, and broader, and wielded a royal power over the messenger, and she was standing by listening to the news, bad news as it was. This is all rather odd, isn't it?
>
> Thursday 26 July 1916 . . . Yesterday I made the professor and another young priest who is with him help to fashion bracelets out of cardboard

18. Sketchbook 2070 TX National Library of Ireland. A line drawing of the scene was issued as a postcard.
19. Brian Boru.

80 *Sketch of Brian Boru and Claud as the Danish envoy*

and gold paper. They were like a particularly gay pair of puppies and jeered at each other's work all the time. The professor found the brown cloak that belongs to my brown national costume and threw it round his tall slender form and admired himself in it. A charming pair together, there's always something rather pathetic about them, I think.

I'm writing this in class, given by the Bull [Seán Tóibín?], who isn't such a bad teacher, tho' rough. In fact he's very good. After our first encounter, he shaved himself – every day – which is rather a triumph and more than Fearghus does, who gives lectures so freely. He gave one to C.C. for going swimming with Maureen, and another to the Bull for being too jocular with Darina and Herif. Those are the names we have given to Mrs. Hone and Mrs. Hopkins which suit them rather well, the first being intended to have a hint of medieval languor, and the other to recall a dryad which the owner of it does. She's the most exquisite creature, last night she had on my white national with the pink scarf widely across her middle under her arms and her hair in two great rolls at each back side of her head, I couldn't take my eyes off her and didn't try, every attitude she took was more spirited and perfect than the last and all so unconscious, which I suppose explains its charm. She's worth having come to college for alone.[20]

20. Herif and Darina are both featured in individual poses in the mural.

81 *Sketch of Darina*

It is splendid as one grows older to feel one's appreciation of beauty deepening and strengthening like this . . . Early in the morning I went out, and saw the sea like a blue pearl and the sky like a pale green one and the golden crescent of the moon above the sea and the golden star of Venus, about three dark clouds on a line, cumulus ones above the horizon. The tide out and flowing. I leaned on the wall and filled my heart with it. It rained yesterday, and there's the most wonderful freshness and new life in the air because it had dried up before.

Later in the morning I went out, and the sun was rising, the sky was pure gold and the sea sapphire and the moon nothing but a pure white thread in the upper air. On the other side there was the characteristic view of Ireland, as I think it, a high royal sky, great clouds, "chunks of cadmium" and a warm blue, and beggars' houses on stretches of fairly monotonous green land. I've done a picture like this, rather fun.[21] Then I went to swim but the tide was going out which made it weedy. But there was such strength in[22] houses and land and the water . . . I did a sketch yesterday morning, and I went to bathe and it came on to rain,

21. Cat. no. 12. A rare landscape from her hand, the picture has not been traced.
22. A thumbnail sketch of huge sky and line of waves is inserted in the text here.

82 *Sketch of Wall at Carrigaholt*

and there were my things left out; and when I dashed out of the water, and [out of] my bathing suit and into a cloak and skirt and back, what would I find but the kind Bull putting them by!. . .

The pageant went off alright. At the last moment I had to be the wise woman. So I made myself up in brown earthy coloured skirt, purple shirt, and brown stuff unshaped fastened at the throat with a brooch and coming into a frayed point on each side, my hair loose and covered with that purple handkerchief. This with my dark sunburnt face, brown braids and bare feet did quite well. Tho' it was a different reading of the part from Ella Young's and from what I meant it at first to be, it did well enough, and I could never have done it her way. I made it into a wild mountainy woman, the earth spirit, not reasoning, but going straight for the truth, instinctively.

A lot of extra boys came from the village and we dressed them all and gave them swords and spears and shields, and they began to fight at once as if they had never done anything else all their lives. First they came out running and playing about together, then the ladies and men courtiers, with the wise woman stalking darkly by herself – and leaned on the wall and stood about talking together and sat on the grass – and then after a bit the king. They all stood up and made a lane, and he passed up preceded by the bard in magnificent green with a gold harp carried by a diminutive person, barelegged with a purple tunic with a blue border and

83 *Sketches of Wall at Currigaholt*

a scarlet cap on his head which he had found somewhere. After some talk, argument and the mountainy woman's skirmish with the old nobleman, the Danish envoy strode in from the gate, head and shoulders taller than anyone else there. Then the blind man with his petition and his complaint . . . (Proinnsias Ó Súilleabháin was Briain, in my blue shirt, Claud's kilt, my belt and a sort of dark rough red sleeveless jacket over it, my brown shoes with the crossed leather lacing and legs so stained and scratched and wounded with vermillion and burnt sienna and earth that the woman of the house wanted to first aid him when first she saw him, his only weapon a naked sword.) He spoke splendidly, and entered into the part as if he had been born to it. . . .

Really the most picturesque part was when we all came back still dressed and sat about on walls and rugs and the grass and gave them a concert. The king sat on his throne in his orange robe and purple cloak fringed with silver and gold crown and gave out the items. The bard began. He had a silver thing on his head and looked fine, and Herif danced, and the boys lay about in long lines on the grass, and the girls sat and listened. Ella and Maureen and Claud made a picturesque group thus: E. on a chair robed in blue, a blue-grey veil on her head very soft and ample, bound with a thin silver chain over her silver hair, Maureen as before described at her right, with her elbow on E's knee. Claud, silver-winged, green-cloaked and shapely, stretched himself lengthily on the ground at her other side and in front of her, his right elbow nearly

84 *Sketch of Claud*

touching M's knees.[23] I sat on the sea wall and made sketches, and explained the play to the people, and felt rather neglected and lonely if the truth must be told. That is the price one pays for the reputation for strength!

After the whole thing was over, and that heart-stirring Co. Derry love-song had been sung, we went and got T. Claud and Móirín were off together as usual, so they didn't get the benefit of my speech which I made to the others . . .

That evening we had a seanchus, still dressed up, and Herif danced a Spanish dance, and P. told stories and Claud sat slightly behind Maureen and leaned his elbow on her chair back, and I made sketches of them and thought my own thoughts.

She had watched the romance between Claud and Móirín maturing quietly since they arrived in Carrigaholt, and was thoroughly in approval if a little

23. Though she placed Ella Young at the centre of the group on the occasion of the pageant, she represents herself in that position as the wise woman in the corresponding mural. Her garments in the mural differ slightly in colouring from the description here – as those of others do. Some colours were changed when the murals were restored.

wistful as she remembered his former passion for herself. Typically, she started on a pair of portraits of the two. That of Móirín, which is in Galway University collection, recalls a small incident in the diary. The first Sunday at Carrigaholt they had missed church because the car hadn't been ordered in time, so they held a little service in the college. 'I made Ella Young and Maureen Fox come, the latter however escaped just before it began. When we came out, . . . as she was a criminal, we had agreed to sacrifice her when we all went to swim. She and Claud went to try and swim to the rocks, three quarters of mile or more . . .'

> and of course she found it much too far, and had to be towed back by him, and then landed prematurely and was held up at each step by him coming out; and Ella and I went along with cloaks and her clothes, and hot milk and whiskey. They've been tremendous friends ever since, and he avoids me studiously which I'm sure to oblige, so of course they're blissfully indifferent, are contented or . . . ! I can't quite believe he'll fall in love with her but I wish he would, they'd suit each other rather well, [tho'] not unless she did with him, of course. I facilitate it in every way I can, and yesterday I had them both cleaning my palette for quite a long time . . .
>
> There was a *sgoraidheacht* [party] last night, and she wore a flame-coloured dress and amber beads in her hair and it hanging down, and they made rather a nice couple, dancing together. It would be an awful thing if she were to fall in love with him alone tho', and I begin to see that she's not nearly so independent a person as I once thought. I wish I could tell her that, or let her know that he was once very devoted to someone . . . so I didn't know whether he might be still, but it'd be so difficult to put it in a way that wouldn't look like a warning!

She painted the portrait of Móirín wearing the Gaelic robe of the dance, a strong radiant likeness, and inscribed on the back "An Íodhbhairt", meaning "The Sacrifice". The pendant portrait of Claud had a more difficult birth. The couple might be blissful, and Móirín had no need of Cesca's concern for her[24]: but a black cloud loomed over what was otherwise a memorably idyllic time. The many petitions to the Government to mitigate Sir Roger Casement's penalty after he had been sentenced for treason had been overruled.

24. Móirín married Claud Chevasse the following year at St. Anne's, Dawson Street, in Dublin. Douglas Hyde and Joseph Hone supported Claud, and Ella Young, Neilí Ní Bhriain, Cesca and Margot Trench supported Maureen – a big Gaelic Protestant occasion. The ceremony was conducted by Feardorcha Ó Conaill ('Conall Cearnach') from Leenane, Co. Galway.

31 July 1916. They say that Roger Casement will be hung on 3 August. I got a letter from Íde Nic N.[25] three days ago. She said, "I'm afraid Roger is having a hell of a time in the place where he is now, and I can't do anything for him. They haven't let any one, nor any friend, go to say goodbye to him. They're worse than the devils in Hell. I would like to get my hands on them" . . .

Cesca continued the story after she had gone on to stay with the Hydes at Ratra, Frenchpark, Roscommon.

15 August 1916 . . . On 3 August I went by myself to the other side of the point at Carrigaholt. I was nearly there when I saw Ella Young standing in front of me. I was running along the straight green walk that goes to the bay with the submerged forest, and I saw a straight figure silhouetted against the dying fires of the sky. It looked misty and blue. "Is that you, druidess?" I called out. We went and sat on the strand. To the right the sun had gone down and the black pointed stumps of the sea stuck up among the sand and stones. Before us the Leap Head lay, dark blue, and the limitless sea and sky. To the left the faint headlands and the thin white line of foam on the low black rocks that run out level into the sea. Nearer to us it was still and clear like glass. There was no sound but the whistling cries of seabirds at intervals, and the movement of swallows who swooped past us as we sat still and silent.

It wasn't suddenly I heard it, but gradually I became conscious of it . . . singing, men's voices, out there in the sea where it meets the sky. It wasn't queer or sad and didn't alarm me or fill me with much wonder or delight, only my soul went out to meet it and the great beings there where the sea meets the sky. It was dusk and the crimson sickle of the moon hid herself in mists as she went down, behind the head. It might have been a dirge for the one that died that morning at 9 o'clock,[26] "strong and erect" as the papers said, but it wasn't sad eno'. It was only the articulate voice of the sea speaking. Ella Young didn't hear it or else I'd say it was human singing, but it came from long long away, and it was like a chorus and it came from the sea . . . Yes that was on the third, there was lightning in my blood . . .[27]

25. Perhaps Íde Nic Néill from the Glens of Antrim, a member of Conradh na Gaeilge.
26. Roger Casement was executed in Pentonville Prison, at 9 A.M. on Thursday, 3 August 1916.
27. This is a reference to the poem, 'Dark Rosaleen', by James Clarence Mangan.

85 *Portrait of Claud Chevasse in a Kilt, 1916*

That morning we could not bear the suspense any longer and I sent a wire to Máighréad to ask had he got a reprieve. All the college knew we had. In the afternoon, as I was painting Claud, I heard the Bull's voice outside. "Is Miss Trench there?" I went outside, he had the envelope in his hand. The message read, *"Níl, beannacht dílis Dé lena anam"*,[28] as I said it out. The Bull took off his hat and said, "Amen". I went within and held it out to Maureen, who had come out from an inner room.

I went on with the picture after a bit. It was rather a jolly one of Claud in his Danish dress, brown tussore tunic, dark green breeches and stockings crossed with green tapes, a short wide green cloak, his throat and strong neck bare, a black raven on a white ground on his breast, and a silver belt and sword, and, best of all, a band of silver with

28. 'No, God have mercy on his soul'.

> great silver wings at each side. He looks perfectly magnificent in it. I fell deeply in love with him the first time I saw him in it, and it was fortunate that I had no opportunity of private speech with him or I should have been capable of I know not what indiscretion. The other portrait is of Maureen in flame dress as I described her. She has a silver spear in her left hand. As the pictures stand they face each other. He has a dagger in his right hand.

It is unknown whether the pendant portrait of Claud in Danish dress has survived; but the portrait of him in his green Irish kilt, slightly larger than the portrait of Móirín in the UCG collection, was probably painted at Carrighaholt the same year.

After the harmonious 'jolly' holiday at Carrigaholt, where the sun seemed to shine all the time and the young people ran wild, Cesca found her stay at Ratra a disappointing contrast. She had been invited by Hyde to his home to make portraits of the family, and the account of her experience there brings her diary to a close.

> [15 August 1916] . . . There's no manner of doubt about it, sunshine does make a lot of difference, and so does sleep. Yesterday I felt so nervy I wanted to slay Nuala and Úna [and] An Craoibhín, only he wasn't there, and then tell Mrs Hyde what I'd done, so I went for a walk on the bog, down by the lake and back across the bog up to my knees once, and nearly always to my ankles, and didn't get in till 7.35, so it was lucky dinner was quarter of an hour late, and my head seemed made of iron pistons which hit me each time I moved it. Mrs. H. was in much the same state so we sat in the study after dinner by the light of a fire without a lamp and made silly jokes at which everyone laughed, at least I did, for solitude had done me good, and Nuala rubbed my head and Una massaged Mrs. H. and An Craoibhín lay on the sofa and petted the white Parrot, and we teased him about his partiality for pretty girls, and he was rather sweet.
>
> It was the thunder the day before yesterday, and not sleeping because of it, and reading, and the way the master was always paying me compliments – this had made me furious, and I summoned up courage to lash out at him half in jest, but more in earnest, and he isn't at all a calming person to lash out at. By jove but he must have been an awfully exciting lover! . . . and such a dear and so kind always, and he was rather pleased with that idea of the play he and I were going to write about the souls at the door of Paradise, and they're not being let in for not knowing Irish . . .

86 *Portrait of Nuala Hyde, 1916*

and [he] said, "Don't put it on the long finger." The chief occupation here is eating gooseberries and shooting, and leisure intervals are occupied by editing Irish manuscripts, writing letters and painting and running the household . . . It's a queer thing that she never learned Irish all these years, it must be rather rotten for him sometimes . . .

24 August 1916. I've done a drawing of An Craoibhín[29] besides one of Nuala and Úna. Mrs. Hyde, he and they two are delighted with it, this unanimity would make me suspicious if nothing else did. Personally I think it's like a greengrocer, so dull and rounded and ordinary-looking, and of course about half way thro' he got into a delightful characteristic pose with his head a little up and on one side, and I wanted to do that fearfully and maybe I shall have another chance. Most oddly shaped head I ever came across.

We went out on the loch on Tuesday and caught fish, a beastly business. He's absolutely crazy about it and indulged in shouts of delight whenever he had got one and directions to us whenever we had, poured out with amazing rapidity and utterly unnecessary . . . They caught a very big pike, white. Mrs Hyde and I were on the island, inhabited only by buachaillín buidhe,[30] bullocks and grouse etc. I never was so annoyed and disgusted with anyone as I was that day, what with being bullied into fishing first, when I didn't want to, and seeing them being killed and all the talk there was about it, and my companion's obvious and expressed dislike of going out fishing at all, and the determination to give away my ragweed when I'd picked it, and the description of the heads after guillotining in the French Revolution, in reference to the big pike's flapping of a fin long after it was supposed to be dead –.

29. See Cat. nos. 52, 53.
30. Ragweed.

Una Duncan
(n.d.)

87 *Cesca in her Wedding Dress*

14
Conclusion

Cesca's diary ends with her visit to the Hydes in August 1916. She knew that the authorities had her under surveillance. One day she was sketching the Metal Bridge from O'Connell Bridge[1] so as to enable her to paint it from memory, and afterwards found herself followed by a drunk. To escape him, she ran into a shop; and when she came out realised he had reported her as a spy. The police then detained her at College Street police station for an hour and a half, threatening her with prosecution, and subsequently they called on her mother and took away her sketch. From then on certain letters and papers in her possession – including the small volumes in which she scribbled her diary – must have had the taint of subversive material, and the last thing she wanted was to bring trouble on her mother and family. At the same time, some of her letters after this contain random but interesting comments on political progress during 1917.

She was more than ever intent now on her artistic career. On leaving the Hyde family at Ratra, she headed north by Sligo and Bundoran. 'And it was on Dr. Douglas Hyde's behalf that I was going about the country sketching,' she wrote to Margot.[2] In September she wrote from Donegal, where she was staying in a cottage opposite Errigal, hoping to get a photograph from Roger Casement's first cousin, a Miss Bannister, so as to paint his portrait. She told

1. NL Sadhbh Trínseach Notebook 2072TX, n.d.
2. Undated letter from Mionabuidhe, Caiseal na gCarr.

88 *Aodh Ó Dubhthaigh, 1916*

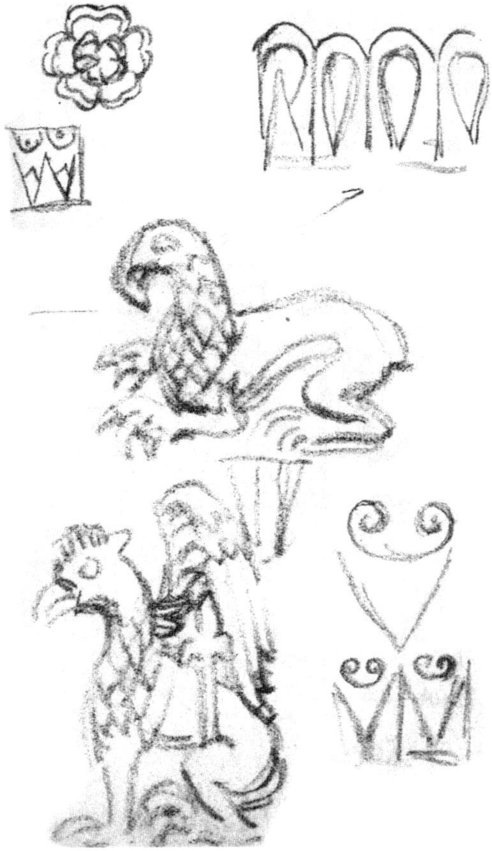

89 *Drawings at Cashel*

Margot that she had done a big charcoal of Casement, and would do several more small ones. The following month she sketched Cormac's Chapel and the medieval Cathedral in Cashel, as well as Aodh Ó Dubhthaigh, 'who put Roger Casement's letters in my beehive at the time of the Rising'. She also sketched the poet James Stephens and some of her Scoil Acla friends.[3]

In Dublin, she continued to draw Celtic artefacts in the National Museum. She was friendly with Miss Gleeson of Dun Emer, who was one of those who attempted to interest her in the Arts Club; and she became involved in a Greek play[4] with Evelyn Gleeson's niece, Kitty MacCormack. Marie Palmer was keen that she should make stained glass windows – study under Miss Purser, who trained young artists in her studio, An Túr Gloine. Cesca preferred the glass of her own contemporary, Harry Clarke, and urged Diarmid and his mother to go and see his windows for the new Honan Chapel in Cork while they were being shown in North Frederick Street. 'They should be good, what I have

3. NL Sadhbh Trínseach Notebook 2071TX, Oct. 1916.
4. To Margot, n.d. c July 1916.'1st rehearsal for the Greek play to begin on Friday . . . Andromache to be Catia MacCormac.'

90 *Conchobhar in 'Deirdre': October 1916*

already seen has been wonderful. They knock anything I have seen by Sarah Purser into a cocked hat! And I have a high opinion of her work.'[5] Cesca herself, however, never attempted this new medium which had attracted other young Irish artists accomplished in illustration and design.[6]

She decided to try for the fáinne, a symbolic gold ring awarded by the Gaelic League for proficiency in the Irish tongue, and was proud to put her name forward at the same time as the revolutionary writer, Piaras Béaslaí, who had commanded a battalion in North King Street during the Rising. She continued to support Cumann Gaelach na hEaglaise events, and made arm badges for the Volunteer Red Cross Division, drilled young members of Cumann na mBan, and began making a collection of songs in Irish and English about the Rising.[7] In December 1916, Kevin O'Shiel of the Irish Nation League, recently founded by nationalists in Ulster opposed to any proposal for the partition of Ireland,[8] wrote to ask her would she design a crest or badge for the League with a woman (Cathleen Ní Houlihan or Róisín Dubh), standing on a rock facing the

5. To Diarmid, 28 April 1917.
6. Beatrice Glenavy worked with An Túr Gloine for a few years. For Wilhelmina Geddes and Ethel Rhind stained glass became a lifetime profession.
7. Undated letter. If this collection came to anything, it has not been traced.
8. See Chief Secretary's Office *Intelligence Notes, 1916*, passim. M.J. Judge, editor of the *Irish Nation*, whom she knew, was a founder member.

91 *Piaras Béaslaí and Another in a Pageant (c. 1914)*

rising sun, her arms – one bound with a piece of broken chain – outstretched. The sunburst was a symbol of the Ancient Fianna, and he wanted the woman to be similar to the graceful female figure on the stamps of the French Republic. Cesca thought that it would be better if the lady faced her own country rather than the 'Land of the Sassenach', and O'Shiel's response was enthusiastic, he was delighted with her design. 'You have put a wonderful expression of relief and power into the lady's face.'[9]

The artist's ties with her friends from the Achill and Carrigaholt summer schools continued as strong as ever. When Claud Chevasse turned up in Temple Hill, she chided him for not leaving his address. 'In he marched with a huge brooch fastening his brat & his hair all long & crumpled by the wind & his cap & a broad cheerful smile . . . saying he had heard we were looking for his address from Mr. Martyn . . . He sat in a large armchair while we scolded him in a trinity of languages.'[10] By October 1917, she was thinking of a subject picture to do with paganism and Christianity for a teachers' scheme organised by

9. Correspondence in Cesca Trench notebook, NL 2069TX.
10. To Margot, n.d. Sunday 1916.

Cormac Mac Fhionnlaigh of Craobh na gCúig gCúigí.[11] Then there was *Red Hugh O'Donnell* – 'Aodh Ruadh Ó Domhhnaill' on horseback in a landscape, head set against a large bright cloud in the sky, his men marching below him with spears. Janet Cunningham was delighted with her seventeenth century hero, writing to Cesca – 'I love the poise & hopeful cloud behind . . . such a joy to me & . . . making an impression too on the Saxon mind which encourages some vain glory in mine'.[12]

Cesca made plans to go to Paris in early 1917[13] – the Germans were retreating, and Raghnal was to be there on 24 February. Gabrielle Genoud warned her[14] that the apartment had been let out until the end of the war (she herself had moved to Barbizon meanwhile), and advised her not to come in February, which would be cold and rainy. In March, however, the whole scene changed. Cesca made up her mind about Diarmid. His proposal to her on St. Patrick's Day was accepted. 'That day will always be to me "a spring day of the soul"', she wrote to him a few days later.[15] Mother or Máighréad would go to France instead of her – she had to remain where her heart was.

She was in County Clare at the Carrigaholt Irish School two months later, starting work on the first of two murals that Neilí Ní Bhriain had commissioned. 'I started on the wall decoration today', she wrote to the Goat on 7 May, 'My God, how many things there are to paint!' Fra (Alfred Palmer), interpreting in a prison camp at Yaltesbury, passed on some useful advice, 'certainly not oil on a white wash . . . Just powder with size & thin painting would do well.' Cesca described the atmosphere of the place to Diarmid, writing her letter from the grass at the top of the strand just below the sea wall where she was sitting with Lennox Robinson,[16] 'the Shannon lying like a lake of glass in front of us & the mountains hidden so you'd think it was the Atlantic, & nothing heard except a few carts collecting *feadhmannach donn*[17] on the strand, & a dog barking at intervals . . . You'd quite love Miss O'B[rien] for getting this lovely sort of life going or making it a possibility . . . We found a quantity of old iron & broken china & glass on the rocks yesterday, & amused ourselves chucking them into the sea below & trying to hit a rock unsuccessfully as far

11. To Diarmid, 29 Oct. 1917.
12. To Cesca, 21 Dec. n.d. See NL Notebook 2069TX.
13. Passport issued 14 Feb. 1917, stamped 17 Feb. for travelling to France.
14. To Cesca, 6 Jan. 1917.
15. 21 Mar. 1917.
16. (1886–1958), dramatist and manager of the Abbey Theatre, he joined the Volunteers in 1914. The following year he left the Abbey for a time to organise the Carnegie Libraries.
17. Brown seaweed.

as I was concerned, & with moderate success as far as Mr. L.R. was. The rocks are all in extraordinarily regular lines like lots of bits of toffee on top of each other that had been bent down here & there by Mananáin.'[18] Brian O h-Uigín and his wife were chatting to each other in Irish.[19]

Diarmid meanwhile was deeply involved in MacLysaght's Convention, working with Colonel Moore and George Russell (Æ) towards some kind of national administration to be agreed upon by representatives of every profession and all shades of Irish opinion, who would meet peacefully around a table, with reasonable realistic attitudes – they hoped. The Government made a public announcement on 21 May that it would summon such a Convention, and Æ quickly assembled thoughts on the matter for circulation as a pamphlet.[20] The initial response appeared encouraging, and the first meeting was arranged for 25 July, to be held in Trinity College, Dublin, with Æ and MacLysaght nominated to speak on behalf of the nationalists. Gavan Duffy of Sinn Féin showed his interest, and Æ arranged further preliminary informal meetings for delegates from the North and their counterparts from the South. The ensuing difficulties were even greater than they had anticipated.

Cesca, who had returned to Carrigaholt in early July to finish the second mural, wrote to Diarmid from Ennis as she waited for the train, sitting in the garden of the hotel where Éamon De Valera's supporters were counting the people coming in to pledge their votes for Sinn Féin in the by-election. She was curious to know where they had got all the petrol for the four large motor cars and the two motor bicycles drawn up in front of the hotel. But, 'when É. De V. speaks, the people hardly make a sound because he speaks quietly and peacefully, not bothering with catch-cries, and if he gets their vote despite this, it'll be a great victory because he will have demonstrated that he has won their minds.'[21]

At the Irish College she weeded and thinned turnips in the garden, or embroidered when the weather was cold and wet – she was solitary, and the suitcase with her paints which she had sent by train hadn't arrived. Despite this, the place continued to be beautiful beyond belief. The sea was so blue, and it was warm enough to sunbathe. Her daily pattern was to rise with the sun. Mass was at 8.30, breakfast at 9, then, after taking a stroll out to look at the sea, she would work till one o'clock when everyone came in from their class. From 1 o'clock until dinner at two, she wrote letters. She told Diarmid

18. Celtic god of the sea.
19. To Diarmid Coffey, 5 May 1917.
20. H. Summerfield, *That Myriad Minded Man: a Biography of G.W. Russell – Æ.* (London, Colin Smythe, 1975) pp. 181–88.
21. To Diarmid Coffey, 7 July 1917.

that she had gone to the village the previous day to buy some delicacies with which to celebrate when they heard how De Valera's vote went. They weren't yet sure about the result, but a priest who had come from Ennis was optimistic. There were things happening that had not been reported in the papers, rumours of ten people knocked to the ground by police and soldiers, and of women in the pay of partitionists attacking De Valera's people. 'Last night at 12, the Volunteers in the village were given a mobilisation order, and they all came here looking for bicycles to go to Ennis to do the policing today.'[22]

The final words of her long letter conjured up the elation of earlier days as a student at Scoil Acla. 'Last night the priests who arrived late had T at the time we're supposed to have supper & we all stood hungrily by the sea-wall in the dusk, till someone started playing *The Soldiers' Song* on a bad old piano. Some of us went in & sang it then. It was wonderful: I wish you'd been there – extraordinarily moving. Brian O h-Uigín standing in a corner near me, his gentle indomitable eyes on the ceiling, Seán Tóibín half sitting on a chair clasping & unclasping large hands, two tall priests in the dusk opposite near white bloused girls, one of the teachers standing holding his girl's hand & singing as tho' he was all voice. I saw these things outwardly, but I never have felt so lifted up out of myself for years & years. All the words were real.'

Writing to Diarmid again she asked had De Valera's majority of 3000 votes surprised him – she and her companions thought at first it must be a mistake for 300, but as soon as they were certain, they raised a green flag with three cheers. There had been 19 bonfires to be seen at one time from Carrigaholt all around the Clare and Kerry Coasts. Éamon De Valera 'reads like a man of sense in the middle of the talkers.' Now she wondered what the outcome would be – she didn't believe Sinn Féin was as united as its English enemies believed and feared – she hoped Diarmid wasn't among those who were angry at the result, because it was being said that this meant the end of the Convention. Impatient with Diarmid's reticence, she begged him to write to her in English. She wanted his opinion on Mr Duke[23] as Chairman of the Convention, and had he heard any more about the possibility of himself as Secretary. Diarmid's reply in English, when it came,[24] was – to say the least – stiff, and riddled with frustration:

> I am rather disappointed at De Valera's speeches and attitude. It seems to me not to lead anywhere as he just talks of an "Irish republic" and

---

22. To Diarmid Coffey, 10 July 1917.
23. Henry Edward Duke (1855–1939), a barrister, was Chief Secretary for Ireland from Aug. 1916 to May 1918.
24. To Cesca, 13 July 1917.

> "going to the peace conference" without shewing in any way how either of those things are to be achieved.
>
> I wish you would talk to your friends on these points as it seems to me that before one throws over every opportunity there is here one ought to have a very clear idea of where one is going. You could do a lot as you know these people and have education and sense. Education I mean in the sense of having been brought up among people who know something of the world and how things like peace conferences are arranged & so on. Going to the peace conference seems to me rather like going to a committee of brewers to settle the drink problem.
>
> I would like to see the Sinn Féin party laying down some solid policy of how they are going to get what they want, as there seems to me to be only two possible ways, one by getting an Irish govt. first through the Convention; the other force of arms, & we never can get physical results by force of arms as long as England has an army bigger than our whole population & endless supplies of material. How I wish you were doing some constructive work of this sort by using your influence to make people think, & discouraging them from mere appeals to sentiment. You could do such a lot!'

De Valera had been released from a British detention camp just one month before the election, and had, as Cesca described, mesmerised the hearts and minds of his constituents in East Clare. Sinn Féin then boycotted the first meeting of the Convention on 25 July, and though the Ulster Unionists attended they did so without any intention of cooperating. It was certainly the death knell to what was a courageous attempt on the behalf of Diarmid and his colleagues to reach a reasonable solution to Ireland's problems.

James Stephens was optimistic for a while, telling his American friend John Quinn after the Convention's second meeting that the Irish situation was rapidly clarifying itself, and a united country was nearer than it had been for a long time – 'All the other ideas have been advanced and have been attacked. Colonial Home Rule has been advanced, and has not been attacked by any one. That is the psychological fact which surrounds the other facts.'[25] Æ and Diarmid continued to visit MacLysaght's home, Raheen, at Tuamgraney in Co. Clare, for talks. But, before the end of the year, despite the beginnings of agreement among the moderates, the Government made it clear that there would be no referendum. First MacLysaght resigned, and shortly afterwards Æ followed suit, with Plunkett accepting that the Convention was yet another political failure.

25. To John Quinn, 8 Aug. 1917. *Letters of James Stephens* edited by Richard J. Finneran. (London, Macmillan, 1974) pp. 225–6.

92 *Æ (George Russell), Portrait of Cesca, 1917*

The Irish party which had fought for Home Rule never recovered. Redmond died a year later, and Arthur Griffith resigned from the leadership of Sinn Féin in De Valera's favour.

Cesca had her own preoccupations. Cousin Maria, so irritatingly unionist and who wouldn't have seen the need to call any Convention, passed away just short of ninety a few days before it first met. Cesca was still very fond of her, and travelled down with Wilbraham to the grand funeral at Millicent, the family home. In September Æ drew an enchanting pastel study of Cesca in profile, and he painted her portrait in oil on 7 October, in front of a draped turquoise curtain.[26] Wearing a lilac hat with veil and a dress of the heather colour she loved, this seems a strangely devout Cesca, hands folded upward to show her ring, a small prayerbook placed on the table before her. Yet her lips twitch impishly, and the iridescent tones and her cascading necklace lend an esoteric opulence to what must have been intended as a wedding portrait.

26. The oil portrait is in the National Gallery of Ireland, no. 4068.

93 *Cesca's Mother, Isabella Trench*

94 *Mrs Joseph Hone (Darina), 1917*

When Russell first visited Cesca at Temple Hill, he said the room reminded him of Miss Young's arrangement, 'a few Gaelic beautifully-coloured pictures on a light wall', she had told Margot. 'He said he'd draw out two symbols some time if I like that would help me to see "fairies". He said anyone could who lived a fairly decent life if they developed the faculty.'[27] Radiance expands from the opalescent void beyond the sitter, illuminating her face. The subject is as warm and earthy as the coarse canvas on which she is painted; but the artist has conjured up the contrasting metaphysical element of the persona too – evidently the aura of the archbishop (who had saved her from the wrath of the authorities during the Troubles) still hung around her.

Cesca had been invited to illustrate *Women in Ancient & Modern Ireland* by C.M. Ní Dubhghaill in 1917, a small book published by the Kenny Press – 'Irish Paper. Irish Ink. Irish Trade Union Labour.' Grace Gifford designed the cover, with a stereotyped head of an ancient princess surmounting a rectangular border composed of Art Nouveau interlace, and Sadhbh pictured 'Emer teaching embroidery to her young companions' and 'Princess Margaret of Ely receiving her guests', as frontispiece and an illustration in the text. The assertive energetic pencil stroke of earlier work has been exchanged here for a regular outline – more in the style of Glenavy, whom she admired, in the *Aids to the Immortality* frieze[28] or of studies for her own murals in Clare. She may have considered the style more in keeping with a modern Ireland. Her Gaelic League greetings cards continued to be produced year by year, coloured by hand. Gab Genoud, writing to her on 6 January 1917, describes a 'ravishing' Adoration scene – the style 'totally unacademic' – a new version of *Nodlaig na nGaedheal;* as well as another card of the Madonna, which she perhaps preferred, 'the embracing gesture with the right arm is so sweet, so maternal, while the other hand holds the hand of the child' – this was the original *Nodlaig*. Cesca's original *Nodlaig na nGaedheal* was published by the Candle Press later the same year as frontispiece to *The Irish Christmas,* and retitled *Nativity in an Irish kitchen.*

Despite the way she was concentrating on her work Cesca was still not ready for an exhibition, and when a Gift Sale in aid of the Volunteer Dependents' Fund was held in the Mansion House in April 1917 (many of the Volunteers were still in prison), and Lily Williams, Tuohy, Ella Young, Katherine MacCormack, Ellen Duncan and other artists were donating pictures, she contributed two pieces of old lace – perhaps hoping they would fetch more money than her paintings.

---

27. Cesca to Margot, 24 Feb. 1916.
28. Which decorates Susan Mitchell's small book of poems (Dublin, Tower Press, 1908).

She may have felt shy when it came to exhibiting, yet Sadhbh Trínseach made an impressive contribution to contemporary art in Dublin in her portraits of family and friends, which are colourful and self-assured and always good likenesses, and in her vivid studies of nationalist personalities. The small half length pastel portraits of her brother Reggie, his wife's sister Amy, and others are delightfully spontaneous. After she had abandoned her journal, she made advances in oil, using an increasingly vibrant brush. A sympathetic oil of the fading Susan Mitchell was painted that same year. Her vivacious manner in subsequent portraits and landscapes bears comparison with the work of her slightly older contemporary Estella Solomons, and, occasionally, in its directness, with the young Augustus John. *Colour Magazine* reproduced a charcoal self-study by her at the same time as another by her friend of Paris days, Alfred Palmer[29] – 'Curious that our two drawings should have come out in the same number of *Colour*,' he wrote to her. 'Yours must have been good but I can see that it has lost a great deal by reproduction. They never seem to be so successful with their black-and-white as with the colour things.'[30] He had had some experience of the new magazine, contributing to it almost from its inception at the outset of war. Cesca's relaxed image depicts the artist standing at her easel, hand on hip. Palmer told her he was working in watercolour and pastel at the time, and was planning the oil of Pagliacci he would paint when the war was over.

Clues to other work by this artist, who has left comparatively little besides pencil sketches, are found in letters and an engagement diary. Since she seldom signed her paintings, there must be quite a number still waiting to be identified. Two pictures in the Oireachtas exhibition of 1915, each simply noted as 'Portrait',[31] may have been self-portraits, of which she made several. Maude Royden showed great appreciation of the now lost portrait drawing she had commissioned from Cesca in 1917;[32] and the large charcoal portrait the artist made of Eoin MacNeill after his return from prison[33] was his wife's favourite likeness of him. Besides Miss Royden's appointment for 5 P.M. on 13 January, there is a note on Easter Monday of the same year, 'draw Wilbraham', and on 12 April 'draw Darina or J. H.' – that is Joseph Hone, the biographer. A page of three studies for a portrait of Mrs Joseph Hone (dubbed 'Darina' at Carrigaholt) is in the National Gallery of Ireland. In December 1917, according

29. *Colour*, June 1917, pp. 140, 146.
30. To Cesca, 24 June 1917.
31. Nos. 117, 118. The exhibition took place in the Technical School.
32. To Cesca, 27 Jan. 1917.
33. After Easter Week he received a sentence of life imprisonment, but he was released in 1917 under the amnesty, and became a Minister in the 1919 Dáil.

95 *Self-Portrait in Colour Magazine, June 1917*

to the engagement diary, she attempted a portrait of Judy Withers, an English student attending Trinity with Margot, who was then working towards a general degree. Two sketches for this show Withers – Margot's lover for a time – as a strong dramatic figure, but the portrait, if she completed it, has not been traced. The diary of January 1918 notes 'Loinseach mac Roibín[34] abt his picture.' Though not stated, one is tempted to think that she was painting his portrait in oil, since he had dined with her a couple of times some months before. She recorded making a sketch of Bláthnaid Salkeld in the summer of 1918, again preserved in the National Gallery of Ireland.

Life for Cesca continued peacefully in the early part of 1918, attending Eoin Mac Neill's lecture at the Rotunda, hearing music at the Arts Club, gardening and planting trees, making posters for a céilí held in Terenure, watching the moon in the early morning of January 27 'like a big yellow plate going down'. She worked on *The Death of Brian* – Brian Boru, king of Munster, of the Carrigaholt pageant, killed by a Dane in the Battle of Clontarf in 1016 as he knelt in joyful prayer after the victory. Æ's portrait of her was now ready, and she brought her mother to see it.

After the Gaelic League flag days on 16 March and St. Patrick's Day, when she collected 3d from a soldier and abundantly from the police, the Trenches

34. The playwright, Lennox Robinson.

96 *Two Studies of Judy Withers, 1917*

were suddenly plunged into deep shock. Clare had sent Cesca a wedding gift of some money from herself and Reggie. Thanking her brother in a letter to the Front, Cesca started on a light note, with banalities, and hoping he could get some leave to be home for the wedding. Forboding news about a recent battle arrived, and she laid down her pen. The tempo in the letter changes as she starts again anxiously on 24 March – 'I do hope we shall get a p.c. or something from you soon to say you're safe. This battle coming just on top of the splendid news of yr 3 months course makes us very anxious. I get my mind full of horrible pictures of you hurt & in want of things & Mother & M. do too & we none of us tell the others but all know & it takes the heart out of our preparations for this wedding business. But we comfort ourselves by Dr. — saying that C.O's are usually bound to be in less danger, except from specially directed shells, aren't they? . . . you simply must get leave to come over for seventeenth, you and Clare. *Do,* please, I want you most awfully badly. It's simply divine here, like summer, & all the daffs: are out & the plum tree that grows outside my studio window is covered with white foam from the blossoms . . . '[35] She and Margot wrote at once to Clare, hoping against hope that he had been taken prisoner. But before Cesca's letter to Raghnall had been sent back two weeks

35. Cesca to Reggie, n.d. and 24 Mar. 1918.

97 *Bláthnaid Salkeld, 1918*

later they knew the worst. He had never received it. He had died on 21 March.[36]

Cesca had planned her wedding as diligently as any of her pageants, sketching out designs months beforehand when writing to Miss Yeats at the Cuala Industries as though she were planning a trousseau for someone else[37]: an embroidered linen surcoat to go over a blue dress; a cloak; a warm brown embroidered dress and a jerkin laced with orange, both made from Grey Abbey silk and poplin; and lastly a 'very simple loose robe, suitable for tall figures'. She and Diarmid were married on 17 April, with Robert Barton (who had served as secretary to Colonel Moore when the Volunteers were first founded) as best man. Barton had joined the British army at the outbreak of war; like others hoping that war would hasten the passing of the Home Rule Bill. Despite the fact that he had resigned in disillusionment after the Rising, he

36. Raghnall had served five years with the Inns of Court Officers Training Corps, remaining in England, irreplaceable in the training of officers. Before going to the Front in 1916, he was unexpectedly sent first to the emergency in Dublin. See 'An officer on the Western Front' by Anthony Fletcher in *History Today* vol. 54 no. 8 (Aug. 2004) pp. 31–37.
37. NL Notebook 2069TX.

98 *Sketches for her Trousseau, from a Notebook, 1918*

99 *An Sinnsear: Robert Barton*

wore his army uniform at the wedding.[38] Cesca made several portrait sketches of him, one inscribed 'An Sinsear [The Elder]' – he was Diarmid's senior by seven years. Margot wrote to her after the ceremony, 'You looked a dream of beauty. Diarmid so handsome & charming.' Not to be outdone she herself had ordered a deep blue opera wrap with a large Chinese dragon worked to look like a clasp in front,[39] which the delighted Cesca was to revel in on her honeymoon, '*Much* too nice only to be seen by the mari. The mari agrees. He made me dress up in it and parade about . . . The maids are in love with it too.'

Writing to Mrs Coffey from the Glenbeigh Hotel in Kerry, she said the proprietress hesitated to give them the *Irish Times* thinking they talked so much Irish they must be nationalists. 'I didn't know any place could be so beautiful, or any person so satisfyingly delightful as Diarmuid. I used to think being engaged very agreeable at times, but it's absolutely nothing compared with this.' The place reminded her of Achill. On 30 April they were in Doire Fionán, they had cycled from Cahirciveen – all the people spoke Irish all the way. 'When we got to the Gap, behold the Moon! Orange colour, nearly full, down over the small sheltered

38. Robert Barton was later arrested and imprisoned for his republicanism. See *Roundwood & District Historical & Folklore Journal* no. 14 (2003) pp. 45–51: 'Letters concerning Robert Barton', by Saive Coffey.
39. E.C.Yeats to Letty, 18 Feb 1918.

bay & islands of this place . . . such a heavenly little place . . . & palms all about & arum lilies growing like herbaceous borders outside cottage doors & there are 200 Volunteers & a just starting branch of C na mB & a Co-Op store started by "Gobnait Ní Bhruadair", and the air so soft, the Great Skellig Rock with a lighthouse on it out to the west.' It was the essence of the New Ireland she had dreamed about. She painted some of her best oils during the honeymoon.

The newly married couple returned to Temple Hill, where they planned to stay until the New Year. Life continued much as it had been, any social activities in the heart of nationalist artistic Dublin. Both corrected exam papers to make ends meet. 'He has started walking into the office in the A.M.,' she wrote to the Goat, '& going out on the road without a hat, and being violently high-spirited even in the middle of all this extra work & when I think of the depressed being there used to be in similar circumstances I rub my hands.' They lived simply, rationing was still in force, but they kept fowl and sold the fruit and vegetables they grew in their spare time, which helped to cover food, rent and servants, with a little over. 'They say we'll have sugar in ten days', Cesca noted in her engagement diary on 13 June. She hoped to get an adjacent field in a Terenure that was largely countrified still, and earn some more by letting it. She wanted many children.

In July they held an Aeridheacht[40] in the garden. Cesca described it to Margot.

> It was quite grey all day & looked as tho' it might rain, & a chill wind, but we went on undiscouraged & put up two tents, one green & brown & purple under a tree, with a mysterious green & purple shrouded lamp beside it, & a small pendant silver one hanging from the tree that formed the back of it inside, & a stool & a low table & Mrs Vanston inside telling fortunes wrapped in an orange scarf & mystery; & another one, an old piece of sacking & a bright green cloak & a lamp & me inside that in an orange blouse & *no* mystery . . . drawing portraits for 1/- a head, - & we had potatoe races 1st . . . & Colm Ó Lochlainn strolled abt piping for the dancers with a blue & yellow handkerchief tied over his head, & after a bit we lit the lamps, one under the big chestnut over the table with T, & one under the Portugal laurel, a big blue one, and one on the walnut, a yellow one with a notice about the concert.
>
> Oh yes the concert. I was drawing away, & raking in shillings, when I became aware of a new colour in the hair, & the softest puff of wind on my cheek. Everyone was enveloped in blue & shadows, a girl near me in

40. An entertainment in the open air in aid of the Gaelic League.

> a grey frock with silver buckles & earrings became a sort of sidhe woman[41] & I looked up & saw stars as bright as silver & wisps of cloud blown from in front of them, thinly spread. Then some one inside the house began to sing. Nugent the chemist, he has a beautiful voice, & I went in to hear him, & when I got to the house people were all sitting on the steps in the faint yellow & blue light, & in the hall when you looked along to the drawing-room you saw only a silhouette in a kilt & heard music . . . – then when people began to go away Diarmuid went swiftly & took the lanterns & hung them on trees on the avenue, & it looked most extra-ordinarily jolly – we made a good bit of money & a lot of Irish was talked & everyone said it was delightful & I know it wasn't a bit like the common or garden aeridheacht which are tiresome affairs on the whole.'[42]

Margot and Cesca then spent a week with Raghnal's widow, Clare, in the Isle of Man, and when she came back Cesca launched into painting again. Her work in oil in the post-Rising period had been going from strength to strength, expressing the riches of her own personality and leading to more adventurous compositions such as her *Self Portrait with Diarmuid Coffey,*[43] and paintings of Margot sitting framed in the window at Temple Hill, and Dora French in a silhouette pose, again in an interior. She wrote to Margot who was in London, 'I was painting Deora today, rather a lark, a slender black figure against a light sofa and wall, holding a reddish statuette tanagra just about the tone of her skin . . .'[44] These portraits with a hint of symbolism courted negative space more overtly than the plein air studies she had made while on honeymoon in Cork and Kerry – a half length of Diarmid in landscape, smoking, and the Caseta in the famous island garden at Glengarriff. Though at no time had she appeared to have any great motivation to paint landscape, she was well able to, judging by the *Caseta* and *Tree at Temple Hill,* both painted with dancing brush and an instinctive understanding of elusive light and the subtlety of colour.

During August of 1918 she was teaching the precocious young Cecil Salkeld[45] at her house, Temple Hill. Already at fourteen he was a prodigy,

41. A fairy woman.
42. Fragment of undated letter to Margot [Aug. 1918].
43. Exh. *Irish Women Artists from the Eighteenth Century to the Present Day* (Dublin, National Gallery of Ireland, 1987) 66 (repro).
44. 12 Aug. 1918. The charcoal study is in a private collection, the oil has not yet been traced.
45. Cecil Salkeld (1904–1969) Cesca and her mother had been friends with his mother for years. Salkeld later trained in Germany under Otto Dix, and made illustrations and painted panels (most notably in Davy Byrne's pub in Dublin) as well as painting portraits and fantasy pictures.

100 *Deora Frínseach on a Sofa, 1918*

shortly to enter the Metropolitan School of Art. She started on his portrait, and one can only speculate how it may have turned out in her flexible oil manner, with its increasing penchant for colour and provocative space. In her engagement diary four visits from Cecil Salkeld are noted, and she was painting him on 21 August. She was also gardening, and on 7 September was at an Aeridheacht at Craobh na gCúig gCúigí. It was on 12 September that she cut her nose fairly seriously, incurring blood poisoning – 'to think you have been so ill, more ill I expect than you really allowed,' Marie Palmer wrote to her rather scoldingly after she had come home in early October, 'how did you get yourself poisoned! . . . You are lucky to start housekeeping with some one like 'Brede' who know all the working of the houses.'[46] Fra had had more pictures published in *Colour*. 'Now one can feel there is some chance of this deadening mantle of war being torn to shreds & one can breathe & plan gaily again.'

Cesca began to revive her interest in the Movement, and to meet with former associates. On 16 October An Craoibhín, with Mrs Hyde and Úna, called on her – poor Nuala had never recovered from her diseased lung, and had died

46. 17 Oct. 1918.

in September. On 17 and 19 October, Cesca attended meetings of Cumann na mBan. The last entry in her engagement diary, on 26 October, notes a Cumann na mBan meeting, a meeting which she never attended.

According to Margot's diary, Cesca had fallen a victim to the dreaded 'flu epidemic that preceded European peace. Very ill on 25 October, she was 'still bad, Temperature 103.4' the next day. Her temperature continued to climb. Mother and Herbert were summoned from London, but cannot have believed that this beautiful vivacious girl, who was so fine and strong only a few days before, was ebbing away from the life she loved so much. Their journey brought them to Temple Hill on 31 October. Cesca had died the day before.

As Sadhbh Trínseach she was mourned in *Fáinne an Lae,* and in *Sinn Féin,* which had carried her sketches of leading persons at the Sinn Féin convention just a year before in their Christmas number. *Sinn Féin* lamented, 'Her life devoted to Gaelic culture and the Irish people . . . Her high artistic ability was invaluable in the movement, and her personality was of that kind which dominated by its attraction.' The Rosary was recited in Irish at her graveside by members of her branch of the Gaelic League, Craobh na gCúig gCúigí. Cumann Gaedhealach na hEaglaise called a special meeting, with Neilí Ní

101 *'Nodlaig na nGaedheal', Frontispiece to 'The Irish Christmas'*

From an original drawing by the late Sadb Trinnseach.

Bhriain in the chair, where a resolution of condolence to the relatives of 'Mrs Coffey (Sadhbh Trinseach)' was carried unanimously.

Everyone in nationalist Dublin was stunned by Cesca's unexpected death, and no one more so than Diarmid, who remained inconsolable for years. In tribute to her, the Candle Press republished the tiny volume, *The Irish Christmas,* the same year, with its selection of poems by Susan Mitchell, Lionel Johnson and Joseph Campbell, the frontispiece by 'the late Sadb Trinnseach'. In this moving study in pen and ink, contrasting dark and light and one of her best drawings in this genre, the Madonna places her hand reassuringly on the arm of the awestruck farmer's wife who stands beside her, a single figure in adoration – in a West of Ireland kitchen.

Catalogue of Sadhbh Trínseach's Known Paintings and Drawings

[This includes works mentioned in the diary which have not been located.]

(1) Oil Paintings

1. *Life* and *Death*
Untraced oils or drawing, measurements unknown
2 Jan. 1914 – 'Ménard said that my *Life and Death* were too symbolic.' Some other subjects Cesca mentions working on are *The Black Abbot* and *Cain and Abel*.

2. *Loie Fuller*
Untraced oil on canvas, measurements unknown
19 Jan. 1914, Cesca mentions starting on a picture of Loie Fuller, the American dancer.

3. *The Cloak* 1914
Untraced oil or drawing, measurements unknown
Exh: 1914 Oct. Gaelic League Exhibition, 7 St. Stephen's Green, Dublin
Lit: *Irish Times* 5 Oct. 1916 'Pictures of Ireland': an exhibition of pictures painted by members of the Gaelic League Branch of 5 Provinces'
Probably bought by Mr Dix, Dublin.

4. *Domrémy Church* 1914
Untraced, probably oil, measurements unknown
Exh: 1914 Oct. Gaelic League Exhibition, 7 St. Stephen's Green, Dublin
Lit: *Irish Times* 5 Oct. 1916 'Pictures of Ireland': an exhibition of pictures painted by members of the Gaelic League Branch of 5 Provinces'
Domrémy in Lorraine, where Joan of Arc was born.

5. *Self-Portrait (1)* 16 Aug. 1914
   Oil on canvas, 27 × 23 cm
   Private Collection
   A portrait by candlelight.

6. *Self-Portrait (2)* 1914–15
   Oil on canvas, 33 × 25 cm
   Private Collection

7. *Portrait of Susan L. Mitchell* 1916
   Signed
   Oil on canvas, 54.5 × 33 cm
   Private Collection

8. *Ella Young with Maureen Fox* June 1916
   Untraced oil, measurements unknown
   Mentioned in Cesca's diary on 5 June 1916: 'I began a picture of the two of them that I think will be a success.'

9. *Portrait of Claud Chevasse in a Kilt* 1916
   Oil on paper laid on cardboard, 76 × 43.5 cm
   National University of Ireland, Galway

10. *Portrait of Móirín Nic Sionnaigh (Maureen Fox)* 1916
    Signed with monogram ST
    Inscribed on reverse: Moirín Nic Sionnaigh ('an Íodhbairt')
    Oil on paper with a strip measuring added to the upper edge laid on cardboard, 60 × 33 cm
    National University of Ireland, Galway
    Painted at Carrigaholt.

11. *Portrait of Claud Chevasse in Danish Dress* 1916
    Untraced, probably oil
    Painted at Carrigaholt Pendant of no. 10.

12. *Landscape* July 1916
    Untraced oil or pastel, measurements unknown
    Painted at Carrigaholt.

13. *Tree at Temple Hill* 1917
    Oil on canvas, 47 × 34.5 cm
    Private Collection

14. *Self-Portrait (3)* c. 1917
    Oil on board, 35.5 × 25.5 cm
    Private Collection

15. *Portrait of Mrs Judy Withers* Dec. 1917
    Untraced, probably oil, measurements unknown
    A sketch for this (see no. 74) is in the National Gallery of Ireland.

16. *Caseta at Glengarriff* Apr. 1918
    Oil on board, 38 × 28 cm
    Private Collection
    A view at Ilnacullin (otherwise Garinish Island).

17. *Portrait of Diarmid Coffey* Apr. 1918
Oil on board, 28 × 36 cm
Private Collection

18. *Portrait of Diarmid* c. 1918
Oil on board, 31 × 24 cm
Reproduced: 'Rediscovering an artist', *Royal Hibernian Academy 173rd Exhibition* 2003, p. 30, fig. 4
Private Collection

19. *Portrait of Margot at Temple Hill* 1918
Oil on canvas, 76 × 71 cm
Private Collection

20. *Self-Portrait with Diarmid Coffey* c. 1918
Oil on canvas, 61 × 51 cm
Exh: 1987 National Gallery of Ireland *Irish Women Artists from the Eighteenth Century to the Present Day* no. 66 (repro p. 112)
Private Collection

21. *Portrait of Cecil Salkeld as a Boy* Aug. 1918
Untraced, probably oil, measurements unknown
Painted at Temple Hill, Dublin.

(2) Pastels

22. *Achill (or Connemara) Landscape* c. 1914
Pastel on paper, 74 × 102 cm
Private Collection

23. *Jesus at the Gates of Jerusalem* n.d., c. 1914
Pastel on paper with a strip added towards the lower edge, 80 × 103 cm
Reproduced: 'Rediscovering an artist', *Royal Hibernian Academy 173rd Exhibition* 2003, p. 31, fig. 5
Private Collection

24. *Reggie Smoking a Pipe* c. 1915
Pastel on paper, 36.8 × 31 cm
Private Collection
Head and shoulders of the artist's brother in uniform. Professor Anthony Fletcher suggests that this pastel and no. 25 date from Cesca's visit to Kent in August 1915.

25. *Head of Amy* c. 1915
Pastel on paper, 36 × 25.5 cm
Private Collection
Amy Howard, sister of Reggie's wife, Clare. Cesca was friendly with her and on a visit to Kent in August 1915 spent a day helping Amy at the hospital where she was a volunteer.

26. *Celtic King and Queen* n.d.
Pastel on paper, 61 × 61 cm
Private Collection
This large pastel must relate to one of the tableaux of Celtic legends that Cesca designed and produced from 1914 on. See sketches of *Deirdre*, Notebook 2071TX, National Library of Ireland.

27. *Girl in orange blouse* n.d.
On reverse *An Rón* (Margot)
Pastel on paper, 44 × 31 cm
Verso inscribed: An Rón
Private Collection

28. *The Death of Brian* 1918
Untraced, probably pastel, measurements unknown
Cesca was working on a composition of this name in January 1918; see also no. 26.

(3) Drawings

29. *View from window, Cill Áirne* Aug. 1908
Watercolour on paper, 7 × 12 cm
Inscribed: View from window, in pouring rain, Aug. 25 1908, Danesfort, Cill Áirne.
National Library of Ireland

30. *Cathleen Ní Houlihan* n.d., c. 1911
Pencil on paper, 19 × 12 cm
Inscribed: Some call me the Poor Old Woman & some there are that call me Cathleen the daughter of Houlihan
Private Collection
The old woman as she leaves the Gillane house, in WB Yeats's play *Cathleen Ni Houlihan*, first performed in 1902. John Butler Yeats's watercolour of Maud Gonne in the role (National Gallery of Ireland) sees her as the old woman she was, while Sadhbh Trínseach anticipates Patrick Gillane's climactic declaration, 'I did not [see an old woman], but I saw a young girl, and she had the walk of a queen.'

31. *Indian Studies: Policeman, Seated Figures and Boat* 1912
Pencil on paper, 23 × 18 cm
Inscribed: Plíasmain [Policeman]
Private Collection

32. *Indian Studies: Pathan and Buachaillín* 1912
Pencil on paper, 23 × 18 cm
Inscribed: Tall & slim & dressed in spotless white. Pathan.
Do bhí an buachaillín seo ag dul 7 ag teacht leis fruit 7 misláin [this little boy was going & coming with fruit & sweets].
Private Collection

33. *Seated Figure Wearing Kilt Identified as An Paorach* n.d., c. 1913
Charcoal on paper, 48 × 33 cm
Private Collection

34. *Claud Chevasse Teaching an Irish Class on Achill Island, Co. Mayo* 1913–14
Charcoal and crayon on watermarked Ingres laid wove paper, 55.7 × 77 cm
National Gallery of Ireland (NGI 3812)

35. *Study for 'Dance' (Nymphs and Satyrs)* (see no. 36) 1914
Charcoal on paper laid on board, 28 × 48 cm
Private Collection

36. *Dance (Nymphs and Satyrs)* 1914
Charcoal on paper, 74 × 104 cm

Exh: 1987 National Gallery of Ireland *Irish Women Artists from the Eighteenth Century to the Present Day* no. 65 (repro p.112)
Private Collection
Cesca was working on this vibrant composition in Ménard's studio in January 1914.

37. *On the Strand* 1914
Untraced oil or drawing, measurements unknown
Exh: 1914 October Gaelic League Exhibition, 7 St. Stephen's Green, Dublin
This was described by the reviewer of the Gaelic League exhibition as 'the only picture in which there is a semblance of mirth' and is probably the joyous *Dance (Nymphs and Satyrs)* no. 36.

38. *The Death of Cuchulain* 1914
Untraced drawing, measurements unknown
On 6 January 1914, Cesca noted 'I am working on *Dance* and *The Death of Cuchulain*'.

39. *Sketch of an Art Class* c. 1914
Charcoal on Ingres paper, 55.7 × 76.7 cm
National Gallery of Ireland (NGI 3821)

40. *Sketches for 'Fergus', 'Cuchulain', and 'Maeve'* Mar. 1914
Untraced drawings, measurements unknown
Cesca notes on 17 March 1914: 'This afternoon I was working in the Palmers' studio. I made couple of sketches for *Fergus*. I made three from the blue eyed American girl another day for *Cuchulain*, and from Julie the day before yesterday for *Maeve*.'

41. *The Pipers* 1914
Untraced, probably charcoal, measurements unknown
Cesca was working on this composition in the Palmers' studio in March 1914.

42. *Christ at the Sea of Galilee* n.d.
On reverse *Two Girls* (perhaps *Self-Sketches*)
Charcoal on paper, 56 × 76 cm
Private Collection

43. *The Flag*
Untraced drawing, measurements unknown
Exh: 1914 October Gaelic League Exhibition, 7 St. Stephen's Green, Dublin
The reviewer in the *Irish Times* noted Cesca's drawing, *The Flag*, as 'out of the ordinary, typifies the spirit of independence rising above the clouds.'

44. *Loch Dan: Iúl 1914: Figures and Cow* July 1914
On reverse *Heads with One Full Length Figure*
Pencil on paper, 8.5 × 6.5 inches
Private Collection

45. *Two Heads of Diarmid Coffey with a Drawing above* c. 1914
Charcoal on paper, 47 × 30.5 cm
Private Collection

46. *Four heads of Diarmid* c. 1914
Pencil on paper, 24 × 19 cm
Inscribed: D. Coffey by ST
Reproduced: 'Rediscovering an artist', *Royal Hibernian Academy 173rd Exhibition* 2003, p. 29, fig. 2

Private Collection

47. *Diarmid Coffey* c. 1914
Pencil on paper, 23 × 18 cm
Inscribed: D. Coffey
Private Collection

48. *George Coffey and Diarmid Coffey Sketched over an Unfinished Sketch* c. 1914
Pencil on paper, 21.5 × 16.5 cm
Private Collection

49. *Milner Meditating the Massacre of the Irish Nation (Diarmuid as Model)* c. 1914
Charcoal on paper, 38 × 56 cm
Inscribed with title
Private Collection

50. *Naomh Máighréad: Guidh ar ár Shon!* c. 1914
Pencil on paper, 35 × 25 cm
Inscribed: Naomh Máirghéad guidh ar ár shon! [Saint Margot, pray for us]
Private Collection

51. *Sadhbh Trinseach: Two Self Sketches with Sketch of Another* n.d., c. 1914
Pen and ink on paper, 19 × 15 cm
Inscribed: ST self sketch
Reproduced: 'Rediscovering an artist', *Royal Hibernian Academy 173rd Exhibition* 2003, p. 28, fig. 1
Private Collection

52. *Two Heads of George Coffey Wearing Hat* July 1914
Pencil on paper, 20 × 15 cm
Inscribed: G. Coffey by S. Trínseach Iúl 1914. Ceanchor.
Private Collection

53. *Portrait of Robert Barton* n.d., c. 1914
On reverse *Early life drawing, with legs of two male nudes* c. 1914
Charcoal on drawing paper with line watermark, 37.3 × 24
National Gallery of Ireland (NGI 3814)

54. *The Master* 1915
Untraced drawing, measurements unknown
In her diary entry of 23 June 1916, Cesca refers to her studio at Temple Hill: '*The Master* is over the head of the bed, the drawing I did of it at the time it was produced.' Pádraic Pearse's one-act play, *The Master*, with William Pearse as Ciarán, was produced at the Irish Theatre, Hardwicke Street, Dublin, at Whitsuntide 1915.

55. *Baby Delle with her mother (Clare Trench)* 1916
Pencil on paper, 26 × 23 cm
Reproduced: 'Rediscovering an artist', *Royal Hibernian Academy 173rd Exhibition* 2003, p. 29, fig. 3
Private Collection
Delle, the artist's niece, daughter of Reggie and Clare, was born 4 November 1915.

56. *Three Studies of Baby Delle* 1916
Pencil on paper, 26 × 23 cm
Inscribed: Delle listening to Granny's singing

Private Collection

57. *Drawings at the Féis: including Seán Beaumont, Deora Frínseach, Cathal Ó Caomhánaigh* n.d., c. 1916
Pen and ink on paper, 35.5 × 25.5 cm
Private Collection
There is another sketch of Seán Beaumont and Deora Frínseach at a meeting in Notebook 2070TX, c. 1916, National Library of Ireland.

58. *Mairéad Ní Ghrádha (Mrs Kissane)* n.d.
On reverse *Portrait of a Gentleman Wearing a Boater*
Charcoal on Ganson & Montgo paper, 32 × 24 cm
National Gallery of Ireland (NGI 3813)

59. *Una Duncan* n.d.
Charcoal on paper with line watermark, 47.6 × 28.2
National Gallery of Ireland (NGI 3815)

60. *Male Head, perhaps of Michael Collins or the artist Fred Morrow* n.d.
On reverse *Unfinished Sketch of a Man with Closed Eyes*
Charcoal on paper, 31.8 × 23.9 cm
National Gallery of Ireland (NGI 3816)

61. *Diombáidh: A Female Head* (Twice) n.d.
Charcoal on Michallet France paper, 61.8 × 47 cm
Inscribed: Diombáidh . . . [the rest illegible]
National Gallery of Ireland (NGI 3817)

62. *Portrait Head and Shoulders of Douglas Hyde* Aug. 1916
Charcoal and chalk on paper, 38 × 28 cm
Signed with monogram
Private Collection

63. *Portrait Head of Douglas Hyde* Aug. 1916
Monochrome wash on paper, measurements unknown
Signed with monogram
Reproduced as frontispiece to *Douglas Hyde: An Craoibhín Aohbinn* by D. Ó Cobhthaigh. (Dublin, Maunsel, 1917)

64. *Portrait of Una Hyde* Aug. 1916
Untraced charcoal, measurements unknown
Made at Raheen where Cesca was staying with the Hydes in the summer of 1916.

65. *Portrait of Nuala Hyde* Aug. 1916
Charcoal with highlights on thin card, 30.5 × 26
Private collection
Douglas Hyde's daughter, Nuala, died in September 1916.

66. *Aodh Ruadh Ó Domhnaill (Red Hugh O'Donnell) on Horseback* n.d.
Untraced, probably charcoal, measurements unknown
Janet Cunningham collection c. 1916

67. *Portrait of Maude Royden* Jan. 1917
Untraced, probably charcoal, measurements unknown
Commissioned by the sitter

68. *Three Heads of Mrs Joseph Hone (Darina)* Apr. 1917
Charcoal and viridian green stain on Michallet France paper, 47.7 × 56.2 cm
National Gallery of Ireland (NGI 3818)

69. *Portrait of Diarmid Coffey* 1917
Charcoal on paper, 37 × 30.5 cm
Private Collection

70. *Portrait (Self Portrait)* 1917
Charcoal, no measurements
Reproduced in *Colour Magazine* June 1917 p. 140

71. *Portrait of Eoin MacNeill* 1917 or 1918
Charcoal on paper, 46.5 × 35 cm
Signed with monogram ST
Reproduced on dust cover of *The Scholar Revolutionary: Eoin Mac Neill, 1867–1945, and the Making of the New Ireland* ed. F.X. Martin and F.J. Byrne (Shannon, Irish University Press, 1973)
Private Collection
Believed by his wife to be the best likeness of MacNeill, who was released from prison on 27 May 1917 and back in Dublin by mid-June, after which this drawing was made. MacNeill is seen sitting in a winged armchair in his study, filling his pipe.

72. *An Sinsear (Robert Barton)* 1917 or 1918
Pencil on paper, 23 × 18 cm
Inscribed: An Sinnsear
Inscription in another hand: (R.C. Barton)
Reproduced: *Roundwood & District Historical & Folklore Journal* no. 14 (2003), p. 46
Private Collection
An Sinsear – Robert Barton was nicknamed 'the elder' as he was Diarmid's senior by seven years – was Diarmid's close friend.

73. *Robert Barton* n.d., 1917 or 1918
Pencil on paper, 23 × 18 cm
Inscription in another hand: R.C. Barton
Reproduced: *Roundwood & District Historical & Folklore Journal* no. 14 (2003), p. 46
Private Collection

74. *'Judy': Mrs Withers* Dec. 1917
On reverse *Three heads on an Arc, Thought to be Anne Cassidy* 22 June 1916
Charcoal on paper with line watermark, 52.2 × 36.5 cm
Recto inscribed with title
The two recto studies were made for the portrait the artist attempted in December 1916, see no.15. Verso is mentioned by Cesca in her diary entry for 23 June 1916: 'I can never get out of her as much as I am sure is there . . . Made 3 rotten little sketches of her.'
National Gallery of Ireland (NGI 3819)

75. *Portrait Sketch (head) of Jane Coffey* c. 1918
Charcoal, 35.5 × 25.5 cm
Private Collection

76. *Study for Oil: Deora Frínseach on a Sofa* Aug. 1918
Charcoal, 48.5 × 84 cm
Private Collection
The artist refers to painting the oil of Deora Frínseach in her diary entry for 12 August 1918.

77. *Bláthnaid Salkeld* Summer 1918
Charcoal on paper with line watermark, 52.3 × 39 cm
Inscribed title on verso
National Gallery of Ireland (NGI 3820)

(4) Published Illustrations

78. *An Claidheamh Soluis* (1) Fashion Illustration: *Cultacha Gaedhealacha I–V,* 22, 29 Nov. 1913, 13, 27 Dec. 1913, 10 Jan. 1914: and perhaps *Culaidh Gaedhealach: 'Cionus an seál do chaitheamh ar an gceann'* 17 Jan. 1914, *'Cóta geimhridh'* 24 Jan. 1914, *'Óigbhean ag dul ag marguidheacht lá gaothmhar'* 28 Feb. 1914, *'Culaith den chaismir uaine Gaedhealach i gcóir an tráthnóna'* 14 Mar. 1914.

79. *An Claidheamh Soluis* (2) Political Cartoons: *'Ceist Hóm Rúil mar atá sé'* 20 Dec. 1913; *'An Dochtúir Séan Buide'* 2 May 1914.

80. Ó Conaire, Pádraic, *An Chéad Chloch: Sgeulta.* (Dublin, 1914). Cover design: *Salome.*

81. Ní Dhubhghaill, C.M. (Doyle, C.), *Women in Ancient and Modern Ireland.* (Dublin, Kenny Press, 1917). Frontispiece: *'Emer teaching embroidery to her young companions'* with another illustration, *'Princess Margaret of Ely receiving her guests'.*

82. O Cobhthaigh, D., *Douglas Hyde: An Craoibhín Aoibhinn.* (Dublin, Maunsel, 1917). Frontispiece: *Portrait of Douglas Hyde.*

83. *The Irish Christmas.* (Dublin, Candle Press, 1917, 1918). Frontispiece: *'Nativity in an Irish kitchen'.*
Taken from the Christmas Card, *Nodlaig na nGaedheal,* no. 84 (3).

(5) Other Artwork

84. Some Conradh na Gaeilge Christmas Cards
Pen and ink, watercolour added when in print.

(1) *Céud Míle Fáilte roimh Rí an Domhain.* 1913 ff.
Signed 'T'.
Reproduced as frontispiece to *An tEaglaiseach Gaelach* vol. 6, Dec. 1925.

(2) *Nodlaig* 1913 ff.
Signed with monogram
Reproduced *An tEaglaiseach Gaelach* vol. 1, Dec. 1919 p. 3 with the inscription: Fáth Do theacht, a Shlánuightheoir, áthas a thabhairt do'n tSaoghal. Tabhair áthas dúinn, a Shlánuightheoir, nach mbaineann leis an tSaoghal. Sadhbh Trínnseach do chum.

(3) *Nodlaig na nGaedheal* (1)
Reproduced as 'Nativity in an Irish kitchen' in *The Irish Christmas.* (Dublin, Candle Press, 1917, 1918).

The woman of the house worships the Christ Child sleeping in her kitchen on his mother's knee.

(4) *Nodlaig na nGaedheal* (2) c 1917
This later version of no. 83 (3) is an *Adoration* which includes the whole family.

85. *Gaelic League Poster* Nov. 1913
Gouache on cartridge paper, 37 × 55 cm
National Museum of Ireland (NM 2671)
Lit: Kenny M., *The Road to Freedom: Photographs and memorabilia from the 1916 Rising and afterwards*. Dublin, National Museum and Country House, 1993
repro p. 18, pl. 2
Cesca recorded how she made the poster in the Paris atelier on 22 November 1913. 'Today I was making a propaganda poster, Gaelic Ireland and West Britain. A dark black-haired girl was posing for me and she held an umbrella like a spear.'

86. *Naomh Brighid (St. Brigid)* Poster Feb. 1915
Medium and measurements unknown
Cesca notes in her diary that she was working at it on 3 February 1915.

87. *Irish Christmas Crib Figures* various dates
Painted plywood, various sizes (St. Joseph 25 × 10, Mary and the Child 13 × 16, shepherd with lamb 16 × 8, kneeling figure 9 × 13, Mary kneeling 15 × 16, cow 12 × 17 cm. The crib surround 30 × 42 × 13 cm).
Note: Several sets of these figures were made
Private Collections

88. *Coláiste Eoghain Uí Chomhraidhe Murals* (Carrigaholt) May–July 1917
Powder with size on prepared walls (the murals have been conserved twice, with occasional divergence from the original colour)
Cesca made the initial sketches in Sketchbook 2070TX (NLI). She wrote in her diary on 19 July 1916, 'The memory strongest in me for some time to come will be the frieze made by the white wall, Ella Young in a blue dress and Maureen Fox in a corn coloured and mauve one sitting on it, Claud Chevasse in his kilt leaning against it, and the woman of the house and Mrs Dix, all of them against a still opal sea and sky and faint blue line of land opposite us in Co. Kerry.'

(6) Portraits of Cesca by other artists

89. *Portrait of Cesca with a Panther* by Georges Cornélius 1914
Untraced, probably oil, measurements unknown
In January 1914 Cesca told her sister Margot that her fellow student at the Atelier Ménard would start on a portrait of her in about a week, 'une petite Irlandaise qui rève la victoire . . . so that there won't be much of me in it, I don't think, he says it's going to be something more of a decorative picture than a portrait & that means he'll take liberties with my appearance.' Cornélius showed Cesca the completed picture on 20 February.

90. *Portrait of Cesca in Blue* by Alfred Palmer 1914
Pastel on paper, 20.5 × 15.5 inches
Private Collection
Alfred Palmer made at least five portraits of Cesca in 1914, see nos. 91–93.

91. *Portrait of Cesca in Orange* by Alfred Palmer 1914
Pastel on paper, measurements unknown
Private collection

92. *Portrait of Cesca in White* by Alfred Palmer 1914
Pastel on paper, measurements unknown
Private collection

93. *Portrait of Cesca Wearing a Black Hat* by Alfred Palmer 1914
Untraced, probably pastel on paper, measurements unknown
The fourth of the five portraits of Cesca by Alfred Palmer has not been traced. In her diary Cesca describes this, the fifth (begun on 22 February 1914), as a standing pose, hands on hips. She wears a black hat, and looks around laughing.

94. *Portrait of Cesca* by Æ (George Russell) Sept. 1917
Pastel on board, 74 × 55.5 cm
Private Collection

95. *Portrait of Cesca* by Æ (George Russell) 1917
Oil on canvas, 61 × 76 cm
National Gallery of Ireland, donated by the Friends of the National Collections of Ireland in 1973.

Select Bibliography

Bowe, N.G., ed., *Art and the National Dream: the search for vernacular expression in turn of century design*. Dublin, Irish Academic Press, 1993

Conlon, Lil, *Cumann na mBan and the Women of Ireland 1913–1925*. Kilkenny, Kilkenny People, 1969

Cullen, M. and Luddy, M., ed., *Female Activists: Irish Women and Change 1900–1960*. Dublin, Woodfield Press, 2001

Czira, S.G. *The Years Flew By: Recollections of Sydney Gifford Czira*. Dublin, Gifford Craven, 1974

Foy, M. and Barton, B., *The Easter Rising*, Stroud, Sutton, 1999

Irish Women Artists from the Eighteenth Century to the Present Day. Dublin, National Gallery of Ireland, Douglas Hyde Gallery, 1987

Kenny, M., *The Road to Freedom; photographs and memorabilia from the 1916 Rising and afterwards*. Dublin, Country House and National Museum, 1993

Larmour, P., *The Arts and Crafts Movement in Ireland*. Belfast, Friar's Bush Press, 1992

Lewis, G., *Eva Gore-Booth and Esther Roper: a biography*. London, Pandora Press, 1988

Macardle, D., *The Irish Republic: a documented chronicle of the Anglo-Irish conflict and the partitioning of Ireland, with a detailed account of the period 1916–1923*. Dublin, Irish Press, 1951 (4th ed.)

MacLysaght, E., *Changing Times: Ireland since 1898*. Gerrards Cross, Colin Smythe, 1978

MacLysaght, E., *Leathanaigh ó mo Dhialann*. Dublin, Clódhanna Teoranta, 1978

Martin, F.X. and Byrne, F.J., *The Scholar Revolutionary*. Shannon, Irish University Press, 1973

Nic Shiubhlaigh, M., *The Splendid Years: recollections of Máire Nic Shiubhlaigh as told to Edward Kenny*. Dublin, James Duffy, 1955

Ní Dheirg, I., *Emily M. Weddall: bunaitheoir Scoil Acla*. Dublin, Coiscéim, 1995

Norway, M.L. and A.H., ed. K. Jeffrey, *The Sinn Féin Rebellion As They Saw It*. Dublin, Irish Academic Press, 1999

1916 Rebellion Handbook. Introduction by Declan Kiberd. Belfast, Mourne River Press, 1998

Ó Ceallaigh, S., *Éamonn Mac Giolla Iasachta 1887–1986*. Dublin, Coiscéim, 2003

Ó Mórdha, M., *Tús agus Fás, Óglách na hÉireann, 1913–1917*. Dublin, Oifig Díolta Foillseacháin Rialtais, 1936

O'Neill, M., *Grace Gifford Plunkett and Irish Freedom: tragic bride of 1916*. Dublin, Irish Academic Press, 2000

Ó Súilleabháin, D., *Conradh na Gaeilge i Londain 1894–1917*. Dublin, Conradh na Gaeilge, 1989

Pyle, H., *'Rediscovering an Artist' in Royal Hibernian Academy: One hundred and Seventy-Third Exhibition*. Dublin, RHA, 2003

Stephens, James, *The Insurrection in Dublin*. Dublin, Maunsel, 1916

Index

Page numbers in italics indicate illustrations and captions